The First Louisiana Special Battalion

The First Louisiana Special Battalion

Wheat's Tigers in the Civil War

GARY SCHRECKENGOST

McFarland & Company, Inc., Publishers
Jefferson, North Carolina

The present work is a reprint of the illustrated case bound edition of The First Louisiana Special Battalion: Wheat's Tigers in the Civil War, *first published in 2008 by McFarland.*

LIBRARY OF CONGRESS CATALOGUING-IN-PUBLICATION DATA

Schreckengost, Gary, 1966–
    The First Louisiana Special Battalion : Wheat's Tigers in the Civil War / Gary Schreckengost.
    p.   cm.
    Includes bibliographical references and index.

    ISBN 978-1-4766-7238-0
    softcover : acid free paper ∞

    1. Confederate States of America. Army. Louisiana Infantry Special Battalion, 1st. 2. Louisiana — History — Civil War, 1861–1865 — Regimental histories. 3. United States — History — Civil War, 1861–1865 — Regimental histories. 4. United States — History — Civil War, 1861–1865 — Campaigns. I. Title.
E565.51st.S36   2017
973.7'463 — dc22   2007041994

BRITISH LIBRARY CATALOGUING DATA ARE AVAILABLE

© 2008 Gary Schreckengost. All rights reserved

No part of this book may be reproduced or transmitted in any form or by any means, electronic or mechanical, including photocopying or recording, or by any information storage and retrieval system, without permission in writing from the publisher.

Front cover: illustration of the arrival of reinforcements for Beauregard, at the camp of the Tiger Zouaves of Louisiana at White Plains, Virginia (*Harper's Weekly*, 1861)

Printed in the United States of America

McFarland & Company, Inc., Publishers
  Box 611, Jefferson, North Carolina 28640
  www.mcfarlandpub.com

To Hap, Spike and Jim

Acknowledgments

A great deal of gratitude is due to those who made this project possible. I would first like to thank my friend and associate, Ross Brooks of the Company of Military Historians, who was quite generous in sharing his valuable research. I'd also like to acknowledge Brandon Danz, John Valori, Meredith Fisher, and Larry Maier, who, like Ross Brooks, carefully read through my manuscript and offered numerous suggestions.

I would also like to recognize Justin Waynick, Thomas Webster, and Brendan Zeigler from the reenactment community, who offered various spirited recommendations during the early stages of the project, and Daniel Barnett and Jim Kistler, who generated the maps and other media.

Special thanks goes out to Colonel "Buddy" Wheat of the U.S. Army War College, a lineal descendent of Roberdeau Wheat's brother, who offered guidance and friendship in the latter stages of the project, Tim Czekanski of New Orleans for sharing his research on the Tigers' accoutrements, and fellow Lancaster Countian Bradley Schmehl for providing his expert artwork.

I would also like to acknowledge the park rangers at the Manassas and Richmond national battlefield parks, "Dewey" Vaughan at the Warren Rifles Confederate Museum in Front Royal, Virginia, the folks at Northeastern Photo in Harrisburg, "Andy" at the Library of Congress, the genteel Shannon Glasheen of the Louisiana State Museum, John Magill and the rest of the fine staff at the Historic New Orleans Collection, Pat Ricci at Confederate Memorial Hall, and the librarians at the Army War College (especially Mike Monahan) and the Lititz and Lancaster public libraries, who helped me collect my sources.

I would also like to thank the editors of *America's Civil War* magazine who published parts of the book before its distribution, greatly adding to its accuracy and opening new channels of communication.

Finally, and most important, I'd like to thank my wife, Kristi, and children, Morgan and Emily, who supported my endeavor and know full well how much time and effort was put into this undertaking.

The 1st Louisiana Special Battalion is simply a beginning, for the story of Wheat's Tigers is not yet complete. I hope that others are spurred by what I have written and seek to reinforce, correct, or clarify the record, for while many people have contributed and assisted in this project, I alone accept the responsibility for any errors of fact.

Table of Contents

Acknowledgments	vii
Preface	1
1. Tiger Roots: The Filibuster Wars to Southernize Latin America	5
2. Formation of "Wheat's Tigers"	32
3. First Blood: Seneca Falls and Matthews' Hill	48
4. Triumph on Henry Hill	68
5. Dishonored Heroes	77
6. Tiger Fury: The Battle of Front Royal	93
7. Give No Quarter to the Damned Yankees: The Battle of First Winchester	108
8. Retreat to the Upper Valley	119
9. The Very Devil in Them: The Battle of Port Republic	129
10. To the Peninsula	139
11. That's Hell in There! The Battle of Gaines' Mill	145
12. Egyptian Darkness: The Battle for Malvern Hill	156
13. A Tiger's Death	167
Appendix I. Service Record of the 1st Louisiana Special Battalion	171
Appendix II. Uniforms and Accoutrements of the Battalion	183
Appendix III. Wheat's Official Report of the Battle of Manassas	186
Chapter Notes	189
Bibliography	203
Index	209

Preface

[The 1st Louisiana Tiger Battalion was] a unique body, representing every grade of society and every kind of man, from the princely gentleman who commanded them down to the thief and cut-throat released from parish prison on condition he would join Wheat.... Such a motley herd of humanity was probably never got together before, and may never be again.
— David French Boyd

On a cold night in December 1861, Private Thomas Lane of the 15th Alabama Regiment was standing guard just outside of Camp Florida, near Centreville, Virginia. The night was quiet, except for the distant sound of crackling fires, an occasional cough from the tents, the crunching of recently fallen snow under his feet, and the whisper of the cold wind. Suddenly, Lane heard a ghostly tone from the dark wood line: "A resurrected tie-ger." Slowly, he pointed his ear toward the sound, drawing his scarf from his face. Again, the words "a resurrected tie-ger" spat forth from the woods. Peering closer, Lane saw a man-sized figure, silhouetted against the moonlight, wearing vertically striped pantaloons. The only men who wore those peculiar trousers were from Major Chatham Roberdeau Wheat's famed "Louisiana Tigers." A few months earlier, two of these Tigers had mugged Lane and had badly beaten him.

Lane cocked his musket and nervously spat out the challenge: "Who goes there?"

"A resurrected tie-ger," was his only response.

Lane reiterated his challenge: "Who goes there?" and then added the threat: "Identify yourself or I'll shoot!"

"A resurrected tie-ger," answered the shadowy figure again, as he began to approach Lane. "A resurrected tie-ger."

Two "Tigers" had been executed a few days before for mutiny; they had been shot by a firing squad drawn from their own company and were buried not far from the camp. Totally overwhelmed with panic, Lane dashed back to camp and called for the sergeant of the guard. Trembling, Lane told the sergeant that he had seen one of the executed Tigers, apparently raised from the grave, in the tree line. Just then, Private Sam Learry, laughing hysterically, came out from under cover and reported to the sergeant that he had borrowed a pair of trousers from one of the Tigers to play a practical joke on Private Lane. It was so funny that the sergeant took no steps toward punishing Lane for leaving his post. From that point on, whenever Lane's company saw anything streaked or striped, they hollered: "Tom Lane, here's your Tiger!" It seemed as though Roberdeau Wheat's infamous band of Louisiana Tigers, even in death, inspired fear in friend and foe alike.

Of all the units that took to the field in defense of Southern rights during the American Civil War, none exceeded the audacity, flair, and combative spirit of the 1st Louisiana Special Battalion, "Wheat's Tigers." Raised from the docks of New Orleans, the Tigers, who were principally Irish immigrant ship hands, dock workers, or veterans of the now-forgotten Filibuster Wars, were as tough, fiery, and resolute as their gallant and genteel commander, Chatham Roberdeau Wheat.

Roberdeau Wheat was one of the greatest filibusters of the antebellum period. Filibusters were implacable North American soldiers of fortune who sought to overthrow Latin American governments and have those countries annexed to the United States as slave states to better secure Southern rights within the Union. Wheat himself had organized and participated in four filibuster expeditions against Cuba, Mexico, and Nicaragua. Eventually, he rose to the rank of brigadier general in the Mexican army and later served on Italian general Giuseppe Garibaldi's staff as an artillery and logistical advisor.

In 1861, when his native South declared its independence, Wheat rushed back to New Orleans from the battlefields of Italy to raise a battalion of infantry. He did so not only to help defend the newly proclaimed Confederate States of America, but also to expand its physical and cultural boundaries into Mexico and Central America. Reestablishing his old recruiting station at 64 Saint Charles Street, near Lafayette Square and across from the prestigious St. Charles Hotel, Wheat raised his own company of volunteers, the Old Dominion Guards. He also attracted four already-forming companies to his banner: Captain Robert Harris's Walker Guards, Captain Alexander White's Tiger Rifles, Captain Henry Gardner's Delta Rangers, and Captain Harry Chaffin's Rough and Ready Rangers.

Wheat's Special Battalion differed from the rest of the Southern military establishment not only because of its filibuster roots but also because one of its companies, the Tiger Rifles, was one of the few Confederate units uniformed in the Zouave fashion. Zouaves were originally Algerian units that had served in the French army; they were considered among the elite fighting forces in the world by 1860. They wore flamboyant uniforms during their French service that inspired a sartorial style that was replicated by a handful of enterprising Americans during the Civil War. Closely matching the gallant Zouaves, the Tiger Rifles' distinctive uniform consisted of dark blue or light brown wool

Zouave jackets with red cotton trim, red flannel fezes with red tassels, red flannel shirts with five white porcelain buttons, outlandish Wedgwood blue and cream one-and-one-half-inch vertically striped cottonade pantaloons, blue and white horizontally striped stockings, and white canvas leggings.

Once Wheat's Tigers took to the field of battle, their dynamic persona was quickly equated by their actions and they rose to become among the most elite — and polemic — formations of the Confederate army. They received accolades at the battle of First Manassas for charging a superior enemy no less than four times with reckless abandon. During Thomas "Stonewall" Jackson's Valley Campaign, they seized key positions at the battles of Front Royal, Winchester, and Port Republic, ensuring Southern victory. During the Seven Days' Battles, the Tigers were among the first of Jackson's command to charge the strong Federal lines at Gaines' Mill and, being thrown into the absolute worst part of the line, were blown to pieces. Wheat himself was killed while leading one final and gallant charge against Union forces.

1

Tiger Roots

The Filibuster Wars to Southernize Latin America

It is time to define what we mean by the term "filibustering": "Wars of conquest waged by the strong against the weak, with little or no provocation."
— George Fitzhugh

The story of "Wheat's Tigers" does not start in New Orleans during the spring of 1861, but in the Caribbean Basin before the Civil War. What made the 1st Louisiana Special Battalion different from the rest of the Confederate military establsihment is that many of its recruits, including Major Roberdeau Wheat, its commander, were veterans of the now-forgotten Filibuster Wars of the 1850s. During these illicit campaigns, Americans, primarily Southerners, tried to overthrow the governments of Mexico, Cuba, and Nicaragua and annex those countries to the U.S. as slave states in order to ensure Southern power within the Union. It is therefore important to briefly summarize these conflicts and contextualize the ideological foundation of "filibustering" or "filibusterism" to better understand the Tigers' fight for Southern independence during the 1860s.

Chatham Roberdeau Wheat, the Tigers' intrepid commander, was born on April 9, 1826, in Alexandria, Virginia, to the Reverend John Thomas and Selina Blair Patten Wheat. As a boy, Roberdeau followed his father to his Episcopal parsonages in Arundel County, Maryland, Wheeling, Virginia, Marietta, Ohio, New Orleans, Louisiana, and Nashville, Tennessee. When he was fifteen, Wheat was sent back to Alexandria to study under the Reverend William Nelson Pendleton, a West Point graduate, former U.S. Army officer, and future artillery chief of Robert E. Lee's Confederate Army of Northern Virginia. In 1842 Wheat returned to Tennessee to live with his family and entered the University of Nashville, where he received his B.A. in 1846.[1]

Soon after his graduation, in May 1846, the U.S. declared war on Mexico and nineteen-year-old Wheat enlisted into Captain William Porter's Company G, 1st Tennessee Mounted Rifles. Because of his education, Wheat was quickly elected the junior lieutenant of his troop and acted as its adjutant. Once mustered into federal service, the Mounted Rifles were sent south to reinforce Maj. Gen. Zachary Taylor's army at Matamoros, Mexico. There, in the hot and bug-infested camps, Wheat became afflicted with the mysterious and sometimes deadly "camp fever." Consigned to the hospital, the young lieutenant quickly attracted the attention of the commanding general's son and volunteer aide, Richard Taylor, who remembered: "[Wheat] was a bright-eyed youth ... wan with disease, but with cheery withal." Subsequently transferred to army headquarters to help him better convalesce and to enliven General Taylor, Wheat became a "pet" of sorts of the headquarters section.[2]

In January 1847 Wheat's regiment was transferred to Brig. Gen. John Quitman's division of volunteers that was, along with two other divisions, ordered to march 400 miles south along the Mexican coast to Tampico, where it was to await the arrival of Maj. Gen. Winfield Scott. Scott was tasked by President James Polk to build up his forces at Tampico and transport them further down the coast by boat to the fortified town of Vera Cruz, take it by siege, and then march 250 miles inland to secure Mexico City. According to Lieutenant George McClellan, a trusted regular army engineer from Philadelphia, Pennsylvania, the volunteers of Scott's army — mostly Southerners — were called "Mohawks" by the regulars for their wild, Indian-like ways. They were dirty, unkempt fellows, McClellan averred, who were "outcasts [who] think nothing of robbing and killing the Mexicans."[3]

In early March, Scott loaded 13,000 of his men, including the Mounted Rifles, aboard transports and landed them just south of Vera Cruz, where they began to lay siege to the town. After a few weeks of bombardment, on March 26, the coastal bastion fell to the Americans and Scott marched his army westward — following Cortez's famous invasion route — and engaged the main Mexican force under Santa Anna at Cerro Gordo Pass. During the fight, in which the volunteers attacked the entrenched Mexicans frontally while the regulars turned their left, Wheat's company carried dispatches

Major Chatham Roberdeau Wheat, commander, 1st Louisiana Special Battalion — "Wheat's Tigers." *Southern Historical Society Papers*

for the general staff. Once the Americans won the hard-fought battle, Scott continued his march toward Mexico City until May 1847, when he was forced to stop at Puebla because most of the volunteers' enlistments, including the 1st Tennessee's, had expired.

While the majority of the men of the regiment chose to return home, Wheat and a hundred others decided to stay in Mexico and continue the fight. Wheat was subsequently elected their captain, and General Quitman, a proud militia officer from Mississippi, recognized Wheat's commission and assigned his independent troop the difficult task of combating partisan raiders who were trying to cut the army's tenuous supply line, which ran from Jalápa to Vera Cruz. Not only was this Wheat's first experience in independent command, but it was also his first taste of guerrilla warfare — warfare that he would come to master. As testament to Wheat's activities in grappling with the elusive partisans, General Quitman later remarked that Roberdeau was "the best natural soldier I ever knew."[4]

After fighting several more desperate battles at Contreras, Churubusco, Molino del Rey, and Chapultepec — conflicts in which Wheat's company did not participate, as it was still fighting a nasty guerrilla war in Scott's rear — the main army captured Mexico City on September 14, 1847. Soon after, Wheat's company, "being well mounted, handsomely uniformed, splendidly equipped and perfect in drill," was transferred to Mexico City to act as provost troops with the District of Columbia Regiment. There they "'did the ornamental' on great occasions for general officers."[5]

In December 1847, "his command having suffered severely in killed and wounded," Wheat was sent home to fill up his ranks with new recruits. These he soon obtained in Nashville, where a flag was presented to his company by "the young ladies of Christ church school; on which occasion the color-bearer had on a complete suit of armor — helmet, breast-plate, &c. of polished brass — taken from one of Santa Anna's body-guards." When Wheat returned to Mexico with his replacements, however, Santa Anna had already surrendered to the United States with the Treaty of Guadalupe-Hidalgo. In the settlement, the Mexican general agreed to cede the northern tier of his country (which included all or parts of the modern-day states of Texas, California, New Mexico, Arizona, and Colorado — the Mexican Cession) to the U.S. in exchange for $18 million and the evacuation of all U.S. troops.[6]

With victory in hand, the state volunteers were mustered out of federal service, and Captain Wheat, now a decorated veteran, settled in New Orleans, the third largest city of the United States. There he opened a law practice and became actively involved in politics, stumping for Whig presidential candidate Zachary Taylor, his former commanding general. Soon after the hotly contested election, which Taylor won, the nation became embroiled over what to do with the Mexican Cession. According to the Missouri Compromise of 1820, all new states below the Thirty-six-Thirty Line (that is, south of Missouri) were to be "slave-choice," and all above would be "no-slave-choice." And because most Southerners felt that the North got the lion's share of the Louisiana Purchase land in 1820, their representatives protected Southern interests by putting a proviso in the compromise that each "no-slave-choice state" which entered the Union would have to be matched by a "slave-choice state." This arrangement had kept a balance in the Senate between the two regions until Taylor became president.[7]

In 1849, the Republic of California, part of the Mexican Cession, applied to join the Union as a no-slave-choice state without a slave-choice partner to complement it. President Taylor desired that California enter the Union on any terms. In the political wrangling that followed, which almost led to the secession of South Carolina and the eventual destruction of Wheat's beloved Whig Party, California was ultimately admitted as a no-slave-choice state, tipping the balance of power in the Senate, at least in the short term, toward Northern interests. As such, Wheat and other Southern partisans saw the writing on the wall: both sections were fighting for control of the national government, and through it were trying to impose themselves on the other. Wheat wanted to make sure that his region was the one that came out on top.[8]

In Wheat's mind, the best way to accomplish this was for the South to expand its particular or "peculiar" culture and institutions—which included the dichotomy of black slavery and white republican society—southward into Old Mexico, Central America, and the Caribbean, lands well-south of the Thirty-six-Thirty Line. This would not only ensure a balance in the Senate, but would also, if need be, give the South enough strength to secede from the United States and form its own nation. To facilitate this lofty goal, as well as that of the reopening of the African slave trade, Wheat and other enterprising Southern brahmins, men such as George Bickley and George Fitzhugh of Virginia, Senator John Breckinridge of Kentucky, Senator Robert Toombs of Georgia, Governor John Quitman of Mississippi, and Louisiana senator and ambassador to Spain Pierre Soulé, formed a clandestine, fraternal organization known as the Knights of the Golden Circle.[9]

The term *Golden Circle* denoted the hope that this new Southern nation would encompass the entire Caribbean region and then some: all of the slave-choice states of the United States, Old Mexico, Central America, the northern portion of South America, and the rich sugar islands of the Caribbean, including Spanish Cuba. In this new tropical empire, the South's institutions would be not only perpetuated, but strengthened. Mississippi senator Albert Gallatin Brown, for example, proclaimed: "I want Cuba, and I know that sooner or later we must have it.... I want Tamaulipas, Potosí, and one or two other Mexican states; and I want them all for the same reason—for the planting and spreading of slavery. And a foothold in Central America will powerfully aid us in acquiring those other States.... Yes, I want these Countries for the spread of slavery."[10]

According to the Knights of the period, Southerners not only possessed the ability to expand their "superior race and culture," but also bore the God-given duty to do so. In a world where it was conquer or be conquered, the "lesser races and cultures," including misdirected Yankees, should be not only dominated and exploited but also guided, assimilated, and enlightened by benevolent white Southerners, or face inevitable natural extinction. This nascent form of social Darwinism was elucidated by future Golden Knight William Walker, who wrote in 1860:

> If we look at Africa in the light of universal history, we see her for more than 5,000 years a mere waif on the waters of the world, fulfilling no part in its destinies, and aiding in no manner the progress of general civilization. Sunk in the depravities of fetishism, and reeking with the blood of human sacrifices, she seemed a satire on man, fit only to provoke the sneer of devils at the wisdom, and justice, and benevolence of the Creator. But America was discovered, and the European found the African a useful auxiliary in subduing the continent for the uses and purposes of civilization. The white man took the Negro from his native wastes, and teaching him the arts of life, bestowed on him the infallible blessings of a true religion.... The labor of inferior races cannot compete with that of the white race unless you give it a white master to direct its energies; and without such protection as slavery affords, the colored races must inevitably succumb in the struggle with white labor.... In [the tropical climes of America] the Negro seems to be in his natural climate. The blacks who have gone thither from Jamaica are healthy, strong and capable of severe labor.... In fact, Negro blood seems to assert its superiority over the indigenous Indians of [the area].... Time presses. If the South wishes to get her institutions into tropical America she must do so before treaties are made by [treacherous Yankees] to embarrass her action and hamper her energy ... in the effort to reestablish slavery in [the Caribbean Region].... The hearts of Southern youth answer to the call of honor, and strong arms and steady eyes are waiting to carry forward the policy which is now the dictate of duty as well as interest.... The true field for the exertion of slavery is in tropical America.[11]

Many Southerners, men like Roberdeau Wheat, apparently agreed with William Walker. Bound by a collective identity, they were seemingly on a mission from God to dominate, "regenerate," "Americanize," or "Southernize" the Western Hemisphere. Modeling this kindred spirit, Wheat progressed to the next logical step when he helped organize and participate in four so-called "filibuster expeditions" during the 1850s. A filibuster was an American soldier of fortune who conducted illicit military operations against Central American countries with which the U.S. was at peace. Although most filibusters, true soldiers of fortune such as Charles Frederick Henningsen, apparently fought for personal gain, at least some men, especially from the Southland, men such as Roberdeau Wheat, fought to spread Southern culture.[12] Noted Southern partisan and Golden Knight George Fitzhugh best articulated the ideological base for what has become known as "filibustering" or "filibusterism" when he wrote the following diatribe in *De Bow's Review* in December 1858:

> For nearly forty years Mexico has been in a state of continually recurring revolution, of misrule, and almost anarchy. She has shown that, left to herself, she is wholly incapable of organizing and sustaining any permanent form of government.

Her highways are infested with robbers, whose known crimes, so far from being punished by public authority, do not affect their social grade, nor exclude them from what is called good society, in their capital. The Indians on her northern frontier are making continual predatory incursions into her territory, and she is powerless to repel them. Her mixed population has all the vices of civilization, with none of its virtues; all the ignorance of barbarism, with none of its hardihood, enterprise, and self-reliance. It is enervate, effeminate, treacherous, false, and fickle. Like the savage and beasts of the forest, its love of liberty is but impatience of control, and hatred of law and government.... Should America, regardless of her interest, her safety, her glory, fail to intervene, France or England will step to avert the sad catastrophe that would celebrate its carnival of blood in the streets of Montezuma.... Yes, should America under the lead or paralysis ... of Northern abolitionism, socialism, and black republicanism, fail in her duty ... forgetful of the Monroe Doctrine ... England will see to it that no war-whoop disturbs the slumbers of the imperial city.... Mexico cannot stand alone. She must become a dependent tributary of some distant European nation, who would not govern her well, because it could not govern her understandingly, or be annexed to our Union, and become a group of free and independent [i.e., slave-choice] states, with all the rights, liberties, and privileges of the now existing states.

"Filibuster." *Frank Leslie's Illustrated Newspaper*

Looking to the mighty benefits resulting to the human race from the annexations of ours, made at comparatively little expense of blood or treasure, can we doubt that there is a "manifest destiny," the finger of Providence in this (so called) filibustering movement of America? After effecting so much good, shall we cease from our labors while so much remains to be done? Shall we be deterred by the epithet of filibustering, or the cant, fanaticism, and mistaken or pretended philanthropy of a part of the North?... Unless we can command all the convenient transit across the Isthmus to California and Oregon, [Mexico and Central America] will annex themselves [to Britain or France].... Filibustering, whether by nations or individuals, is not like avarice — selfish, sordid, and narrow — but has always public good for its object. It proceeds from ambition; and ambition, rightly directed, is the noblest of human passions. It sacrifices, very often, all the endearments of home and country, encounters privation and suffering, and perils health and life, to benefit country or mankind, as asks only reputation and fame as its pay and recompense. It warms the missionary's zeal, impels him to deeds of greater daring than a soldier ever undertook, carries him into midst of cannibal savages, where the foot of the white man has never before trodden....

The learned, accomplished, and pious bishop of the Virginia diocese, maintains that the Negro slave-trade, and slavery in America, were means and agencies intended and provided by Deity to civilize and Christianize the blacks. This surely was filibustering; but the most needful of filibustering; for modern experience has demonstrated it to be the only means sufficiently coercive to civilize and Christianize the Negro....

It is time to define what we mean by the term "filibustering." [Viz.:] "Wars of conquest waged by the strong against the weak, with little or no provocation," fulfills our idea of filibustering.

Alexander the Great was a filibuster, for, without provocation or pretext of injury or offence, he conquered a large part of Asia, and part of Africa and Europe. Yet he was a benefactor of mankind, for he diffused Greek civilization — the highest form of civilization — throughout many countries, whose civilization, always very low grade, was then rapidly decaying.

Julius Caesar was also a filibuster, for he conquered Gaul pretty much on his own hook, alleging the flimsiest pretexts for his conduct. But he civilized and Latinized Gaul, and the civilization which he planted and engrafted remains to this day.... Mohammed was a filibuster....

All savage races which cannot be domesticated and enslaved, will be gradually exterminated. Many will fall by the sword, but more by their inability to compete in the field of industry with the more laborious, provident, and skillful whites. While we lament the fate that awaits them, we would not avert it by inflicting far greater evils on the whites.[13]

William Walker, another implacable filibuster of the period, echoed Mr. Fitzhugh's sentiments but was much more succinct:

That which you ignorantly call "filibusterism" is not the offspring of hasty passion or ill-regulated desire; it is the fruit of the sure, unerring instincts which act in accordance with laws as old as creation. They are but drivellers [i.e., fools] who speak of fixed relations between the pure white American race, as it exists in the United States, and the mixed Hispano-Indian race, as it exists in Mexico and Central America, without employment of force. The history of the world presents no such utopian vision as that of an inferior race yielding meekly and peacefully to the controlling influence of a superior people.[14]

The first filibuster expedition in which Wheat participated was commanded by the rebel Spanish general Narciso López. Born in Venezuela to well-born parents, López was commissioned in the Spanish army and had fought against Simón Bolívar during the 1820s. By 1840 López had become a trusted minister to the governor of Cuba. In 1848, on the heels of the U.S.'s conquest of Mexico and the revolutions that were sweeping Europe, López, fearing a liberalization of the empire, joined a group of ultraconservative planters who were working to make the island an independent country with the institution of Negro slavery intact. When Spanish authorities exposed the conspirators, however, López fled to the U.S. to escape execution as a traitor to the crown.[15]

Undeterred, López set forth to recruit various Cuban exiles and American veterans of the Mexican War to launch an invasion of the island, foment a rebellion, build an army of like-minded Cubans, conduct a *coup d'état*, and install himself as president of a sovereign Cuba. To garner further support, he insinuated the possibility of having the island annexed to the U.S. as a slave-choice state as Texas had been in 1846.[16]

Once López declared this, he immediately obtained support from the Knights of the Golden Circle. Mississippi governor John Quitman led the charge to aid López as much as possible by supplying money, equipment, expertise, and over 500 volunteers, mostly young men from Mississippi and Louisiana. Wheat himself was commissioned a colonel in López's filibuster army and was put in charge of the Louisiana Battalion, which consisted primarily of "worthless characters and rowdies" from the levees and boweries of New Orleans.[17]

On the night of May 2, 1849, López's filibusters, which included Callender Fayssoux, Achilles and Albert Kewan, Theodore O'Hara, Louis Schlessinger, Donatien Augustin, John Pickett, J.R. Hayden, Thomas Theodore Hawkins, W.H. Bell, M.J. Bunch, Peter Smith, Ambrosio Gonzales, and Roberdeau Wheat, quietly slipped out of New Orleans aboard the packed steamer *Creole*. Two weeks later, on May 19, the dilettante filibusters landed near the Cuban town of Cárdenas and forced their way into the square. After a bloody daylong fight, López's men defeated some 700 Spanish regulars and a hundred or so machete-wielding Cuban peasants.[18]

With Cárdenas secured, López loaded his victorious army back aboard the *Creole* to move down the coast to continue his destabilization program. On its way out of the harbor, however, the *Creole* ran aground and damaged its hull. To avoid sinking, the filibusters were forced to dump their arms, equipment, and ammunition overboard. They consequently decided to return to the U.S. to refit and reorganize.[19]

Two days later, on May 21, about forty miles from Key West, the limping filibuster vessel was sighted by the Spanish warship *Pizarro*, seeking retribution for the sacking of Cárdenas. In the race that followed, the *Creole* barely made it to Key West ahead of the Spanish frigate. To add insult to injury, once the defeated mercenaries came ashore, they were forced to scatter to evade capture by federal authorities.[20]

After this humbling first experience in filibustering, Wheat made his way to his family's new home in Chapel Hill, where his father was a faculty member of the University of North Carolina. Wheat hid out there until he was arrested by federal marshals for breaking the Neutrality Law of 1818 and shipped off to face trial in New Orleans. Other men who were indicted included Mississippi governor John Quitman, John O'Sullivan, editor of the New York *Democratic Review*, who had originally coined the phrase "Manifest Destiny," and Laurent J. Sigur, editor of the militant New Orleans *Daily Delta*.[21]

By March 1851, after a spirited exercise in American jurisprudence, all charges against Quitman, Wheat, and the others were dropped when a New Orleans grand jury refused to even bring the case to trial. "If the evidence against [the conspirators] were a thousand fold stronger," proclaimed the New Orleans *Orleanian*, "no jury could be impaneled to convict him because public opinion makes law."[22]

Emboldened by the findings of the court, Wheat joined Colonel José Carvajal's band of Mexican insurgents who were out to finish the job started by the U.S. in the last war by stripping the northern Mexican provinces of Tamaulipas, Nuevo León, and Coahuila from the Mexican Union and declaring them an independent federation called the Republic of Sierra Madre, with slave-choice reintroduced to spur American immigration. Because the South, Mexico, and the "world at large" would benefit from such a transaction, Wheat readily offered his services. Ever since the close of the last war, Wheat had been convinced that although Mexico was the "finest country in the world ... the present occupants [of Mexico] were as incompetent to develop its resources as the Indians whom the Spaniards had supplanted." He therefore thought that it would "be a charitable proceeding, as in the interest of civilization and reformed Christianity" to smash the "corrupt church in Mexico ... the curse of the country" and replace it with Anglo-American institutions. Becoming Carvajal's artillery chief (commanding but one tiny six-pounder smoothbore), Wheat and his 500 fellow insurrectionists, including Captain John "Rest in Peace" Ford's troop of Colt revolver–wielding Texas Rangers, continually harassed Santa Anna's forces in true guerrilla fashion. In October, the enterprising filibusters went so far as to attack the key Mexican Army post at Matamoros, only to be driven back. After a few more months of conducting illicit operations, "Carvajal's Rebellion" ran out of steam and Wheat, frustrated, snuck back across the border into Texas and returned to New Orleans.[23]

In 1852, with his fame as a Southern partisan firmly secured, the local Whig Party bosses asked Wheat to run for the Louisiana State House. Having party backing, he easily won the election and served in Baton Rouge for one term. In 1854, apparently bored with the banality of state politics, Wheat joined insurgent general Juan Álvarez of Mexico who intended, unlike Colonel Carvajal, to completely overthrow Santa Anna's government, establish himself as president, and give Mexico a constitution more like America's, thus opening the way for better relations with the United States. Wheat was commissioned a brigadier general in Alvalrez's army and was assigned to command its artillery forces. For the next several months, General Wheat campaigned with the rebels in the central mountains of Mexico, slowly but surely wearing down the paltry forces which were still loyal to Santa Anna. Finally on November 14, 1855, the insurgents took Mexico City and installed Álvarez as the new president.[24]

This crowning achievement should have been the pinnacle of Wheat's life. He was a general officer, the owner of a magnificent subtropical estate in "the finest country in the world," and a close confidant to the president of Mexico. But for Wheat, this was not enough. In July 1856 he gave it all up and returned to New Orleans to organize a relief expedition to help save fellow filibuster William Walker, who had overthrown the government of Nicaragua and installed himself as president the year before, making him the greatest filibuster of the period. And for many of the men of the soon-to-be organized 1st Louisiana Special Battalion, especially those from Company A, the Walker Guards, William Walker would serve as the Tigers' knight exemplar of how and why to expand Southern culture.[25]

In 1855, while Wheat was fighting against Santa Anna in Mexico, Walker was enlisted by the second-wealthiest man in America, Cornelius Vanderbilt, to help rebel general Francisco Castellón overthrow President Fruto Chamorro's "Legitimate" government in Nicaragua. After winning its independence from Spain in 1821, Nicaragua had gone through no less than thirteen revolutions. By 1855, after yet another upheaval, two factions controlled the country. In the east, with their capital at Granada, were President Chamorro's "Legitimists" or "Whites," who were quietly backed by Britain and France. In the west, with their capital at León, were Francisco Castellón's "Rebels" or "Reds." They were quietly backed by Honduras, El Salvador, and Cornelius Vanderbilt.[26] In the February 1858 issue of *De Bow's Review*, the political situation in Nicaragua was explained as follows:

William Walker, the "Grey-eyed Man of Destiny." *Leslie's*

Since the tripartite union of the states of Nicaragua, San Salvador, and Honduras under the title of "the National Representation of Central America," in 1849, and the disorders consequent thereupon, a comparative political quiet had prevailed throughout the country in 1854, when a revolution in Nicaragua, involving to some extent the other States took place.... The revolution first broke out on the occasion of the presidential election in Nicaragua in the fall of 1853; but, although the riots at the polls was its starting point, it was in all respects a struggle between two political faiths in Central America that had been in conflict for thirty years.

The candidates for the office of president, which had been vacated by the death of [Laureano] Pineda, and for which an election was held in the fall of 1853, were Fruto Chamorro, of Grenada, and Francisco Castellón, of León. The former was ultra-servile [i.e., conservative] in his politics, and particularly inimical to the immigration of foreigners; while the latter was distinguished for the liberal political education which he had acquired by extensive travel in Europe, having been minister to England and France, as well as for his position in the liberal party.... When the day of the election came, Chamorro, who was ... in command of the army, besieged the polls with his soldiers, and in the riots which ensued some of the Castellón men were killed, and it was said that others were bayoneted in cold blood for refusing to vote on the side of the army. By such violence, and by an alleged fraud in the returns, Chamorro claimed that he had been elected. He commenced his administration by abrogating the constitutional privileges of the people, and by banishing Castellón ... to Honduras.... After a brief recuperation, Castellón returned to Nicaragua and landed at Realejo on the fourth of May, 1854, at the head of about two hundred men. They were received with [the] usual boundless demonstrations. Nearly the entire population pronounced for Castellón; and he was made Director of the provisional republic.... [Chamorro then went after Castellón] ... and the war continued with various success.[27]

The linchpin to Nicaragua, the primary reason for Vanderbilt's interest, was its "Accessory Transit Route." Vanderbilt wanted to build a canal along this route to link the east and west coasts of the United States. The overland route to California was long, costly, and dangerous, and the sea route around the tip of South America was equally as bad. The locomotive across the Isthmus of Panama was promising, but an all-water route through Nicaragua was even better.[28]

During the 1850s Nicaragua was the most feasible place to build a transcontinental canal. On its eastern coast, the San Juan River snaked about 120 miles through the jungle and into Lake Nicaragua, which was about seventy miles wide. On the western side of the lake was the town of Virgin Bay; from there, a good road, the Accessory

Cornelius Vanderbilt, antebellum business tycoon from New York who facilitated and then destroyed William Walker's filibuster expedition to Nicaragua. *Library of Congress*

Transit Route, twisted a mere twelve miles through the jungle and over the coastal mountain to the town of San Juan del Sur and the Pacific Ocean. Vanderbilt and his American Atlantic and Pacific Ship and Canal Company intended to build a canal along this twelve-mile-long track. Vanderbilt even went so far as to build a fleet of steamers, like the *Star of the West*, to transport passengers and cargo from the east coast of the U.S. to San Juan del Norte, which was near the mouth of the San Juan River.[29]

In 1851, however, the British seized San Juan del Norte, renamed it Greytown, and cut off all shipping up the San Juan River. When Vanderbilt protested through legal channels without satisfaction, he hired William Walker to aid Castellón's Reds in overthrowing Chamorro's British-backed Whites in exchange for free access to the Transit Route. To entice enlistment, all American volunteers, or "colonizers" as they were shrewdly called, would be salaried and given "five hundred acres of prime Nicaraguan land" if their mission was successful.[30]

Although he was only able to muster fifty-seven adventurers, Walker was not disheartened since his own brothers, John and Norwell Walker, as well as eight veteran mercenaries rallied to his banner: Tim Crocker, C.C. Hornsby, Frank Anderson, Charles Doubleday, Thomas Fisher, Doctor Alexander Jones, and Achilles and Albert Kewan. He outfitted his filibusters in baggy red or blue flannel battle shirts with red cotton scarves, white cottonade trousers, leather

Star of the West. Leslie's

"Filibuster Company." *Leslie's*

boots, and wide-brimmed hats wrapped with red ribbons (to match Castellón's forces). He also ensured that his men were armed with the most current firearms—repeating pistols and breech-loading carbines—and less-sophisticated machetes or bowie knives for jungle survival and close-quarter combat.[31]

On May 3, 1855, Walker's Fifty-seven Immortals, as they came to be called, quietly steamed out of San Francisco aboard the S.S. *Vesta*, posing as colonizers to Nicaragua. On June 1, Walker's 'busters landed at Realejo, Nicaragua, marking, as Walker later proclaimed, "a new epoch, not only for Nicaragua, but all of Central America," and made their way through the jungle to Chinandega and then León, Castellón's capital, which numbered about 25,000 souls. There Walker and his Fifty-seven were welcomed with open arms by the native population, who thought they were sent by God himself to help free Nicaragua from Chamorro's thugs. Walker was subsequently commissioned a colonel in Castellón's army, and his mercenaries were mustered into service as *la Falange Americana* (the American Phalanx) with Achilles Kewan as Walker's lieutenant colonel and Tim Crocker as his major.[32]

Once the filibusters were settled in, Walker was briefed that Chamorro was gathering a superior force at Rivas, on Lake Nicaragua, to crush the Reds.

Realejo. *Leslie's*

Chinandega. *Leslie's*

Walker devised a plan to hit the Whites first, however, and to gain control of the all-important Transit Route as per Vanderbilt's secret instructions. On June 23, 1855, he sailed the Phalanx, reinforced by a hundred or so of Castellón's rebels under Colonels Félix Ramírez and Mariano Méndez, down the coast to the uninhabited promontory of Punta Gigante, about eighteen miles north of San Juan del Sur. From there, Walker pushed inland, up and over the coastal mountains, and through a dark and rain-soaked jungle.[33]

León, the Red capital. *Leslie's*

After marching several days, the filibusters encamped at a deserted adobe house not far from the mountain village of Tola, nine miles northwest of Rivas. There, Walker's men, with "thick and heavy beards [which] gave to most of the body a wild and dangerous air," were allowed to eat and rest while Méndez's scouts were sent on ahead. Walker later remembered:

> As soon as the sentries were posted, the Americans began to dispose of their crackers and cold meat, washed down in some instances by a draught from a liquor canteen; while the native soldiers opened their supplies of cheese and tortillas, winding up with a little tiste — a mixture of chocolate, sugar, and corn meal, diluted in water — from the fantastically carved jicaras they carried tied with a string run through the button holes of their jackets or trowsers [sic].[34]

Méndez's scouts reported that a small body of Legitimist horsemen, about ten in all, occupied the village. Walker ordered an immediate attack, and twenty of his men, using the rain to mask their approach, stormed Tola, killing or wounding most of the enemy with only two or three escaping to warn the main body at Rivas of the filibusters' approach. The next morning, June 29, 1855, the Phalanx, "eager for a fight, pressed forward briskly" and attacked the Legitimist stronghold.[35]

Several cocoa plantations and mansion houses, places such as Santa Ursula and Maleano, surrounded Rivas, one of Nicaragua's premier lakeside towns. The town itself, which had a Spanish central plaza and several government buildings, was defended by about 500 of Castellón's best troops. The plan was for Captain Hornsby and his company to storm Santa Ursula and the

Walker attacks Rivas. *Leslie's*

commanding heights above Rivas. Then Colonel Walker, Lieutenant Colonel Kewan, Major Crocker, and Captain Anderson, with the main body, reinforced by Colonel Méndez's contingent, were to charge down the main street, driving the enemy before them, and take the central plaza while Hornsby's men, on the heights, provided covering fire. Colonel Ramirez, following with most of the native contingent, was to shadow the filibusters and protect their flanks and rear.[36]

In the attack which followed, Walker's men charged down the main street, red banners waving, and fought their way through the narrow and muddy streets which lined the plaza. Walker, riding forward on his horse, cajoled the filibusters to move forward and finish the job. Major Crocker, his chin bleeding from the graze of a bullet and one arm hanging useless from another bullet wound, exclaimed: "Colonel, the men falter; I cannot get them on!" Looking back for Ramirez, Walker was stunned to find that he had fled from the battle, leaving him and Méndez to fend for themselves.[37]

The situation was now critical for Walker. While his men had killed or wounded over 200 of the white-ribboned enemy who were now strewn about the muddy streets or within the squalid adobe houses, he had lost fifteen of his own men, including the fearless Colonel Kewan and, before long, Major

Crocker. To make matters even worse, Walker's forty or so surviving filibusters were up against a superior enemy that was growing hourly from reinforcements marching up from Virgin Bay. Walker therefore reluctantly ordered a retreat, and his men fought their way up from the plaza to Santa Ursula and temporary safety.[38]

Now cut off and alone in the jungle, Walker, with the help of Méndez, led what was left of his filibusters south for the Transit Route, reaching it the next day. There he learned through Méndez's scouts that San Juan del Sur, only a few miles to the west, was clear of all troops, White or Red, and marched into the town. He later remembered: "A few minutes after sunset, the people of San Juan del Sur beheld about forty-five men, several of them wounded — some without hats, others without shoes — all of them travel-stained and clinging to their rifles, defile through the streets of the town and take up their quarters in the barracks near the beach."[39]

Wanting to get as far away from Rivas as possible, the filibusters hijacked the Costa Rican schooner *San Jose*, sailed back to Realejo, and then marched on to Chinandega to recuperate. There they were disheartened to hear that General Castellón, Vanderbilt's ally, had died of cholera, and that they were now

Filibusters resting in Chinandega. *Leslie's*

expected to follow the dictates of General José Muñoz, a man who both Méndez and Walker despised. Fortuitously, during this upheaval, Captain Bruno von Natzmer, a former Prussian cavalryman, and twenty-five more fair-skinned adventurers who also disliked Muñoz, joined Walker.[40]

Natzmer would prove invaluable to Walker. He had lived in Nicaragua for six years as a businessman and knew the ins and outs of local politics. The German entreated Walker to snub Muñoz and to instead install himself as Nicaragua's president, which could be easily done if he made the proper alliances with various factions of the country. These included a few key plantation owners, men such as José Valle, and the peasantry, who were sick of the war and depressed economic conditions.[41]

As the situation rapidly developed, Walker accepted Méndez's and Natzmer's counsel and determined to take control of the country. He would still overthrow the British-backed Whites as originally planned, but would instead install himself as president, seize the Transit Route, and build the proposed canal, thus gaining control of American east-west travel. Under Walker's tutelage, it was thought, Nicaragua would become the gem of the Caribbean. And with the added power, Walker could then expand his filibuster kingdom to include all of Central America.[42]

Like Roberdeau Wheat, William Walker believed that he had a destiny to fulfill; that his life would be great, and that he would do great things for his beloved South. Walker would, as alluded to earlier, "regenerate"—that is, "Americanize" or "Southernize"—all of Central America by establishing and maintaining a "powerful and compact Southern federation, based on military principles." He would create a region in which like-minded American colonizers would become the new benevolent landowners who would lead Central America out of the dark ages. The "mixed Hispanic population" would be exterminated by "natural selection," the Indians would work for the "ruling race" (i.e., whites) as free laborers, and the whites would be rooted or "fixed" to the soil by importing African slaves.[43] Walker wrote:

> If Spain, then, failed to leave her colonies with the internal force or system capable of reorganizing their independent society, the plan immediately suggests itself of applying to them the rules which have constructed a firm and harmonious civilization where the Anglo-American has found himself on the same soil with one of the colored races. The introduction of Negro-slavery into Nicaragua would furnish a supply of constant and reliable labor requisite for the cultivation of tropical products. With the Negro-slave as his companion, the white man would become fixed to the soil; and they would together destroy the power of the mixed race which is the bane of the country. The pure Indian would readily fall into the new social organization; for he does not aim at political power, and only asks to be protected in the fruits of his industry. The Indian of Nicaragua, in his fidelity and docility, as well as in his capacity for labor, approaches nearly the Negroes of the United States; and he would readily assume the manners and habits of the latter. In fact, the manners of the Indian toward the ruling race are now more submissive than those of the American Negro toward his master.[44]

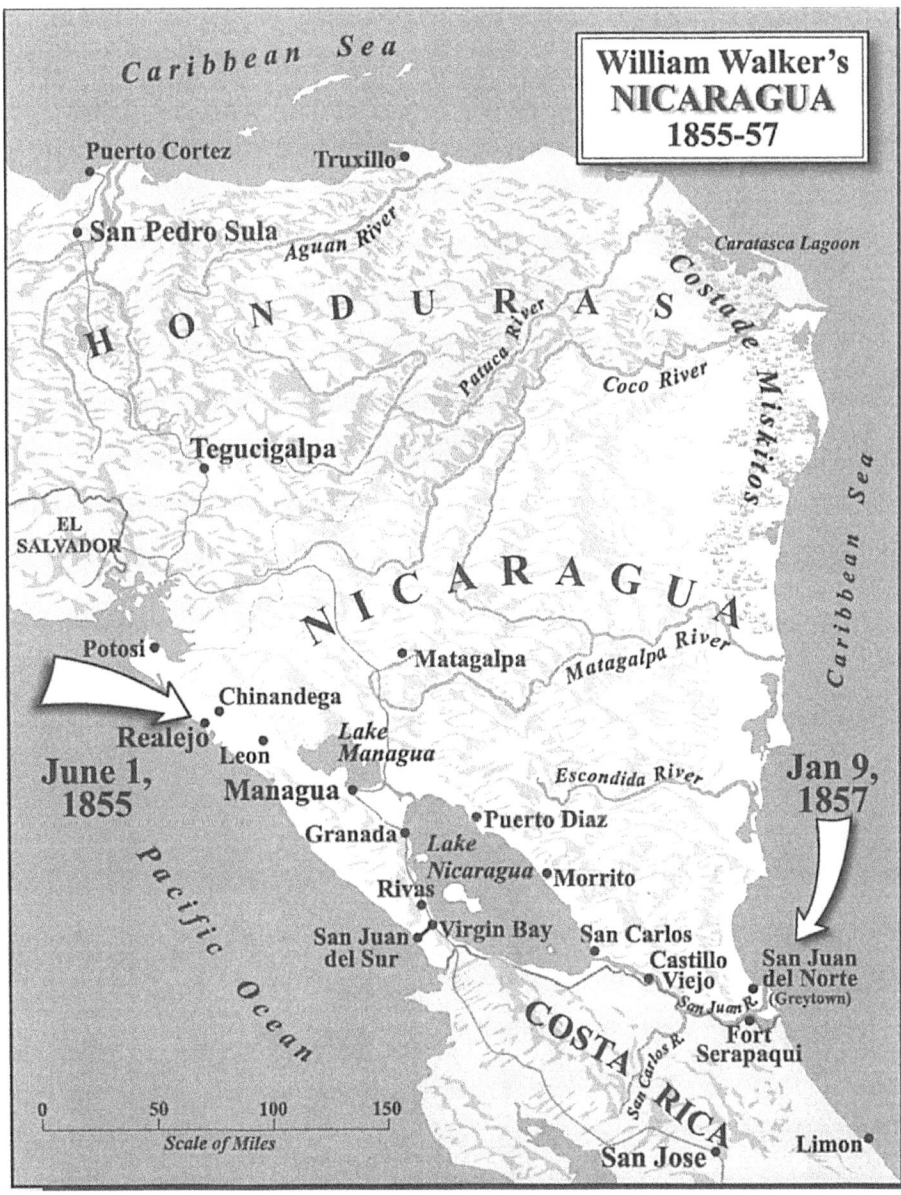

With all this in mind, Walker's daring filibusters ignored General Muñoz and sailed back down to San Juan del Sur. With control of this important port town, Walker now had a link to the outside world and was able to get word back to San Francisco of his ambitious plan. The newspapers proclaimed Walker as "the destined conqueror of Central America" and compared him to Cortés and Pizarro. About one hundred men, fortune seekers mostly, but mixed with a few veteran mercenaries such as Charles Frederick Henningsen, Charles Gilman, Parker French, George Davidson, Callender Fayssoux, Archibald Brewster, John Waters, Thomas Dolan, George Caston, William Williamson, Theodore O'Hara, Louis Schlessinger, and John Walton, flocked to Walker's banner in San Juan del Sur.[45]

With almost 250 well-armed and equipped filibusters and a similar number of native troops now at his disposal, and having received the exciting news that President Chamorro, like General Castellón, had recently died of cholera, Walker resolved to push up the Transit Route, take Virgin Bay, shanghai one of Vanderbilt's lake steamers, and storm Granada, the White capital.[46] On October 11, 1855, the filibusters easily captured the bay as the Whites had by and large abandoned the place after Chamorro's death. Once Walker's zealots consolidated their position, they waited until nightfall, hijacked the S.S. *Virgin* (which flew the U.S. flag), and piled aboard for the fifty-mile journey to Granada. Arriving soon after midnight the next evening, the filibusters disembarked about three miles north of the town and headed for their objective through the noisy, wet, and foreboding jungle.[47]

The epic battle for Granada didn't last long; a few shots, if that. In fact, disheartened Legitimists, "completely taken by surprise, threw off their [white]

Walker takes Virgin Bay. *Leslie's*

1. *Tiger Roots*   25

Filibuster army in Virgin Bay. *Leslie's*

Filibuster army on Lake Nicaragua. *Leslie's*

Walker's victory march in Granada, the White capital. *Leslie's*

coats ... dropped their blankets [and ran away]." With the town now in his hands, the puritanical Walker quickly declared martial law and threatened strict punishment for rape, looting, drunkenness, or abuse, especially by his own men. Impressed by his benevolence, some of the more stalwart white leaders of the town, including one Irena O'Hara, who eventually became Walker's lover and confidante, joined the filibusters. On June 29, 1856, after a few more months of intrigue, Walker was elected president of Nicaragua with a vote of 16,000 for and 7,000 against. Among his first acts as chief executive, Walker terminated Nicaragua's membership in the "National Representation of Central America" and opened the country to American colonization (going so far as sending land agents to California and Louisiana). He also reinstated slave choice, seized all land to benefit the filibusters and future American settlers, publicly announced his intent to pursue an *entente cordiale* with the U.S. to help keep the French and British out of the region, and nationalized (i.e., confiscated) the Accessory Transit Company, proclaiming Nicaragua a "truly sovereign Republic."[48]

It was the last point that drew the attention of Cornelius Vanderbilt. He was not about to allow a girlish, upstart freebooter to take over his operations in Nicaragua. Marshaling the resources of the United States (Democrat Franklin Pierce was president), Costa Rica, El Salvador, Honduras, Guatemala, and what was left of Muñoz's forces in Nicaragua, Vanderbilt moved to destroy Walker, his own creation, once and for all. In September 1856, almost a year after Walker's coup, the armies of Vanderbilt's Central American allies invaded Nicaragua by landing at San Juan del Sur and del Norte, both ends of the country. From these points they moved inland and headed for Grenada.[49] President Walker, pleading to fellow Americans for support, commented:

> You have, doubtless, learned from newspaper how pacific was the policy Nicaragua proposed to pursue towards the other states of Central America. Notwithstanding all our overtures of peace, the neighboring governments showed themselves, if not positively, at least negatively, hostile to [my] administration. It [has been] constantly asserted not only here, but also throughout Central America, that the states were stimulated by English and French agents against the government of Nicaragua. The government of Costa Rica has yet to declare war against Nicaragua; yet it has invaded our territories, and has murdered American citizens who have never forfeited the protection of the U.S. Government. Costa Rica says Americans shall not immigrate to Nicaragua, and take arms in her service. It remains to be seen whether she can sustain herself in so singular a position.
> In such a war as they are now waging against us, there can be one result. They may destroy my whole force — a circumstance which I deem almost or quite impossible — they may now kill every American now in Nicaragua, but the seed is sown, and not all the forces of Spanish America can prevent the fruit from coming to maturity. The more savage the nature of the war they wage against us, the more certain the result, the more terrible the consequences. I may not live to see the end, but I feel that my countrymen will not permit the result to be doubtful. I know that the great honor and interests of our great country, which, despite of the foreign service I am engaged in, I still love to call my own, are involved in the present struggle. That honor must be preserved is inviolate, and those interests must be jealously maintained. Nothing but our own sense of justice of the cause we are engaged in, and of its importance to the country of our birth, has enabled us to struggle on as far as we have done. We may perish in the work we have undertaken, and our cause may not be for a time lost, but if we fall, it is in the path of honor. And what is life, or what is success, in comparison with the consciousness of having performed a duty, and of being co-operated, no matter how slightly, in the cause of improvement and progress![50]

By the end of the year, after fighting many desperate defensive battles— in which Chinandega, León, and Granada were razed, countless villages were burned, and hundreds of peasants were killed, raped, or terrorized — it did seem as though Walker would not live to see the end, as the allies had driven his defiant little army to Rivas, surrounding it. Before the jaws snapped totally shut, however, Walker was able to send out one last urgent plea for reinforcement, one like William Travis's at the Alamo twenty years before. This is when Roberdeau Wheat and many of the soon-to-be members of the 1st Louisiana Special Battalion entered the scene.[51]

Samuel Lockridge, Frank Anderson, and Charles Doubleday, three of Walker's original "Fifty-seven"; Roberdeau Wheat, the renowned soldier of fortune from Mexico; and Henry Titus, a Missouri Border Ruffian who had been fighting Yankee "Jay hawkers" in Kansas, answered Walker's clarion call and led a relief expedition of 300 adventurous souls from New York and another 800 from New Orleans. Embarking on the steam ships *Orizaba*, *James Adger*, and *Texas*, Lockridge's and Wheat's filibusters took Greytown on January 9, 1857, and proceeded to fight their way up the San Juan River toward San Carlos and Virgin Bay, taking out a few Costa Rican strong points, such as Fort Serapaqui, along the way. During these operations, which Walker described as being "haphazard and ineffectual," Wheat acted as Lockridge's artillery chief, commanding two captured light guns. By February, the filibusters were working on Castillo Viejo, "Old Fort," when two U.S. Navy steam frigates under Commodore Hiram Paulding, sent by newly-elected Democratic president James Buchanan to rescue Walker from the clutches of Vanderbilt's allies, sailed up the river to extinguish Lockridge's and Wheat's relief efforts.[52]

To facilitate the removal of these American freebooters, Buchanan wisely offered free passage and freedom from prosecution to the filibusters if they agreed to leave Nicaragua post haste. The outgunned crusaders, including Wheat, reluctantly took up the president's offer and embarked on the American steamer *Illinois*, arriving in New York City on April 29, 1857.[53]

With Lockridge and Wheat out of his hair, Paulding was able to forge a

San Juan River. *Leslie's*

tenuous agreement between the allies and Walker's besieged army. The allies would be allowed to establish a new government in Nicaragua, and, in return, Walker's men were to surrender directly to Commodore Paulding, and not to the Central Americans. Once all agreed to the terms, what was left of Walker's army, about four hundred half-starved and disease-stricken men, were loaded aboard several American steamers for transit to New Orleans or New York City.[54]

Arriving in New Orleans on May 27, 1857, Walker was welcomed as a conquering hero, a man who had been betrayed by his own government. In a speech given at the upscale Saint Charles Hotel in front of a crowd that reportedly numbered almost 10,000, Walker extolled the well-wishers to keep the faith and pledged to outfit another expedition.[55] He proclaimed:

> I call upon you, therefore, to execute this mission ... to regenerate the amalgamated race ... to Americanize Central America.... I feel that my duty calls upon me to return to [Nicaragua]. All who are nearest and dearest to me are there ... those who lie dead beneath the jungle foliage, in the mango groves, in the sugar cane, or in the rubble of Rivas.... There sleep the men, soldiers, and officers whose rights I cannot fail to have respected.... I call upon you then, fellow-citizens, male and female, whose friends and relatives have perished, to lend your aid; upon the men to assist ... in carrying out and perfecting the Americanization of Central America.[56]

While Walker traveled throughout the rest of the South to further his goals, Wheat, still up in New York City and most probably embarrassed by the fiasco, abandoned the filibusters' cause. He instead accepted a job to market inventor James Haskell's breech-loading "Accelerating Cannon" to the U.S. Army and Navy and to governments that were friendly to the United States. Wheat was even able to sell a few of these intricate weapons to his old friend in Mexico, President Álvarez.[57]

While Wheat was dealing in arms, in November 1857 Walker had raised enough filibusters, just under 300, including Hornsby, Anderson, Natzmer, and Fayssoux, and embarked from Mobile, Alabama, aboard the steamer *Fashion* for his second expedition to Nicaragua. One militant Southerner, hopeful of Walker's success, proclaimed: "Thousands of hearts are throbbing with anxiety for [Walker's] success as it is believed that the establishment of Anglo-Saxon rule in Nicaragua will add to the commercial prosperity of the South and the extension and safety of our peculiar institutions."[58]

Taking Greytown and the Old Fort, Walker continued up the San Juan River toward San Carlos and Lake Nicaragua when his former savior, Commodore Paulding, captured him and his army. Walker was subsequently shipped back to New Orleans where he, like Wheat a few years before, was tried in federal court for breaking the 1818 Neutrality Law. This time Walker was defended by New Orleans attorney Pierre Soulé, a fellow Golden Knight and a one-time ambassador to Spain. In the short trial that followed, a jury acquitted Walker of all charges.[59]

In 1860 Walker embarked on his third and final filibuster expedition to Nicaragua. Sailing past the Mosquito Coast of British Honduras, Walker was snagged by the Royal Navy and, surprisingly, handed over to Honduran authorities. On September 12, 1860, the "Grey-Eyed Man of Destiny" was unceremoniously executed by a native firing squad in Truxillo.[60]

In the wake of Walker's death, Roberdeau Wheat once again left the country to sell his services. This time he took a steamer bound for Europe to join General Giuseppe Garibaldi, who was in the process of helping his king, Victor-Emmanuel II of Piedmont-Sardinia, unify the Italian peninsula. At this stage of the War of Italian Unification, Victor-Emmanuel and Garibaldi, with French help, had driven the hated Austrians out of the northern Italian principality of Lombardy and had annexed it to Piedmont-Sardinia. They were now going after the rest of the Italy: Naples and Sicily, Tuscany, Parma, Modena, Romagna, Marches, Umbria, Venetia, and Rome.[61]

This was not to be a war of conquest, the king promised, but one of freedom and unity. The new and larger kingdom would be a constitutional monarchy, one with a parliament, elected by the citizenry, which would restrict the king's powers. There had been a growing Italian Republican movement for years, and these men, discreetly spread throughout Italy, pledged to help Victor-Emmanuel in his unification efforts. In the spring of 1860, southern Italian Bersagliari, spurred by King Emmanuel's successes in the north, rebelled against the Spanish-supported king of Naples and Sicily. In order to support these insurgents, Victor Emmanuel sent General Garibaldi and his now-famous "Gallant One Thousand" to the island, where they landed at Marsala on May 11, 1860. There the red-shirted Garibaldinis pushed inland, gathering nearly 800 native Bersagliari, and defeated forces loyal to the Neapolitan king at the battles of Calatafimi and Milazzo, securing the island for the Republican cause. In August, with the help of the British navy, Garibaldi crossed the Straits of Messina and marched on Naples. Gathering even more volunteers, creating an army of over 20,000, Garibaldi took the city on September 7. He then drove north into Umbria, defeating the enemy at Castelfidardo on September 18 and at the Volturno River on October 2, 1860.[62]

After these important victories, Roberdeau Wheat and some 600 British, Irish, or American volunteers, including Robert Going Atkins, an Irish adventurer and soon-to-be member of Wheat's 1st Louisiana Special Battalion, landed in Naples to reinforce the Republican army. Although the war by this time was nearly over, the English-speaking volunteers were enthusiastically accepted into Garibaldi's fold. Wheat himself was commissioned a brigadier general in the Italian army and was present at Victor-Emmanuel's coronation ceremony, which formally declared him king of Italy, in November 1860.[63]

As Victor-Emmanuel was crowned king of a unified Italy, the United States was being ripped apart in the wake of Abraham Lincoln's election as president. Incensed that Lincoln was against the spread of slavery into the western territories, seven Southern states—South Carolina, Mississippi, Georgia, Alabama, Florida, Louisiana, and Texas—brazenly declared their independence from the United States and began forming their own nation, the Confederate States of America. Expecting that this would no doubt start a war and offer employment for the errant soldiers of fortune who were serving in Italy, men such as Philip Kearny, Gustav Paul Cluseret, Felix Agnus, Valery Sulakowski, Percy Wyndham, and Roberdeau Wheat boarded various packets to America to sell their services to the constituent sides. For Wheat, ardent Southern patriot that he was, there was no question as to which side he'd fight for, as he undoubtedly relished the chance to filibuster the U.S. government out of his native South. Sailing to New York, Wheat made his way down to New Orleans and reopened his old recruiting station. This new conflict, the War for Southern Independence, would be the climax of Roberdeau Wheat's life and career: the ultimate filibuster.[64]

Pierre Soulé, Louisiana senator and U.S. ambassador to Spain, who defended William Walker in Federal court. He, along with ambassador to Britain James Buchanan, authored the notorious Ostend Manifesto, which threatened war with Spain unless it ceded Cuba to the United States. *Library of Congress*

2

Formation of "Wheat's Tigers"

> *I got my first glimpse at Wheat's battalion from New Orleans. They were all Irish and were dressed in Zouave dress, and were familiarly known as "Tigers," and tigers they were too in human form. I was actually afraid of them, afraid I would meet them somewhere in camp and that they would do to me like they did to Tom Lane of my company — knock me down and stamp me half to death.*
>
> — William McClendon

By the time Wheat made it back to New Orleans in early April 1861, all forts, arsenals, and other federal offices in Louisiana had been seized by the insurgent Confederate government. These included Forts Jackson and St. Philip on the lower Mississippi, Forts Pike and Macomb on the Rigolets, just north of New Orleans, and the Federal Arsenal at Baton Rouge, which contained over 50,000 small arms. Existing home guard militia units that were not already mobilized were called up, and entirely new volunteer formations were raised. At the time, the standard practice was for a man of ability or position to recruit, uniform, and train a company of one hundred volunteers, men from the same locale, and muster them into state and then national service for an extended period of time — usually one year. A company, whether it be infantry, artillery, or cavalry, generally consisted of one captain, one first lieutenant, two second lieutenants, four sergeants, four corporals, two musicians, and eighty or so privates. The men elected all leadership positions, including captain.[1]

The selected captain was expected to uniform his volunteers through local contractors. This was called the commutation system. Because there were no set regulations at the time, each company created its own uniform design. While most Louisiana volunteer units chose to clothe themselves in gray wool short jackets, trousers, and kepis trimmed with black or blue cotton tape, others, especially from New Orleans, with its strong French influence, chose to model themselves after the French army with blue wool frock coats, red wool trousers, and red kepis.[2] A visitor to New Orleans remembered:

> It is scarcely possible to imagine a more heterogeneous-looking body of men; the variety of uniform, of clothing and of accouterments were as great as if a specimen

squad had been taken from the battalions of [*la Grande Armée*] of 1812. The general effect of the men and of their habiliments is decidedly French.... The streets are full of Turcos, Zouaves, Chasseurs; walls are covered with placards of volunteer companies.... In fact, New Orleans looks like a suburb of the camp of Chalons. Tailors are busy night and day making uniforms.[3]

Without doubt the most exotic units raised in New Orleans during the early months of the war were Zouave formations. Zouaves (pronounced zwav) were originally select units of the French army which, by 1861, were considered among the elite fighting forces of the world. When France took control of the Arab city of Algiers in 1830, it had enlisted the support of a fiercely independent mountain tribe which called itself the *Zouaoua* (pronounced ZWA-wa). These native Zouaves were organized into two battalions under French officers to maintain order among the Arab population. By 1835 the Zouave battalions evolved to consist of four companies of native Zouaves and two companies of Frenchmen, all uniformed in traditional Zouave dress. By 1841 the native Zouaves were segregated out by government decree to form *Tirailleurs Algériens* or Turco battalions, and the so-called Zouave battalions thereafter consisted only of Frenchmen. In 1852 three French Zouave regiments of three battalions each were raised; the 1st Regiment was posted in Blidah, the 2nd in Oran, and the 3rd in Constantine.[4]

The French Zouave uniform generally consisted of a red fez, a short blue wool jacket, red wool pantaloons, and white canvas leggings. The fez itself, called a *chechia*, was made of red felt and had a dark blue wool tassel attached to its top. The jacket was made of the same dark blue wool as other French uniforms but was cut shorter and made to be worn open. It was trimmed with one-half inch cotton tape that formed an ornate design consisting of a loop leading into a trefoil, which the French called a *tombeau* (pronounced tom-BOW). The color of the tombeau distinguished the Zouave regiments from one another, that is, red for the 1st, white for the 2nd, and blue for the 3rd. In 1855 a fourth Zouave regiment was raised, drawing the best soldiers from the other three, and it was added to the French Imperial Guard. Both its tassel and *tombeau* were yellow.[5]

Under the jacket, French Zouaves wore a collarless vest, called a *gilet* (zhee-LAY) that was made from a thinner grade of blue wool. It was trimmed around the collar and down the front with the same color *tombeau* as the jacket. Over the vest, the Zouaves wore a light blue sash ten feet long by ten inches wide, called a *ceinture*, that served three purposes: to help carry heavy packs, to act as a wrap around during cold desert nights, and to help support their distinctive loose fitting trousers, called *serouel*, which were made of dark red wool. The *serouel* were tucked into white canvas leggings which were fastened with buttons. To help hold the leggings up, the Zouaves would often strap on a pair of leather grieves, called *jambières* (zhawm-bee-AIR), just below the knees.[6]

French Zouaves were trained primarily in light infantry tactics collectively referred to as *chasseur à pied*. Proponents of this tactic believed that, with the increased range and use of the rifle musket, battlefield success could only be achieved through quick maneuver, malleable formations, and aggressive action. Zouaves were thus taught to begin engaging targets at about three hundred yards, load while they advanced fifty yards at a time at the double quick, kneel, aim, and fire again. They were to do this until they reached about one hundred yards from the opposing line where they were to fire their last volley, concentrate, charge, and smash the enemy with their expert use of the bayonet. The salient points of *chasseur à pied*, then, were rapid movement and aggressive action rather than simply standing still one hundred yards from the enemy and exchanging volleys. Maneuver, fire, and charge decisively: these, as in the days of the Roman legions, were the keys to victory.[7]

During the Crimean War (1854–55) and the War for Italian Unification (1858–59), French Zouaves proved themselves to the world by using these aggressive tactics at the battles of Alma, Inkerman, Sebastopol, the Malakoff, Magenta, and Solferino. U.S. Army captain George McClellan, who had been sent by the American government to observe the Crimean War, stated in 1855: "[Zouaves are the] finest light infantry that Europe can produce ... the *beau idéal* of a soldier."[8]

Inspired by these gallant warriors, two groups, Colonel Elmer Ellsworth's Zouave Cadets, a Chicago-based militia unit, and an acting troupe, shrewdly calling itself the "Inkerman Zouaves," were formed to show off the French Zouaves' distinctive uniform and drill to American audiences. Touring throughout the country, the genteel style and impressive drill of these sartorial *Zouave d'Afrique* captivated thousands and inspired several standing militia organizations to convert over to the Zouave concept, uniform and all. The Inkerman Zouaves, for example, who often performed in New Orleans, so moved Anatole Avegno, a wealthy Italian immigrant, that he converted his existing six-company home guard militia battalion, part of the Governor's Guard, into a Zouave formation.[9]

Closely copying the Inkerman Zouaves, Avegno's gentlemen uniformed themselves in "soft red cotton flannel skull caps with dark blue tassels that hung down behind instead of on the side," dark blue wool Zouave jackets trimmed with red cotton tape (but no *tombeau*), dark blue wool *gilet* trimmed in red, French blue sashes, brick red *serouel*, black leather *jambières*, and white canvas leggings. Following in Avegno's footsteps with Louisiana's secession several months later, another immigrant, George Auguste Gaston de Coppens from French Martinique, raised his own battalion of Zouaves, the 1st Louisiana Zouave Battalion, and offered it up for Confederate service in March 1861.[10]

Soon after Coppens's formation was raised, Roberdeau Wheat returned to New Orleans with the intent to raise a company and then a full regiment for Confederate service. And once he proved his mettle in battle, he hoped to gain

"New Orleans and Vicinity." The five base companies of Wheat's Battalion were initially assembled at Camp Davis, which is near the docks, middle left, along the broad avenue called Common Street. The suburbs of Algiers, MacDonough, and Belleville are across the Mississippi River to the right. The Gulf of Mexico, the Ringolets and Lakes Pontchartrain and Borgne are in the background. *USAMHI*

a brigadier's star.[11] On April 18, 1861, just a few days after U.S. Fort Sumter was attacked by Confederate forces in an expression of their sovereign rights, the New Orleans *Daily Crescent* carried the following announcement:

> We understand that our friend, Gen. C.R. Wheat, is about to raise a company of volunteers, to serve in the Army of Louisiana. His headquarters are on 64 [Saint] Charles [Street], where we advise all friends of a glorious cause to repair and enlist.[12]

Wheat called his company the Old Dominion Guards to commemorate his native state's recent secession from the United States and adjunction with the Southern Confederacy. With the help of Obedia Plummer Miller, a well-established New Orleans attorney, Wheat quickly recruited fifty or so men to his company, mostly expatriate Virginians, men such as Henry S. Carey, a relative of Thomas Jefferson's, Richard Dickinson, who would become Wheat's adjutant, and Bruce Putnam, a towering man who became Wheat's intimidating sergeant major. While Miller, Carey, Dickinson, and Putnam continued recruiting for the Guards, Wheat was able to attract four already-forming companies to his banner—Captain Robert Harris's Walker Guards, Captain Alexander White's Tiger Rifles, Captain Henry Gardner's Delta Rangers, and Captain

Harry Chaffin's Rough and Ready Rangers—which were assembling a few blocks away at Camp Davis on the grounds of the "Old Marine Hospital/Insane Asylum/Iron Works" between Common and Gravier streets at South Broad (today's Camp) Street. Many of the men of these precocious units, unlike those from the more upscale Old Dominion Guards, were former filibusters who had served with Wheat or Walker in Nicaragua. Since the late campaigns, they had slipped back into their old jobs as shiphands, stokers, dock workers, watermen, draymen, screwmen, stevedores, or simple laborers on the New Orleans waterfront. As such, they were considered to be the lowest members of white Southern society. One disgusted observer proclaimed that many of Wheat's recruits were "the lowest scum of the lower Mississippi ... adventurous wharf rats, thieves, and outcasts ... and bad characters generally."[13]

When work was available, these men, mostly recent Irish immigrants, were often relegated to do the most dangerous of tasks, such as servicing decrepit steam engines on Mississippi River packets or digging canals or drainage ditches in the fetid swamps of the lower Mississippi because slaves were too valuable to lose. "The Niggers are worth too much to be risked," recounted one calculating steamboat pilot. "If the Paddies are knocked overboard or get their backs broke nobody loses anything." Another boat pilot explained that the reason why slaves were not used as stokers on the aged packets was because "every time a boiler bursts [the owners] would lose so many dollars' worth of slaves; whereas by getting Irishmen at a dollar-a-day they pay for the article [the Irish worker] as they get it, and if it's blown up, they get another."[14]

In this social hierarchy, Irish laborers, stevedores, and dock workers were at the very bottom. Immediately above them were the ship hands, watermen, and stokers, followed by the draymen, who hauled bales of cotton or barrels of sugar, molasses, pork, or flour from the Mississippi docks to the numerous warehouses of New Orleans. Because screwmen were skilled laborers, they received higher wages than stevedores or ship hands and were considered to be at the top of societal ladder. Working in gangs of five, many of them exclusively Irish, the screwmen went into the holds of the cotton ships where they used large jackscrews to compress the bales into the smallest possible size. This was a dangerous way of earning a living, for in the cramped quarters below deck a screwman had little space to dodge a wayward bale. Broken limbs were common, and occasionally a heavy bale crushed the life out of a worker.[15]

The Walker Guards were raised under the auspices of Robert Harris, one of Wheat's former comrades in the Filibuster Wars. As the name denotes, many of Harris's recruits had "smelt powder ... saw the elephant ... [and] felt bullets" in Nicaragua. Since the late war, Harris reportedly had become the operator of a bawdy gambling establishment along the waterfront. The Tiger Rifles, the Delta Rangers, and the Rough and Ready Rangers, however, Wheat's other cohorts, made no special claim to fame. All that is known about them, other than the fact that they were largely Irish shiphands, dock workers, stevedores,

One of the many docks along Front Levee. Note the bails of cotton, the drivers, and the Mississippi River steam boats. Captain White's company of Tiger Rifles was exclusively recruited from this bustling area. *Louisiana State Museum*

or draymen, is that the commander of the Rangers, Henry Gardner, had signed a petition which called on the governor of Louisiana to convene a secession convention and declared that the intrepid commander of the Tiger Rifles, Alexander White, was a known felon and river pilot. Similar to William Walker in stature, the fiery "White," if that was his real name, was reportedly "the son of a one-time Southern governor," supposedly from Kentucky. Gardner claimed that, during a game of high-stakes poker in his youth, White had shot a man who accused him of cheating. Through the influence of his supposed family, he was able to escape prosecution as long as he left the state and went underground. Fleeing to New Orleans, the vast Southern metropolis where it was easy to get lost, White purportedly gambled, conned, and boozed his way through life until the war with Mexico, when he enlisted in the U.S. Navy to pilot men and material down to Corpus Christi, Tampico, or Vera Cruz. After his five-year enlistment was up, he settled down, got married, and became the captain of the steamer *Magnolia*, which hauled goods between New Orleans and Vicksburg. During this time White once again lost his temper, severely pistol-whipped a passenger on his steamer, was arrested and convicted, and as a result, ended up in the Louisiana State Penitentiary in Baton Rouge. By March 1861, with Louisiana's secession and the subsequent U.S. blockade, White began to form a company of volunteers around his crew and was even able to rent prime space for a recruiting station at 29 Front Levee, between Gravier and Poydras streets, near the Custom House and Camp Davis.[16]

Wheat, using his gentlemanly appeal, was apparently able to talk Harris, White, Gardner, and Chaffin into forming a battalion under his command with the assurance that all involved would better be able to control their destinies if they acted as one. And with Wheat's eminent stature as a Mexican War veteran, a Southern partisan, a former assemblyman, and a general officer in two foreign armies, they would no doubt get the choice assignments and equipment. So, on April 23, 1861, the *Daily Crescent* carried the following announcement:

> Gen. C.R. Wheat, with reference to raising a battalion, invites such of our friends and citizens generally, as feel an interest in the cause, to call at No. 29 Front Levee

"The [Federal] Custom-House at New Orleans, Seized by the State." The Custom House was on Levee and Canal streets, in the vicinity of Camp Davis. *Louisiana State Museum*

Street, where they will find the material for the first battalion of the States, and one that will make its mark when called upon.[17]

With the deal cut, all commands, including the Old Dominion Guards (originally assembled across from the prestigious St. Charles Hotel), moved their constituent recruiting stations to Captain White's on Front Levee Street, and recruitment became a shared task. To attract even more bellicose souls to

The St. Charles Hotel near Lafayette Square is where filibuster William Walker reportedly preached to 10,000 people in 1857 and where Wheat, across the street, recruited his upscale Old Dominion Guards for the 1st Louisiana Special Battalion in 1861. *Louisiana State Museum*

"The Rowdy in the New Orleans Bar-room." This scene captures the spirit of many of Wheat's recruits who were garnered from such locales. Robert Harris, captain of the Walker Guards, was known to have operated such an establishment. *Leslie's*

his nascent battalion, men who "were actuated more by a spirit of adventure and love of plunder than by love of country," or who filibuster General Henningsen once proclaimed "thought little of charging a battery, pistol in hand," Wheat christened his command "the Tiger Battalion." He then extolled his volunteers—led by Captain White's large company of Tiger Rifles, who had "painted a motto or picture of some sort on [their] ... broad brimmed ... hat[s] such as: A picture of Mose, preparing to let fly with his left hand and fend with his right, and the words, 'Before I Was a Tiger'"—to continue to comb the docks, thoroughfares, alleyways, hotels, poor houses, and jails of the New Orleans waterfront for more recruits. Other slogans that the Tiger Rifles painted on their hats included: "Tiger Bound for Happy Land," "Tiger Will Never Surrender," "A Tiger Forever," "Tiger in Search of a Black Republican," or "Lincoln's Life or a Tiger's Death."[18]

While the men of the ad hoc battalion continued to attract more recruits—and in some instances impressing "known Yankees" into service, shaving their heads—Wheat worked through the Ladies Volunteer Aid Association of New Orleans to help uniform the Walker Guards, the Delta Rangers, and the Old Dominion Guards in red flannel "battle" or "Garibaldi" shirts and jean-wool trousers "of the mixed color known as pepper and salt." For headgear, the men apparently retained their own broad brimmed hats of various earthy tones (except Henry Gardner's Delta Rangers, who were reportedly presented with gray or blue wool kepis and white cotton havelocks). Harry Chaffin's Rough and Ready Rangers were ostensibly uniformed in light gray wool jackets and trousers with matching kepis.[19]

The Tiger Rifles received their uniforms from A. Keene Richards, a wealthy New Orleans businessman. Because he was "so impressed by their drill and appearance" at Camp Davis, Richards elected to outfit White's company in the Zouave fashion: dark blue or light brown wool Zouave jackets (the 1st platoon was apparently outfitted in blue and the 2nd platoon in brown) with red cotton trim, distinctive red flannel fezzes with red tassels, red flannel band-collar shirts with five white porcelain buttons, and outlandish "Wedgwood blue and cream" one-and-one-half-inch vertically striped cottonade pantaloons that would become their signature. They were also provided with blue and white horizontally striped stockings and white canvas leggings.[20]

Most of the lieutenants and captains of the battalion more than likely uniformed themselves in gray wool single breasted frock coats or short jackets with matching trousers, gray or blue wool kepis with stiff black leather bills, red officers' sashes, and white canvas leggings worn over or under the trousers. The officers of the Tiger Rifles probably wore blue wool single-breasted short jackets with red wool trousers, white canvas leggings, and red wool kepis. Wheat chose to wear the uniform of a field grade officer in the Louisiana Volunteer Militia: a red kepi bedecked with appropriate Austrian gold lace, a double-breasted dark blue wool frock coat with brass shoulder scales, and red wool trousers. He also sported a buff general's sash, no doubt to commemorate his past commissions in the Mexican and Italian armies.[21]

While Wheat, Richards, and the ladies were gathering the uniforms, the company commanders arranged to have guidons, banners, or full-blown battle flags made for their units. The Walker Guards' banner was made of "blue silk with a white crescent in the center." The Tiger Rifles' flag consisted of a "gamboling lamb" device with "Gentle As" written derisively above it. The

These "unidentified Confederate soldiers from the Louisiana Tigers Brigade," although more than likely not from Wheat's Battalion, exemplify the persona of the "original Tigers" from the Delta Rangers with their jaunty battle shirts, trousers, kepis, and Irish countenance. *Chicago Historical Society*

Delta Rangers' flag, which became the battalion's color at the battle of Manassas by "the luck of the draw," was a rectangular silk "Stars and Bars" with eight celestial points in a circular pattern.[22]

As the five companies were being filled and uniformed, Wheat moved his volunteers to Camp Walker at the Metairie (pronounced met-are-E) Race Course and Fairgrounds in the center of the city near Carondolet Canal and Bayou John. On May 10, 1861, Wheat was elected major by his fellow company commanders (Obedia Miller becoming captain of the Old Dominion Guards), and state officials officially recognized his battalion. On May 14 the battalion was moved eighty miles north by rail to Camp Moore in Saint Helena Parish,

Above left: "Tiger Drummer." ***Battles and Leaders of the Civil War.*** *Right:* French-born Captain León Joseph Frémaux, Co. A, 8th Louisiana painted the famous "Tiger Rifles" watercolor. The battle shirt that Frémaux is wearing closely matches the type that was issued to the Walker Guards, the Delta Rangers, and the Old Dominion Guards of Wheat's Battalion in 1861. *USAMHI*

near the town of Tangipahoa and the Mississippi border. The encampment, named after Louisiana's secessionist governor Thomas Overton Moore, was the central depot for organizing, training, and mustering Louisiana volunteer units for Confederate service.

Upon arrival, the Tigers were issued newly-fabricated Louisiana Pelican

Left: Captain Alexander White, commander of the Tiger Rifles, holds a cane in his right hand, wears an open double-breasted gray short jacket, and sports Austrian lace on his left sleeve. His red kepi has a fairly large Bengal Tiger device and the brass letters "RIFLES" across its front. This photo was probably taken in the winter of 1861-62. Photographed by Claude Levet. *Confederate Memorial Hall, New Orleans*

Above: The Delta Rangers' Stars and Bars was used as the battalion's colors at the battle of Manassas by "luck of the draw." The color bearer, Lt. Austin Eastman, ripped this flag from its staff and draped it over Wheat, who was horribly wounded. The bloodstains are still discernible. Photographed by Claude Levet *Confederate Memorial Hall, New Orleans*

2. Formation of "Wheat's Tigers"

Camp Walker on the grounds of Metairie Racecourse/Fairgrounds. Located east of the docks near Bayou Jean, Camp Walker became the primary mustering station of all New Orleans units for Confederate service. Here is where Wheat was elected major and his battalion was officially recognized by the state. The track's grandstand is in the background. Photographed by Claude Levet. *Confederate Memorial Hall, New Orleans*

Plate or fork-tongue belts, cartridge boxes, cap boxes, and knapsacks which were manufactured by the New Orleans–based Magee and Kneass or James Cosgrove Leather Companies. They were also issued their weapons. While the Walker Guards, the Delta Rangers, the Old Dominion Guards, and the Rough and Ready Rangers seem to have been issued either M1842 muskets or aged M1816 conversion muskets with socket bayonets, the men of the Tiger Rifles, Wheat's chosen skirmishers, were issued the coveted M1841 "Mississippi" Rifle, made by the Robbins and Lawrence Gun Company of Connecticut. Governor Moore's insurgents had seized these accurate weapons, among the best in service at the time, from the Federal Arsenal at Baton Rouge in January 1861.[23]

The M1841, originally manufactured in Harpers Ferry, Virginia, was America's first military percussion rifle and had many different names. Its most famous, "Mississippi," was derived from its successful use in repelling a full-scale Mexican attack at the battle of Buena Vista by Colonel Jefferson Davis's

1st Mississippi Regiment (and then charging with bowie knives). The rifle was also called the Windsor Rifle, the Harpers Ferry Rifle, and the Yaeger Rifle. The M1841 was a muzzle-loading, percussion cap, .54 caliber rifle that measured 48.5 inches in length and weighed about ten pounds. Since it was designed to be a light infantry or skirmishing weapon, the barrel was browned and no bayonet lug was affixed. To offset their absence of bayonets, the Tigers were either issued or brought along their own bowie-style knives, implements which were described as "murderous-looking ... with heavy blades ... twenty inches long with double edged points ... and solid long handles."[24]

With their weapons and equipment in hand, the men of Wheat's Battalion were trained in the latest light and heavy infantry techniques by the Old Filibuster himself in the pine stands which surrounded Camp Moore. Once their exhausting and sometimes frustrating sessions were over, many of the Tigers often drank, played cards, and got into fights with themselves or other units. One man scoffed that the Tigers were "the worst men I ever saw.... I understand that they are mostly wharf rats from New Orleans, and Major Wheat is the only man who can do anything with them. They were constantly fighting with each other. They were always ready to fight, and it made little difference to them who they fought." Private William Trahern of the up-country Tensas Rifles (soon-to-be Company D, 6th Louisiana) claimed that he once heard Wheat declare: "If you don't get to your places, and behave as soldiers should, I will cut your hands off with this sword!" One man was in fact so afraid of Wheat's belligerent filibusters that he stayed as far away from their encampment as possible. He later wrote: "I got my first glimpse at Wheat's battalion from New Orleans. They were all Irish and were dressed in Zouave dress [sic], and were familiarly known as 'Tigers,' and tigers they were too in human form. I was actually afraid of them, afraid I would meet them somewhere in camp and that they would do to me like they did to Tom Lane of my company — knock me down and stamp me half to death."[25]

As the Tiger Battalion meshed at Camp Moore, five other men with less military experience than Wheat were commissioned colonels, and their assembled companies were mobilized into regiments for Confederate service. No doubt embarrassed and frustrated, Wheat was spurred to desperate action. On June 6, 1861, he made a creative deal with the state to officially commission him a major of volunteers and to recognize his five companies temporarily as the "1st *Special* Battalion, Louisiana Volunteers." With the special or temporary status secured, Wheat hoped to attract four or five more companies and become the colonel of the soon-to-be organized 8th Louisiana Regiment.[26]

In the political wrangling that followed, Wheat's rowdy dock workers seem to have repelled potential allies to their cause as Henry Kelly, a retired U.S. Army officer from northern Louisiana, became the commander of the 8th Regiment. With Kelly's ascension, on or about June 8, Captain Jonathan W. Buhoup's company of Catahoula Guerrillas voted to leave Kelly's command

and threw in its lot with the Tiger Battalion. As the Guerrillas were primarily the sons of native-born planters or were doctors, lawyers, farmers, overseers, or artisans from Catahoula Parish in northern Louisiana, they were complete social opposites from the majority of the members of Wheat's Battalion. Originally intending to become part of a cavalry regiment, the Guerrillas outfitted themselves in gray wool short jackets, matching mounted trousers, gray wool kepis, and riding boots, and, like the Tiger Rifles, were armed with stout Mississippi Rifles, looking much like dismounted dragoons.[27] Buhoup had lobbied hard for John R. Liddell, a prominent Catahoula Parish planter, to be colonel of the 8th Regiment with himself as its lieutenant colonel. When he and Liddell failed in their bids to gain field commissions, however, Buhoup used what was left of his political leverage to have his company transferred to the Special Battalion, where he hoped to gain a field commission once it was converted into a full regiment.[28]

With six companies now under his belt — an interesting cross-section of Louisiana society which David French Boyd of the soon-to-be organized 9th Louisiana perceptively described as being "a unique body, representing every grade of society and every kind of man, from the princely gentleman who commanded them down to the thief and cutthroat released from parish prison on condition he would join Wheat ... a motley herd of humanity" — Wheat resolved to get his menagerie to Virginia, the seat of war, as soon as possible. Six other Louisiana infantry formations, the 1st, 2nd, 5th, 6th, 7th, and 8th regiments, had already been dispatched from the Pelican State to the Old Dominion, and Wheat did not want to miss the grand battle that was supposed to win Southern independence in one fell swoop.[29]

On June 13, 1861, not a week after his battalion's formal organization, Wheat loaded five of his six companies (the Rough and Ready Rangers were retained at Camp Moore because it failed to sufficiently fill its ranks) aboard a freight train that was bound for Manassas Junction, a major staging area for the gathering Confederate army in Virginia. In so doing, Wheat gave up his bid to form a regiment from the special battalion, at least for the time being, and his unit was officially named the "2nd Battalion, Louisiana Volunteers" by the state. To the officers and men of the battalion, however, they would always be known as the 1st Louisiana Special Battalion, the Special Battalion, Wheat's Battalion, the Tiger Battalion, the Star Battalion, Wheat's Louisiana Battalion, the New Orleans Battalion, or simply as Wheat's Tigers.[30]

En route, the Special Battalion passed through Holly Springs, Jackson, Granada, and Corinth, Mississippi; Chattanooga and Knoxville, Tennessee; and Lynchburg, Charlottesville, Gordonsville, and Culpeper, Virginia. Their first battle would not only be a test of moral and physical courage, but would also propel the "motley herd" to become true heroes of the Southern nation.[31]

3

First Blood

Seneca Falls and Matthews' Hill

Wheat's charge seemed to me to be the most terrible moment of this terrific contest.
— Sam English

On June 20, after a week of tedious train travel across the Southern Confederacy, the Special Battalion pulled into Manassas Junction, Virginia, the designated assembly area for Brig. Gen. Pierre Gustave Toutant Beauregard's Confederate Army of the Potomac. As the colorful Tigers disembarked at the depot, some soldiers from the 18th Virginia noticed that "one freight car was pretty nearly full of [so-called] Louisiana 'Tigers' under arrest for disorderly conduct, drunkenness, etc., most of which were bucked and gagged as some of my men reported who were at the station when they arrived." The rambunctious battalion was subsequently assigned to Colonel Philip St. George Cocke's brigade, stationed in Centreville, just north of Manassas. Upon arrival, Wheat requested the honor of holding the most advanced position of the Confederate army. Cocke obliged and sent the Star Battalion up to Frying Pan Church, south of the Potomac River between Leesburg and Alexandria, near Washington City.[1]

There the Tigers were assigned to Colonel Nathan "Shanks" Evans's command, which consisted of two companies of Virginia cavalry, Captain John Alexander's and Captain William Terry's, and one regiment of infantry, Colonel John B. Sloan's 4th South Carolina. While at Frying Pan Church, the Tigers and others were tasked with patrolling the south bank of the Potomac, the proclaimed northern boundary of the Southern Confederacy and, when able, with

Opposite: Brig. Gen. Pierre Gustave Toutant Beauregard, commander, Confederate Army of the Potomac, 1861. Former U.S. Army officer and West Point instructor, Beauregard commanded the Confederate force which attacked Fort Sumter in April 1861. He rose to become the highest-ranking Louisianan in Confederate service. He is wearing the blue uniform that he donned at the battle of Manassas. *USAMHI*

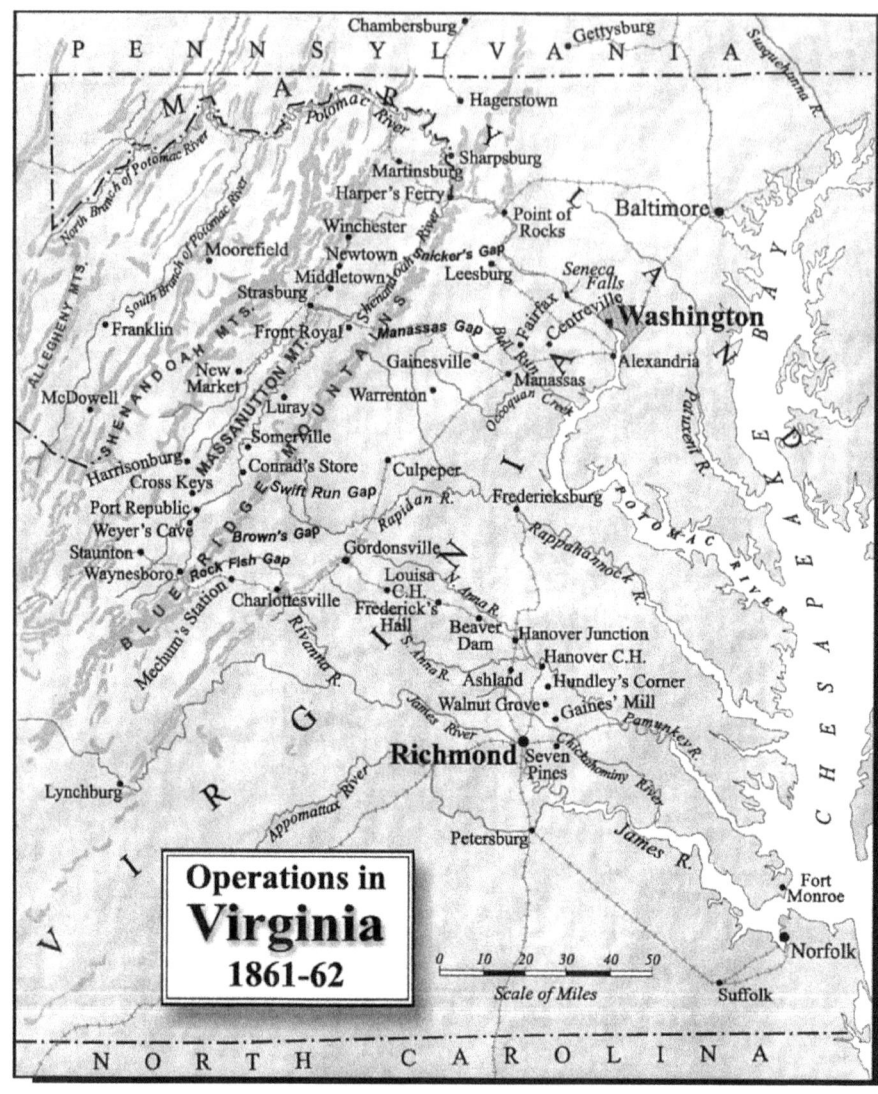

harassing the Federal troops who guarded its crossings. Evans's insurgents, according to Colonel Charles Stone of the 14th U.S. Infantry, engaged in "the unsoldierlike practice of firing at pickets across the river." Private Drury Gibson of the Catahoula Guerrillas, Wheat's Battalion, similarly remembered: "Completely exhausted, we [were] lying in ambush and marching around for two weeks, without tents or anything to cover us, save the canopy of heaven, it raining part of the time and with nothing to eat." In conducting these bold but limited offensive operations, Wheat was not only able to better ease the Tigers into battle by striking the nervous Yankee pickets, many of whom were demoralized by the aggressive Confederate probes, but was also able to instill confidence in his men and indoctrinate them in the spirit of attack—to hit the enemy often and at leisure. During this pivotal period for the Tigers, Robert Going Atkins, the Irish soldier of fortune who had served with Wheat in Italy, joined the Special Battalion and was made aide-de-camp by the Old Filibuster, who was hoping to eventually secure for Atkins a regular commission in the Confederate army.[2]

On June 28, 1861, on the heels of numerous successful and casualty-free raids, Captain White's company of Tiger Rifles was ordered to hit the "8th Battalion, District of Columbia Volunteers," who were posted at Seneca Falls, about fifteen miles upriver from Washington. The Tigers "had a nice little skirmish," Wheat reported, "killing three of the enemy and [their] loss was one man shot in the leg." Private James Burnes was the unlucky Zouave who was wounded in the engagement, making him the first of many battle casualties of the Special Battalion. His leg was "amputated at the thigh" by Dr. Samuel Fisher.[3]

On July 16 General Beauregard ordered Colonel Evans to withdraw from the Potomac crossings and redeploy behind Bull Run Creek with the rest of the army. Evans's command, now designated the 7th Brigade, Army of the Potomac, was assigned the important task of guarding the extreme left of the Confederate line astride the Alexandria-Warrenton Pike at Stone Bridge. Locating his headquarters at the Van Pelt House or "Avon," Evans tasked Captain Alexander's troop with guarding nearby Poplar and Farm fords and deployed Wheat's Battalion and the 4th South Carolina along Van Pelt Ridge, which was about 600 yards west of Stone Bridge. Two 4.62-inch Field Howitzers from Captain H. Gray Latham's Lynchburg (Virginia) Artillery, commanded by Lieutenant George Davidson, were posted on the south side of the pike, holding Evans's right.[4]

Evans had his men dig several rifle pits along the ridge and fell trees along the west side of the creek to not only clear a better field of fire but also "obstruct [the enemy's] passage over the flat except by the defile of the bridge and road." As the enlisted men toiled, Colonel Evans had a local resident, Dr. Bronaugh, take himself and his officers on a reconnaissance to become better acquainted with their surroundings. The good doctor showed them that the country road that led north from the pike just behind their position led in many different directions. It snaked past "Avon," Evans's headquarters, and wrapped around the ridge to the left. About 400 yards northwest of the house a path angled back to the right, to Farm Ford. Continuing along the road for another 500 yards, a path from Poplar Ford angled in from the northeast. The ford itself was about 1,500 yards from this point. Off to the northwest, continuing up the main road, was the imposing Carter Mansion, which was located on the left, or south side of the road. The mansion, a Georgian-style house named "Pittsylvania," was on the northeastern slope of a ridge that continued in a southwesterly direction toward the Sudley-Manassas Road. Another 500 yards or so, beyond the man-

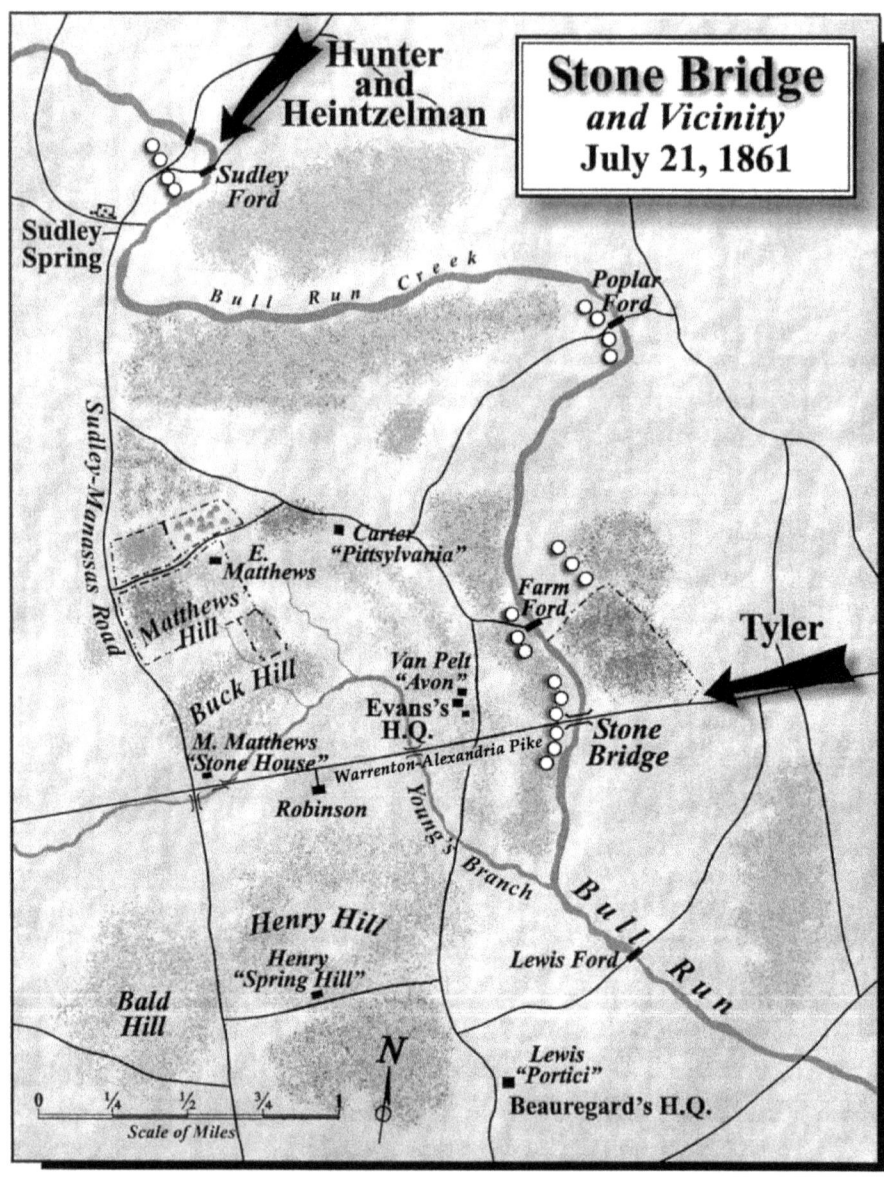

sion, the road forked again; to the right it led off to the northwest, toward Sudley Ford, on the Sudley-Manassas Road. To the left it led southwest atop the ridgeline, past a quaint house owned by Edgar Matthews and then on to the Sudley-Manassas Road. The distance from Pittsylvania to Matthews's house was about a thousand yards.[5]

On July 18, a week after the Tigers settled into their positions along Van Pelt Ridge, the expected Federal attack began when part of Brig. Gen. Irvin McDowell's 30,000-man Army of Northeastern Virginia, sent down from Alexandria to disperse Beauregard's Army of the Potomac, launched a reconnaissance-in-force against the Confederate right at Mitchell's and Blackburn's fords, well south of the pike. Once it was determined that the Louisiana Creole had in fact moved some of his forces to meet the threat, McDowell began to shift the bulk of his army to the north and west and attacked Beauregard's left on Sunday, July 21, 1861.[6]

Brig. Gen. Irvin McDowell, commander, U.S. Army of Northeastern Virginia at the battle of Bull Run (later promoted to major general). *Library of Congress*

While Colonel Israel Richardson's 4th Brigade, Brig. Gen. Daniel Tyler's 1st Division, was kept at Blackburn's and Mitchell's fords to hold the Confederate right, three divisions were to conduct an *en echelon* attack against the Confederate left. Two of these divisions, Brig. Gen. David Hunter's 2nd and Brig. Gen. Samuel P. Heintzelman's 3rd, were to cross Bull Run at Sudley Ford and march down the Manassas Road, flanking Evans's dug-in brigade at Stone Bridge. Once Evans was turned, the bulk of Brig. Gen. Daniel Tyler's 1st Division, previously demonstrating at Stone Bridge, was to force a crossing and link up with Hunter and Heintzelman. All three divisions, commanded by McDowell himself, would then drive south, link up with Richardson, disperse the rebel army, capture Manassas Junction, and continue on to Richmond, quelling the "slaveholder's insurrection."[7]

The battle resumed just after 4:15 A.M. when skirmishers from Tyler's 1st Division stumbled into some of Evans's pickets who were posted along the pike on the east side of Bull Run. Alerted to the Federal approach, Evans mobilized

The Alexandria-Warrenton "stone bridge" looking west toward the Van Pelt house (background). The 4th South Carolina and Wheat's Battalion were on the right side of the pike and Davidson's two howitzers were on the left. *Library of Congress*

his brigade, reinforced the rifle pits along Van Pelt Ridge, and kept two companies from Sloan's 4th South Carolina behind the hill as a reserve. About an hour later, Tyler made his "appearance in line of battle on the east side of the stone bridge, about 1,500 yards in front of [the Tigers' position]," and opened fire with a massive 4.67-inch Parrott Rifle commanded by Lieutenant Peter Haines of Battery G, 1st U.S. Artillery. Private Drury Gibson of the Catahoula Guerrillas, manning part of Evans's works, remembered, "We were anxious to meet the enemy, in fact our hearts jumped for joy when we saw their bayonets through the distant forest."[8]

Haines's gun, planted on the north side of the pike, was soon joined by Captain James Carlisle's Battery E, 2nd U.S., and together they "commenced firing at intervals at different directions [in an effort to make Evans] show his position, which was still concealed." Knowing that he was more than likely outnumbered, Evans chose to keep his men hidden and ordered all of them, including Davidson's well-camouflaged cannon, to hold their fire until the Federals made an actual push across the creek. After about an hour of incidental shelling, Tyler advanced

Col. Nathan "Shanks" Evans. Later promoted to brigadier general. *USAMHI*

"a considerable force of skirmishers" from the wood line toward the bridge. To match them, Evans dispatched the Calhoun Mountaineers and the Confederate Guards from the 4th South Carolina and the Tiger Rifles from Wheat's Battalion to advance from their rifle pits and make their way down through the slashing to challenge the Federal push.[9]

As the skirmishing intensified, Wheat, with "characteristic daring and restlessness" crossed Bull Run at Farm Ford to investigate with some Tiger Zouaves and Virginia cavalrymen in tow. Riding along a cornfield to a clump of trees, Old Filibuster carefully watched some Federals who were about 500 yards distant. After a full hour of fighting, Wheat thought, Tyler should have been advancing his entire force across the pasture in an attempt to storm Evans's position, and not merely fiddling with a few skirmishers. Riding closer to get a better look, the Yankees finally spotted the Tiger commander, fired at him, and forced him and his patrol to withdraw.[10]

As Wheat and his entourage splashed back across the creek, Colonel Evans received a report from Captain John Alexander at Poplar Ford that a "large enemy force" was marching up the country road north and east of his position. Another report, the one that apparently sealed it for Evans, came from Captain E. Porter Alexander, the army's principal signal officer, who spotted "the reflection of the sun from a brass cannon" several miles to the north, near Sudley Ford. "Look out for your left," Alexander warned, "you are turned."[11]

The Stone Bridge looking north towards Farm Ford. The cornfield that Wheat traversed is in the background. *USAMHI*

With Wheat's and the Alexanders' information in hand, Evans correctly deduced that the action to his front was merely a ruse and boldly decided to "quit his position and meet the enemy in his flank movement." Informing Beauregard and Cocke of his intentions and leaving but four companies from the 4th South Carolina and Lieutenant Thomas Adrian's platoon of Tiger Rifles to hold Van Pelt Ridge, Evans ordered the bulk of his brigade, ten and a half companies of infantry, Alexander's troop of cavalry, and Davidson's yet-to-be-fired howitzers—about 900 men total—to head up toward Pittsylvania to try to stop or at least slow the advancing Federal column.[12]

Following Alexander's horsemen, Wheat's Tigers trotted along the country road to the Carter Mansion, where Evans deployed them in a field located northeast of the house. As the 4th South Carolina and Davidson's guns came into line on their left, Shanks ordered Wheat and Alexander to ride up the road in the direction of Sudley Ford to seek out the enemy. About fifteen minutes later, the cavalry scouts came galloping back with the exciting news that the Federals were in fact marching down the Sudley-Manassas Road and headed toward the pike. Evans agreed to move his men once again, farther to the left, to try to block the now-important crossroads.[13]

With Alexander's troop and the Tiger Battalion once again in the van, Evans led his command along the southern base of the ridge that stretched from Pittsylvania to the Manassas Road. As the Tigers marched along a small valley between Matthews' and Buck hills, about 600 yards from the road, Evans directed Wheat to deploy his battalion "on the right by files into line" and move forward up Matthews' Hill. In the meantime, Sloan was to continue his march to the road where he was to stop, deploy his six-company battalion into line, and adjoin with Wheat's left. Evans kept Alexander's troop in the valley, behind a pine thicket, as his only reserve. Trusting that Sloan and Wheat would properly enjoin their battalions atop Matthews' Hill, Evans rode down to the pike to grab Davidson's guns and have them deploy atop Buck Hill, about 200 yards south of the oak patch.[14]

Wheat cautiously led his battalion through a cornfield to a fence where he paused to assess the situation. He was at the bottom of an undulating ridge that ran northeast to southwest. To his left front was a large "scrub field" that was

Edgar Matthews's house looking toward the Sudley-Manassas Road. Maj. Wheat led the Catahoula Guerrillas and Capt. White's platoon of blue-clad Tiger Rifles across the property from left to right, running into Col. John Slocum's 2nd Rhode Island, thus initiating the battle for Matthews' Hill. *USAMHI*

enclosed by a split-rail fence, to his immediate left was the pine thicket, and to his right was a thin patch of woods cordoned off by a fence. To his immediate front, about fifty yards away, was a swale or "covert," as he called it, and beyond the swale, continuing up the open slope another 300 yards or so, Matthews' Hill topped off. There, at its crest, the hill was bisected by a fence-enclosed farm lane that connected the Sudley-Manassas Road with Edgar Matthews's house.[15]

Wheat decided to keep the Delta Rangers and the Walker and Old Dominion Guards in the covert while he led White's platoon of Tiger Rifles and Buhoup's company of Catahoula Guerrillas up the slope in skirmish formation. As he did so, however, Sloan also sent out his own company of skirmishers, Captain James Hawthorne's Saludia Guards, up through the thicket in search of the Star Battalion. Creeping through the tangled pines, unable to see more than twenty yards, some of the Carolinians spotted movement to their right front, on the other side of the woods.[16]

Apparently forgetting that Wheat had a company of Zouaves with him, the nervous South Carolina skirmishers fired into the backs of White's blue-clad Tiger Zouaves who were just exiting the covert. In the salvo of friendly fire that followed, Sloan's men mortally wounded Privates Hugh McDonald and James Wilson. Aroused, the Tigers turned about and returned fire. A small battle could have ensued right then and there if Wheat had not rushed into the woods and straightened the matter out with Captain Hawthorne.[17]

Soon after this unfortunate incident, at about 10:00 A.M., Wheat ushered his Zouaves to the top of the hill to join the Guerrillas who were deployed along Matthews Lane. The Tiger commander was no doubt ready to order up the rest of the battalion when the Guerrillas spotted several Federals spilling out of the woods to their front, about 100 yards away. Wheat instantly reined in his horse and ordered the men to take cover behind the fence along the north side of the lane and open fire with their accurate Mississippi Rifles.[18]

The stalking Federals belonged to Colonel John Slocum's 2nd Rhode Island Regiment of Colonel Ambrose Burnside's 2nd Brigade, Hunter's 2nd Division, the lead element of McDowell's main column. Behind the 2nd Rhode Island, stacked up on the Sudley-Manassas Road, was Captain William Reynolds's Battery A, 1st Rhode Island Light Artillery, the 2nd New Hampshire, the 71st New York, and the 1st Rhode Island. Behind the Rhode Islanders was Colonel Andrew Porter's 1st Brigade, which consisted of Captain Charles Griffin's Battery D, 5th U.S., a battalion of recently-recruited U.S. Marines, the 8th, 14th, and 27th New York State Militia regiments, and a battalion each of regular army infantry and cavalry.[19]

Not giving Wheat enough time to bring up the rest of his battalion, the 2nd Rhode Island quickly formed from column into line, absorbed its skirmishers, and advanced up the hill with fixed bayonets. Faced with a full-blown regimental attack, one of the first seen on American soil in over forty years, Wheat

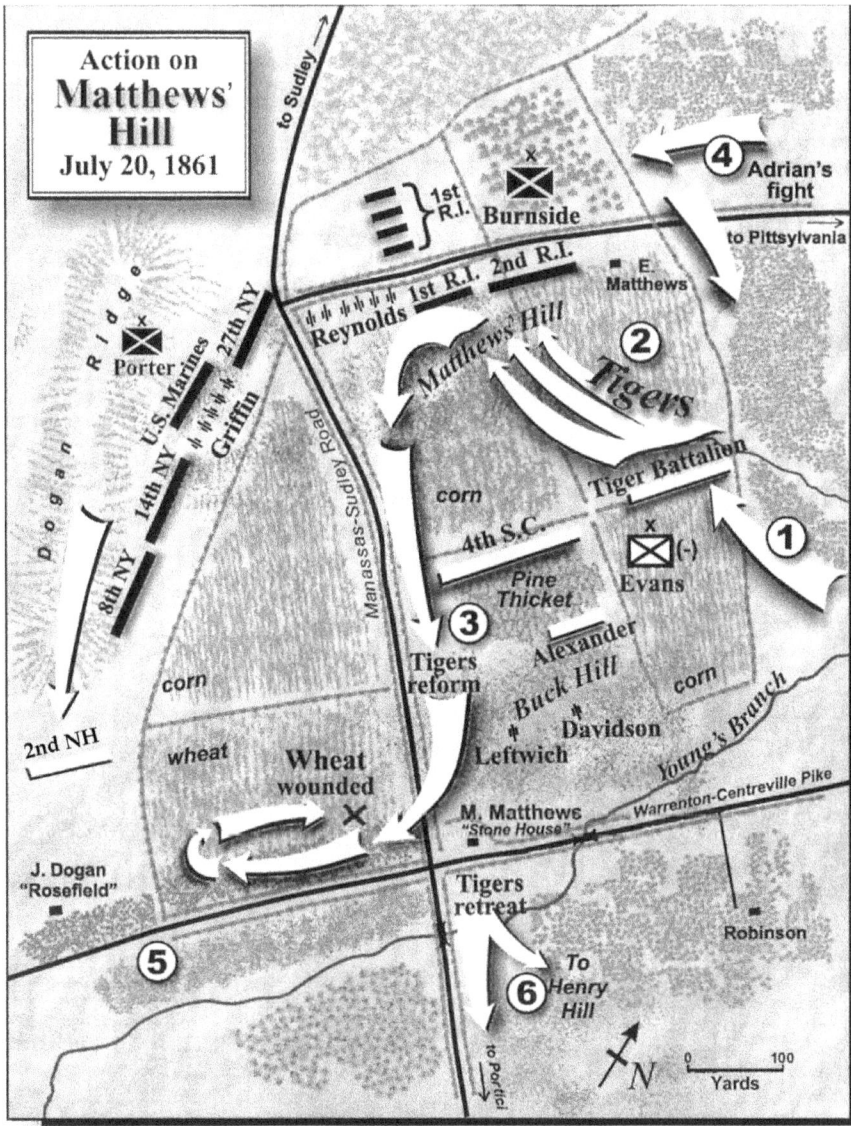

judiciously ordered his skirmish companies to fall back and reform on the flanks of the battalion that was still in the covert.[20]

When the 2nd Rhode Island swept across the top of Matthews' Hill on the heels of the Tiger skirmishers, Evans's entire line, including Davidson's guns, let them have it. "A perfect hail storm of bullets, round shot and shell was poured into us," remembered Private Sam English of the 2nd Rhode Island, "tearing through the ranks and scattering death and confusion everywhere."

Left: Col. John S. Slocum, commander, 2nd Rhode Island Regiment. Slocum was killed while fighting the Tigers and others on Matthews' Hill. *USAMHI. Right:* Col. Ambrose E. Burnside commanded the brigade that tangled with the Tigers on Matthews' Hill. He is wearing the famous "Burnside blouse" that the Rhode Islanders of his brigade donned at Manassas. Burnside later went on to command corps and army-sized elements. *USAMHI*

The well-directed fire momentarily stunned the Rhode Islanders, and they pulled back from the crest to await reinforcement.[21]

Hunter quickly ordered his next unit, Captain William Reynolds's company of six 3.8-inch bronze James Rifles, to deploy to the right of the 2nd Rhode Island. For the next half-hour or so, from 10:15 to 10:45 A.M., the two lines of apprentice soldiers blazed away at each other at close range.[22] Private Drury Gibson of the Catahoula Guerrillas remembered:

> The balls came as thick as hail, grape, bomb and canister [into] our ranks every minute.... Poor Hall [i.e., William] Stone and Elias Stone [from the Catahoula Guerrillas] got killed.... They were both mess-mates of mine. I very much regretted their untimely and premature deaths. Elias fell on the field during the action. When I saw that he was shot I asked him if he was badly wounded. He said yes but I will give them another shot. He run his hand in his [cartridge] box and fell dead in the act of loading his gun. Hall was mortally wounded, but lived two days. Poor fellow, he struggled so hard against death. I never saw anyone take death so hard, he said he wanted to live to revenge the death of Elias who fell by his side.[23]

By 10:45, Matthews' Hill was enveloped in thick smoke and visibility was cut to a mere fifty yards. Wheat knew that his tiny command could not stay where it was lest it get slaughtered; that the Federals would eventually garner enough strength and gumption to renew their attack down the slope and force his Tigers to yield the valuable pike to the Unionists. Since retreat was not an option for America's premier soldier of fortune, the Old Filibuster decided to hit the Yankees first. One audacious charge, Wheat thought, should send the Federals packing.[24]

His target would be the spot where the 2nd Rhode Island and Reynolds's battery were adjoined. If his men could break through there, they would surely be able to knock the Federals from the crest and allow Sloan's Carolinians, currently pinned down by the Federal cannon, to advance and help hold the hilltop. With this in mind, Wheat ordered his Tigers to move from their sheltered position and advance up the hill, guiding diagonally to the left over the fence and into the enshrouded field, which would partially mask their forward movement.[25]

Considering Wheat's vast combat experience, his timing could have been better. He should have launched his counter-attack soon after the 2nd Rhode Island was thrown back by the Confederate fusillade that had scattered "death and confusion everywhere." Now, however, a little before 11:00 A.M., the 2nd Rhode Island was not only fully recovered from its shock, but was also finally being supported by its sister regiment, the 1st Rhode Island.[26]

Unaware of the Federal reinforcements, the intrepid Tigers from Louisiana charged up the hill as Federal musketry, shot, and shell buzzed over their heads or smacked into their advancing ranks. About fifty yards from the Yankee line, to the right front of the forming 1st Rhode Island, the Tiger Rifles paused and fired at Reynolds's gun crew, killing several of them. Just then, the red-shirted filibusters from Captain Harris's Walker Guards, in the center of the line, came up, fired their last round, and ran full-bore at the 2nd Rhode Island in the same fashion they had attacked Central Americans in Nicaragua five years before. To one member of the 2nd Rhode Island, a man who had never before faced a bayonet charge let alone wild-eyed filibusters or Tiger Zouaves, Wheat's charge "seemed to be the most terrible moment of this terrific contest."[27]

These two rugged volunteers from Col. Slocum's 2nd Rhode Island, photographed in camp on the eve of the battle of Manassas, engaged Wheat's Tigers on Matthews' Hill. Note their distinctive "Burnside blouses." *USAMHI*

When the men of the Special Battalion got to within twenty yards of the Federal line, however, the Rhode Islanders gave "the most hideous scream" and raked them with a volley of musketry. The frenzied fire at close range was enough to stop the Tigers' charge cold and forced them to retreat back down the hill and seek shelter behind the pine thicket. "Never will I forget," proclaimed one of Reynolds's artillerymen, "how that Rebel flag [the Delta Rangers' Stars and Bars] looked as it bobbed out of sight under the hill." Three hapless Tigers, Privates Thomas Hayes of the Delta Rangers, John Kuntz of the Old Dominion Guards (who was wounded in the back), and Chester Woods of the Catahoula Guerrillas, were reportedly snagged during the retreat by members of the 2nd Rhode Island. A few other unfortunates from the Special Battalion were left dead or mortally wounded at the feet of Burnside's victorious New Englanders.[28]

Reforming his battalion to the left and rear of Sloan, Wheat watched in dismay as Burnside deployed his entire brigade atop Matthews' Hill. The stalwart Rhode Island regiments held the right, out past the house; the 71st New York and its two Dahlgren boat howitzers held the center; and Reynolds's battery held the left, near the road, which was directly in front of Wheat's Tigers and Sloan's Carolinians.[29]

Position of Reynolds's Rhode Island battery atop Matthews' Hill looking south toward Henry Hill. Wheat's Battalion charged up from the left, from the now-overgrown pine thicket where a patch of oak used to be. The trees that bisect the field did not exist in 1861.

While Evans and Burnside continued to hammer away at each other, Brig. Gen. Barnard Bee, sent up from Manassas to support "Shanks," was deploying his Confederate command about a thousand yards south of Matthews' Hill along the northern slope of Henry Hill. Bee had with him two regiments of infantry, Colonel Egbert Jones's 4th Alabama and Colonel William Falkner's 2nd Mississippi, and one battery of light artillery, Captain John Imboden's.[30]

Seeing that Evans was holding out against incredible odds, Bee rode down to the pressed South Carolinian to urge him to fall back to Henry Hill, a stronger position. But Evans, not recognizing Bee's authority (he was from Joe Johnston's Army of the Shenandoah, recently arrived by rail), balked and instead dared him to move toward and support his men, who were bravely holding their ground against the contemptible Yankees. Faced with Evans's obduracy, Bee rode back up to Henry Hill and ordered his two regiments to take up a position to the right of the 4th South Carolina, where Wheat's Battalion was originally deployed. "Here is the battlefield," Bee cried, "and we are in for it!"[31]

Once reinforced by Bee's regiments, Wheat asked Evans if he could swing his battalion around to the left and take Reynolds's guns in flank. Once the dreaded battery was silenced, he argued, the 4th South Carolina, the 2nd Mississippi, and the 4th Alabama could charge up the slope and drive Burnside's infantry back from the dominating crest. Inspired by Old Filibuster's bold scheme, Evans consented.[32]

Wheat led his Tigers west across the Manassas Road and into a "line of scrub oak and pine" that paralleled the pike. As he did so, however, Colonel Gilman Marston's gray-clad 2nd New Hampshire Regiment, Burnside's brigade, sent to guard Reynolds's right, had been mistakenly directed by Hunter to march all the way down Dogan's Ridge to "Rosefield," the same landmark that Wheat was shooting for. The New Hampshire men and the Tigers therefore collided in a field of haystacks near the Dogan House, and a nasty fight ensued. Marston's regiment, already in line and on higher ground, held the clear advantage and proceeded to savage the Tigers with musketry. Seeing that some of his men had "by mistake crossed the open field and suffered severely from the fire of the enemy," Wheat rode back across the field to rally them. As he ran the Federal gauntlet, however, a bullet that was claimed to have been fired by a sergeant in the 2nd New Hampshire nailed the Tiger commander and knocked him from his horse.[33] Wheat remembered:

> Advancing from the wood with a portion of my command, I reached some haystacks under cover of which I was enabled to damage the enemy very much. While in the act of bringing up the rest of my command to this position, I was put *hors de combat* by a Minie Ball passing through my body.[34]

The New Hampshire sergeant's bullet clipped Wheat's left arm, drilled into his left side "immediately under and a little in front of the armpits" and "perforated one of his lungs" before passing out the other side. Falling heavily to the ground near the line of trees, the Tiger commander was quickly sur-

"Colonel Burnside's Brigade, 1st and 2nd Rhode Island, and 71st New York Regiments, with their artillery, attacking the Rebel batteries at Bull Run. Sketched on the spot by A. Waud." This depicts the battle for Matthews' Hill soon after Wheat's first abortive charge. Reynolds's battery is in the background as well as Porter's brigade, assembling atop Dogan's Ridge. Wheat's battalion charged up from the left and retreated back toward the trees. *Library of Congress*

rounded by several men of his battalion who, "by the judicious management of Captain Buhoup," rolled him onto a blanket. The loyal Tigers then began to lug their burly commander (he weighed over 250 pounds and topped six feet) into the wood line. The enemy fire was so terrific that Wheat reportedly shouted: "Lay me down, boys, you must save yourselves!" His pleas were ignored.[35]

As Wheat was dragged into the woods, Lieutenant Austin Eastman of the Delta Rangers ripped the battalion colors from its staff and threw it over Old Filibuster to help stop his profuse bleeding. The Tigers then frantically searched for a way to evacuate their horribly wounded commander and before long snatched up a "mounted staff officer" who was riding up the pike. The sympathetic officer draped Wheat across his horse like a bag of meal and taxied him down the Manassas Road to a field hospital that was located at the New Market crossroads, just north of the junction.[36]

Wheat's wounding proved momentous. The once-brave Tigers, all alone on the far left, under intense enemy fire, and without the guiding hand of their charismatic leader, scattered in the face of the 2nd New Hampshire and inglo-

Henry and Jane Matthews' "Stone House" at the corner of the Warrenton Pike and Manassas Road. Buck and Matthews' hills are in the background. After Wheat's wounding on the foot of Dogan's Ridge (to the left), some of the Tigers assembled around this sturdy structure before they retreated south to Portici. *Library of Congress*

riously fled for the rear. Most of them didn't stop running until they reached the plantation of Portici, Beauregard's headquarters, or Camp Pickens, near Manassas, which were well away from the battle area.[37]

Soon after the Tiger Battalion scattered, Dan Tyler's Federal division began its much-anticipated advance across Bull Run at Farm Ford and Stone Bridge. Also outflanked and overwhelmed, the last organized unit of the Special Battalion, Lieutenant Adrian's brown-clad platoon of Tiger Zouaves, abandoned its position along Van Pelt Ridge and hoofed it up past Pittsylvania, intending to join the rest of the battalion. As the wayward Zouaves pressed up the road, however, they inadvertently stumbled upon the left flank of the 2nd Rhode Island, near the Matthews House. This was too good to be true. Adrian, a stalwart filibuster who reportedly "loved war," resolved to inflict harm on these unfortunate Yankees. As he maneuvered his platoon into position, however, one alert blue coat spotted him and fired, "wounding him slightly." Undaunted,

Adrian and his men returned fire and "gave the enemy much trouble, killing an officer and many of his men." After firing a few more rounds, Adrian's Tigers "were compelled to abandon their position to him [and] fell back, having sustaining much loss." Thrown back, the red- and brown-clad Zouaves headed south through the woods toward Young's Branch, where they fell in with the 4th Alabama of Bee's brigade.[38]

Possibly wanting to support Wheat's second attack, Evans and Bee, now reinforced by Lt. Col. William Gardner's 8th Georgia Regiment of Colonel Francis Bartow's brigade, Army of the Shenandoah, ordered their men to charge Burnside's line around 11:45. In the course of leading his troops in the abortive charge, however, Adrian, fighting with the 4th Alabama, was once again wounded, this time in the thigh. Seeing his Tigers' subsequent hesitation in their advance up the hill, Adrian, who was lying in a pool of his own blood, shouted, "Tigers, go in once more, go in my sons, I'll be great gloriously God-damned if the sons of bitches can ever whip the Tigers!" Inspired by Adrian's plea, the small band of Confederate Zouaves continued their bold assault up the slope and from "a point near the top of the hill, and not far from Matthews's house" delivered "sharp and destructive fire" until they, like their brethren an hour before, were forced to retreat.[39]

Soon after the last Confederate attack on Matthews' Hill was thrown back, Colonel Andrew Porter's 1st Brigade, Hunter's 2nd Division, and Colonel William B. Franklin's 1st Brigade, Heintzelman's 3rd Division, were finally brought up to support Burnside's brigade. This reinforcement included twelve guns from Captains James Ricketts's and Charles Griffin's batteries of regular army artillery. With overwhelming force now on the field, the Federals charged down both sides of the Sudley Manassas Road and crushed Bartow's, Bee's, and Evans's commands, forcing them to retreat across the pike and onto Henry Hill.[40]

4

Triumph on Henry Hill

Our blood was on fire. Life was valueless. The boys fired one volley, then rushed upon the foe with clubbed rifles beating down their guard.... I have been in battle several times before, but such fighting never was done, I do believe as was done for the next half hour; it did not seem as though men were fighting, it were devils mingling in the conflict, cursing, yelling, cutting, and shrieking.
— Robert Richie

As the Tigers and others retreated south across the Warrenton-Alexandria Pike, Brig. Gen. Thomas Jackson, sent up from Camp Pickens to stem the Federal attack, approached Henry Hill with an odd collection of nine regiments of infantry and thirteen pieces of artillery from Beauregard's and Johnston's armies. After a quick gaze across the pike from the northeastern edge of the grassy eminence, the phlegmatic Jackson, sensing the Federal commander's intent, deployed most of his forces, which eventually became known as "Jackson's Stone Wall," perpendicular to the Federal line (facing west) and not parallel to it (facing north).[1]

Jackson formed an inverted "L" along the northern and eastern slopes of Henry Hill. The left wing, which Jackson weighted, faced west across Henry Hill and consisted of the thirteen cannon and six Virginia regiments. Jackson's right wing, comprised of Wade Hampton's South Carolina Legion, Eppa Hunton's 8th and William "Extra Billy" Smith's 49th Virginia regiments from Colonel St. George Cocke's 5th Brigade, Army of the Potomac, was situated to directly face the Federals who were massing north of the pike. Because these units were in an exposed position, they came under intense artillery fire from the eighteen Federal guns that were massed along Matthews' Hill and Dogan's Ridge.[2]

Jackson hoped that the Federals would try to flank his exposed right by attacking it from the west, thus coming smack into his main line, which was held by his artillery forces and six regiments of infantry. And if more forces could be garnered, the belt of trees along the southern edge of Henry Hill could also be utilized and the Federals would walk into a giant "Z-shaped" ambush.

As Jackson completed his masterpiece, General Beauregard arrived on the field, took over command, and helped Bartow, Bee, and Evans consolidate their brigades behind Jackson's sobriquet stone wall.[3]

Like Wheat's Battalion, Sloan's 4th South Carolina was scattered after its fight on Matthews' Hill and Stone Bridge. What was left of five of its companies attached themselves to Hampton's Legion. The other four companies, one-time defenders of Matthews' Hill, fell back to Beauregard's headquarters at Portici, about a mile east of Henry Hill near Ball's Ford, where they were adjoined with the "New Orleans Zouaves and some Alabamians." Once assembled, Colonel Francis Thomas, a Maryland ordnance officer from the general staff, took command of this "makeshift battalion."[4]

While Beauregard and Jackson were busily constructing an entirely new line atop Henry Hill, General McDowell also arrived on the field and conferred with his principal lieutenants atop Matthews' Hill. Happy with how the battle had evolved thus far, McDowell decided to press the attack south toward Manassas Junction with Ricketts's and Griffin's batteries of regular artillery and five brigades of infantry from Tyler's 1st, Hunter's 2nd (now commanded by Porter), and Heintzelman's 3rd divisions. In directing the attack, however, McDowell curiously instructed his artillery chief, Major William Barry, to order Ricketts and Griffin to displace their guns from Dogan's Ridge and move them in advance of the infantry to Henry Hill.[5]

Ricketts and Griffin received McDowell's orders in total disbelief. They both scanned the hill where they were ordered to go. It was just behind the area in which Imboden's guns had been recently driven off. Ricketts protested the order, stating that the area was not only void of friendly infantry support, but was also in easy musket and canister range of the forming enemy line that was discernible through the haze. It would be better, he argued, if the long-range rifles were massed along Matthews' Hill and Chinn Ridge, thus bringing converging fire onto the massing Confederates atop Henry Hill. He further argued that the only advantage his three-inch rifles had over the larger-mouthed smoothbores he faced was in standoff range. His guns could easily engage the Confederates at 2,000 yards while they could only return fire at 1,500 yards.[6]

Writing after the war, Confederate Captain John Imboden of the Staunton (Virginia) Artillery concurred with Ricketts's insightful analysis. "It was at this time that McDowell committed, as I think, the fatal blunder of the day, by ordering both Ricketts's and Griffin's batteries to cease firing and move across the turnpike to the top of Henry Hill.... The short time required to effect the change enabled Beauregard to arrange his new line of battle on the highest crest of the hill." In retrospect, it probably would have been better if Ricketts's, Griffin's, and Reynolds's batteries had massed on Matthews' Hill and Chinn Ridge. There their long-range guns would have had Henry Hill in a complete cross fire. With this cover, Tyler's 1st Division could have attacked up the east side of Henry Hill from Stone Bridge, Heintzelman's 3rd could have attacked

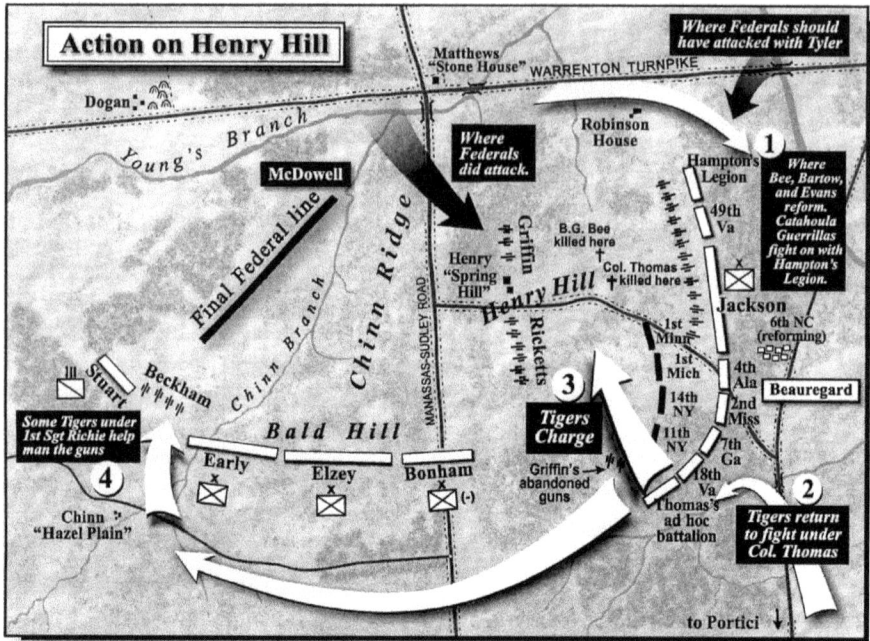

directly south across the pike, and elements of Porter's 2nd Division could have swung around Chinn Ridge and hit the Confederates atop Henry Hill from the west. If this had been done, the Federals would more than likely have won the battle, Richmond would have fallen, and the war might have ended right then and there.[7]

But instead of heeding Griffin's and Ricketts's sensible arguments, Barry inexcusably instructed the batteries to go forward anyway, arguing that "the general has ordered it." Disgusted, Ricketts and Griffin limbered their perspective batteries and moved in advance of the infantry to the western face of Henry Hill. There they deployed on both sides of "Spring Hill," Judith Henry's house; and their nine rifles and two smoothbores, not 300 yards from thirteen Confederate smoothbores, were met by a horrifying fusillade of shot and shell from Jackson's well-placed line. Captain Imboden later remarked, "I venture the opinion, after a good deal of observation during the war, that in open ground, at 1,000 yards, a ... battery of smooth guns ... well handled, will in one hour discomfit double the number of the best rifles ever put in the field."[8]

In the wake of his now-outgunned artillery, McDowell dispatched his battalion of Marines from Porter's 2nd Division and Noah Farnham's 11th New York, Elmer Ellsworth's famous "Fire Zouaves," and Willis Gorman's 1st Minnesota Regiment from Samuel Heintzelman's 3rd Division to support the guns and begin the assault. Once arrived, the infantrymen and Marines deployed to the right and rear of the cannon, shielded by the western slope of Henry Hill.[9]

4. Triumph on Henry Hill

After fifteen minutes or so, at about 2:30 P.M., General Heintzelman ordered the 1st Minnesota and the 11th New York to move further down the road and skirt the woods on the south side of the hill in order to roll up Beauregard's left. As the Minnesotans and Fire Zouaves moved onto the plateau, however, they were unexpectedly hit by musketry from Arthur Cummings's 33rd Virginia Regiment from Jackson's 1st Brigade, Army of the Shenandoah. In the confusing fight that followed, the Federals broke and retreated back up the Sudley Road. As they did so, from the south, two troops from Lt. Col. James Ewell Brown "Jeb" Stuart's 1st Virginia Cavalry, Army of the Shenandoah, charged into their disorganized mass — routing them — and drove them further up the road. The untried Marines, seeing this conflagration developing to their right and rear, bolted as well, leaving Ricketts and Griffin totally unsupported.[10]

At this juncture, Lieutenant Charles Hazlett, one of Griffin's section leaders, suggested that the exposed battery should be withdrawn to Chinn Ridge, about 500 yards to the rear. From there, the guns would not only be farther from the dangerous Confederate smoothbores, but would also be safe from an infantry counter-attack. Although Griffin agreed with Hazlett in theory, he refused to withdraw. His orders were clear — no matter how unsound — and he instead decided to maneuver his two field guns to the very place where the Fire Zouaves and the Minnesotans were driven off in order to enfilade the Confederate cannon that were wreaking havoc on his battery. Unlimbering atop a small knoll, but a hundred yards from the rebels, Griffin fired two salvos of solid shot into the Confederate gun line. A few minutes later, to his right front, about 200 yards through the thick gray smoke, Griffin noticed a line of "dust-covered" infantry heading toward his rear. Correctly thinking that these were Confederates, the old regular had promptly ordered his cannon to swing over to the right and switch to canister when Major Barry rode up to inform him — mistakenly — that the men below were in fact advancing Federals from Heintzelman's 3rd Division. Barry therefore ordered Griffin to change back to solid shot and continue his well-placed enfilade fire against the rebel guns. Again Griffin protested Barry's orders. "They are Confederates," he argued, "as certain as the world, they are Confederates!" Barry answered, "No *captain*, they are your battery support!"[11]

After a few more tense minutes, the yet-to-be-identified line of infantry moved to within seventy yards of the right rear of Griffin's guns, fired a volley into the Federal artillerists, and then charged up the slope. The "dust-covered" men were in fact from Arthur Cummings's 33rd Virginia, Jackson's brigade, and they quickly overran the Federal cannon. When the surviving members of the doomed gun section retreated back to the Henry House, Griffin snidely asked Barry, "Do you think that was our support?" The artillery chief answered, "I was mistaken." "Yes," Griffin snapped, "you were mistaken all around."[12]

Soon after Griffin's smoothbores were captured, Alfred Wood's 14th New York State Militia Regiment, the "Red-Legged Devils" from Porter's 2nd Division, charged up from the Sudley-Manassas Road, slammed into the 33rd Virginia's left, and drove it back into the woods, retaking Griffin's cannon. The emboldened New Yorkers then continued forward, intent on taking Beauregard's entire gun line in flank. As they advanced north, across the front of the Confederate-held woods, however, Jackson's 4th and 27th Virginia regiments ripped several volleys into their right, charged them, and forced them to retreat back behind Ricketts's battery. Again, Griffin's and Ricketts's guns were left unsupported.[13]

Seizing this rare opportunity, at about 3:00 P.M., Beauregard ordered his entire line to advance and take the Federal cannon. While elements from the 2nd, 4th, 27th, and 33rd Virginia regiments from Jackson's brigade, in the center, were to sweep across the field and take Ricketts's battery, the 49th Virginia, joined by the 2nd Mississippi and the blue-clad 6th North Carolina Regiment from Bee's 3rd Brigade, Army of the Shenandoah, were to retake Griffin's field guns on the left. After a brief fight — a gallant charge — the advancing Confederate infantry took all eight Federal pieces.[14]

But not for long, for down below, on the Manassas Road, Brig. Gen. William B. Franklin, commander of Heintzelman's 1st Brigade, led his fresh 5th and 11th Massachusetts regiments onto the hill, exchanged several volleys with Jackson's Virginians, charged them, and drove them from Ricketts's battery. At the same time, the scattered remnants from the 1st Minnesota and the 11th and 14th New York renewed their attack against the Confederate left and drove the rebels away from Griffin's abandoned section.[15]

During this back-and-forth fighting across Henry Hill, Colonel Robert Withers's 18th Virginia Regiment from Cocke's 5th Brigade, like the 49th Virginia before it, was ordered to remove itself from Lewis Ford and reinforce Beauregard's embryonic line on Henry Hill. On his way to the front, Colonel Withers noticed several stragglers heading out of the battle area. Among them were two Zouaves from the Tiger Rifles. Unlike the other fugitives who refused Withers's pleadings to rejoin the fight, the combative Tigers agreed and fell in with the 18th Virginia for the rest of the battle. Withers remembered:

> We pushed on past the [Lewis] House in the direction of Henry House, when we netted a string of wounded men and stragglers, streaming to the rear. As many of these were unhurt, I urged them to go back with us into the fight, all refused except two "Tigers," who, from their brogue were evidently Irish. They fell into line and we passed through some pines and emerged on the open plateau near the Henry House, where most of the fighting had been done, some skirmishing was going on between a mob of disorganized men on my left and some of the enemy beyond the [Sudley-Manassas Road], who were invisible to us. No other troops being in sight, I told the men to lie down until I could ascertain something of my surroundings, expecting each moment to see the other regiments of the brigade emerge from the pines. Just then, one of the "Tigers" who had joined us ran up the slope to an orchard occupied by the skirmishers, got behind an apple tree, and fired two or three times, when he was shot through both legs. He squatted down, and turning his head over his shoulder called to his comrade: "I say, Dennis

[Corcoran of the Tiger Rifles?], come up here and give them hell, for they've got me!"[16]

With more forces now at his disposal, Beauregard ordered his line to once again advance and drive the Federals from Henry Hill. For this attack, several red-shirted filibusters from the Walker Guards, the Delta Rangers, and the Old Dominion Guards, coupled with some colorful New Orleans Zouaves from the Tiger Rifles, just arrived with Colonel Thomas from Portici, were again asked to charge the enemy uphill and at close range. Griffin's guns, the Tigers' immediate objective, were still situated on a small clear knoll about a hundred yards above their position. Once they "emptied their rifles in a fateful discharge at close quarters," the Tigers bolted out from the tree line "with a terrible shout" and charged up the steep slope. The Federals, who were posted above, shot withering fire into their ranks and downed many officers and men in the process.[17]

Despite the odds, the Tigers and others continued their attack up the smoky knoll and into the faces of the enemy. Plunging unmercifully into the New York Fire Zouaves and Brooklyn Chasseurs, the Tiger Zouaves reportedly dropped their rifles, unsheathed their "murderous-looking" bowie knives, and "by dexterous blows, beat down the bristling bayonets before them [and] began to hack their antagonists to pieces. A dreadful carnage ensued." The New Orleans *Commercial Bulletin* reported that Captain White and Lieutenant Adrian were "disgusted with their Mississippi Rifles (without bayonets)" and when ordered to charge, "threw away the rifles and charged with Bowie Knives, as the enemy say like demons, and put all to flight before them." The New Orleans *Daily Delta* similarly reported that, "upon reaching the enemy's column, [the Tiger Rifles] threw down their rifles (having no bayonets), drew their bowie knives, and cut their way through the enemy, with a loss of two thirds of the company."[18] Robert Richie, the Tiger Rifles' tough first sergeant, similarly remembered:

> Our blood was on fire. Life was valueless. The boys fired one volley, then rushed upon the foe with clubbed rifles beating down their guard; then they closed upon them with their knives, "Greek had met Greek"; the tug of war had come. I have been in battle several times before [in Nicaragua?], but such fighting never was done, I do believe as was done for the next half hour; it did not seem as though men were fighting, it were devils mingling in the conflict, cursing, yelling, cutting, and shrieking.[19]

This final and dramatic charge of the 1st Louisiana Special Battalion — bowie knives and all — at the battle of Manassas forever placed Wheat's "adventurous wharf rats, thieves, and outcasts" among the pantheon of Southern gods. The October 1861 issue of the widely read *Southern Literary Messenger* wrote:

> Among the accounts of the battle of Manassas, mention is made of the Tiger Rifles of Louisiana, one of those capacious names, perhaps, that were common among the Roman legions.... They fought after the Roman manner with some improvements of their own. The regiment which they charged received them with a murderous fire. They divided the distance which separated them by falling upon their faces and so

waiting for a few moments. Then rising, they delivered their fire, and with a terrible shout rushed forward. They clubbed their rifles, beat down the bristling bayonets before them, and unsheathing their long and heavy Bowie knives (a weapon somewhat similar to the Roman sword) they began to hack their antagonists to pieces. A dreadful carnage ensued. They performed prodigies of valour and made good their claim to the sobriquet "the Tigers," which they had assumed.[20]

As the Tigers consolidated around Griffin's captured guns, McDowell's last available unit, Colonel William Tecumseh Sherman's 3rd Brigade, 1st Division, swept across the plateau and headed for Ricketts's guns. After another thirty minutes of intense fighting, Sherman's 13th, 38th, 69th, and 79th New York regiments, supported by the gray-clad 2nd Wisconsin Volunteers, were able to boot the 5th Virginia and Hampton's Legion from the battery and drive them back. The tough survivors from the Special Battalion, over near Griffin's guns with what was left of the 4th Alabama, the 2nd Mississippi, the 7th Georgia, and the 18th Virginia, were now left in an exposed position.[21]

Luckily for them, at about 4:00 P.M., the 2nd and 8th South Carolina regiments from Brig. Gen. Milledge Bonham's 1st Brigade, Army of the Potomac, marching up the Manassas Road, arrived at the southern base of Henry Hill and slammed into Sherman's right, driving his brigade from Ricketts's battery. This enabled Jackson to sweep across the plateau with his command and finally seize or drive away all of Ricketts's and Griffin's guns. Bonham's regiments were soon followed by Colonel Jubal A. Early's 6th Brigade, Army of the Potomac, which began to deploy atop Bald Hill, elongating the Confederate left. No doubt inspired by this turn of events, 1st Sergeant Richie led what remained of his Tiger Zouaves across the road and to the far left of Early's brigade, where Lieutenant Robert Beckham's Culpeper (Virginia) Artillery was going into battery just above "Hazel Plain." The Tigers reportedly helped the pressed Virginia artillerists man their pieces.[22]

Inspired by the intrepid Tigers, Colonel Harry Hays of the 7th Louisiana, Early's brigade, yelled, "Hurrah for the Tigers! Charge for the Tigers and for Louisiana!" These troops—Beauregard's last—finally tipped the scales against McDowell's forces that were now surrounded on two sides by advancing rebel infantry and well-placed Confederate artillery. Before long, after another gallant Confederate charge (in which General Bee and Colonels Bartow and Thomas were killed), the Federals were driven from Chinn Ridge, and ultimately, from the field of battle itself.[23]

As the beaten Union army pulled back toward the Bull Run crossings, some men from the 79th New York of Sherman's 3rd Brigade, 1st Division, were surprised to find an unidentified Tiger Zouave "prisoner" (who later escaped) in their ranks. Private William Todd of the 79th New York remembered:

> Considerable astonishment as well as amusement was caused by the presence in our retreating ranks of a solitary prisoner, who plodded along with us and entertained us by his quaint remarks. His uniform attracted our attention: a Zouave cap of red, and jacket of blue, with baggy trousers made of blue and white striped material,

and white leggings, gave him a rather rakish appearance; he announced himself as a member of the Louisiana Tiger Battalion, Major Wheat commanding.[24]

By dusk, McDowell had reached Centreville, and the next day the remainder of his army retreated all the way back to Alexandria, its starting point. The first great contest of the war, the battle of Manassas, thus ended in Southern victory. Needless to say, Wheat's intrepid battalion, as part of Evans's brigade, was instrumental in bringing about the coup. Its actions on Matthews' Hill and Dogan's Ridge, for example, gave General Beauregard time to shuffle over enough forces to make a stand on Henry Hill. And on Henry and Bald hills, the places where the Federals were ultimately driven back, the Tigers again distinguished themselves, charging and then holding Griffin's section of guns (Bowie knoves and all), serving Beckham's artillery, and participating in the final attack.[25] General Beauregard himself noted that the Tigers "maintained their stand with almost matchless tenacity ... dauntless courage and imperturbable coolness," and cited Wheat for his "brilliant courage." The Louisiana general went on to say, "In the desperate, unequal contest, to which these brave gentlemen were for a time necessarily exposed, the behavior of the officers and men was worthy of the highest admiration, and assuredly hereafter all those present may proudly say: 'We were that band who fought the first hour of the battle of Manassas.'"[26]

What is even more remarkable is the fact that even though the Special Battalion was scattered after its active defense of Matthews' Hill, losing most of its command structure, the men fought on in small groups. Led by company commanders, sergeants, or even privates, the Tigers continued to display their

"First Battle of Bull Run." *Leslie's*

valor across the entire battlefield. Their dynamic experiences along the Potomac River, under Wheat's guiding hand a few weeks before, had apparently paid off. As such, the Tigers were always looking for the fight — always choosing to renew their attacks against an enemy they did not fear.

All told, the 1st Louisiana Special Battalion officially listed forty-seven casualties (thirty-one wounded, twelve killed, three captured, and one wounded and captured) at the battle of Manassas. Its commander, Major Chatham Roberdeau Wheat, was wounded in the left arm and breast and shot through a lung. His adjutant, Lieutenant Robert Dickinson, was wounded in the leg: "His horse having been killed under him, he was on foot with sword in one hand and revolver in the other, about fifty yards from the enemy when a Minnie ball struck him. He fell and lay over an hour, when ... Capt. McCausland [one of Evans's staff officers] passed. The generous McCausland dismounted and placed Dickinson on his horse." Captain Alexander White was supposedly "stunned" when his horse was shot out from under him during the first charge on Matthews' Hill; Captain Obedia Miller of the Old Dominion Guards was wounded in the ankle; Lieutenant Thomas Adrian of the Tiger Rifles was wounded in the thigh; and Lieutenant Henry S. Carey of the Old Dominion Guards was "shot in the foot, and when lying on the field stabbed through the thigh by a Yankee officer, whom he killed."[27]

The Tiger Rifles suffered ten casualties, paying the highest price of the battalion with seven men killed and three wounded. The Walker Guards took seven casualties (all wounded); the Delta Rangers lost six men (five wounded and one captured), and the Catahoula Guerrillas lost four men killed, three wounded, and one captured. The Old Dominion Guards took the most casualties in the battalion with one killed, twelve wounded, and one wounded and captured (total of fourteen). Most of the battalion's known casualties were the result of fourteen leg wounds, followed by four head wounds. There were two shoulder wounds, two arm or hand wounds, and three back wounds.[28]

When Wheat was brought to the field hospital after getting mangled at the foot of Dogan's Ridge, the surgeons who examined him declared his wound to be mortal. But Old Filibuster defied their grim forecast by spouting: "I don't feel like dying yet." One surgeon then sadly relayed that he knew of "no instance on record of recovery from such a wound." "Well then," Wheat gurgled as he spat up blood from his punctured lung; "I will put my case upon record."[29] To echo this tenacity, on July 23, 1861, the editor of the New Orleans *Daily Picayune* wrote:

> In every corner of this land, and at every capital in Europe, [the battle of Manassas] will be relived as the emphatic and exulting endorsement, by a young and unconquerable nation, of the lofty assurance President Davis spread before the world on the very eve of battle, that the noble race of freemen who inherit these States will, whatever may be the proportions of the war may assure, renew their sacrifices and their services from year to year, until they have made good to the uttermost their right to self government. The day of battle shows how they redeemed this pledge for them, and in adversity as in victory, it is the undying pledge of all.[30]

5

Dishonored Heroes

Today I witnessed the most effecting sight and heart rending affair that has transpired during the campaign. It was the public execution of Denis Cochrane and Mik O'Brian (two of the New Orleans Tigers).... They met their fate without a sigh, without a murmur. They neither feared God, man nor the Devil.
— Zachary Gilmer

With the Federal rout at Manassas, the men of the Special Battalion were able to supplement their Louisiana-made equipment with Yankee-made packs, blankets, gum blankets, canteens, and haversacks that had been discarded during their retreat. One reporter from the New Orleans *Daily Delta*, for example, stated: "[I noticed] that the knapsacks and haversacks of our Bengalese friends were all marked in large letter 'U.S.' I inquired what the letters meant. 'A few weeks ago,' was the ready reply, 'they meant 'Uncle Sam,' now they mean 'us.'" And as for Major Wheat, he did indeed defy the doctors' grim prognosis of death and slowly recovered from his horrid wounds. Francis Shober, Wheat's brother-in-law from North Carolina, was the first to reach Old Filibuster's bedside in a cabin not far from the railroad depot at Manassas. Arriving on July 25, Shober found Wheat "still improving and ... rallying very rapidly.... His life seems to be a charmed one and he is still full of vitality and strength."[1]

While bedridden, the Tiger commander received a steady flow of visitors, consisting mostly officers and men from his battalion. On one occasion, he saw a Tiger Zouave peering through a window into his room with "an expression of great anxiety on his face." Wheat invited him in and when the Tiger came to his bedside, Old Filibuster, struggling to raise his right hand, said: "Come here my Royal Bengal, and let me shake your paw." General Beauregard also visited the bedridden filibuster, assuring him that the gallant actions of he and his men at Manassas would "not be forgotten."[2]

While Wheat recovered from his wounds in Camp Pickens, "a serious rift" arose between Captain Alexander White of the Tiger Rifles and Captain William McCausland of Colonel Evans's staff. McCausland apparently called White a coward for failing to rise from the ground when "his horse was shot under him" during the Tigers' charge up Henry Hill. White of course denied the accusation and called McCausland a liar. McCausland retorted, and the argument escalated to the point where White answered McCausland's slander by challenging him to a duel. The weapons chosen for the subsequent test of honor were "Mississippi rifles at short range." White, the faster of the two, mortally wounded McCausland, who was "bored through the hips." Briefly arrested for the matter, White was quietly sent back to New Orleans not only to reduce tensions within the brigade, but also to escort the wounded Obedia Miller back to his home and recruit more idle but patriotic lads to help fill the ranks of the now-famous Tiger Battalion.[3]

On August 3 Wheat was well enough to be moved to Culpeper, thirty miles below Manassas, for his convalescence. This he spent in the home of James Barbour, an old family friend. While there, Barbour and Wheat had several discussions concerning Roberdeau's military service. Barbour believed that Wheat could serve the Confederate cause in a much greater capacity than as major of a battalion of infantry. On August 12 he wrote to Virginia governor John Letcher to press the Confederate government to promote Old Filibuster to a rank more commensurate to his abilities. He wrote:

> Dear Sir:
> Major Roberdeau Wheat who was severely wounded in the battle ... at Manassas ... will be ready for active service in a week or two. As he is a native of our state ... it is appropriate to present to you ... the past career of this remarkable man.... An intense ambition for military distinction has been the controlling influence in his life and has made his life a career of rich and bold adventure.... He was educated at the Military High School under Reverend now Colonel Pendleton. He served in the Mexican War under Scott as a Captain of Cavalry. He commanded a Louisiana regiment in López's expedition against Cuba. He was for ten years a brigadier general in the Mexican Service.
> He held an artillery command in Walker's Nicaraguan Expedition. He was with Garibaldi in Italy being volunteer aid to Avezano second in command to Garibaldi. He raised a battalion in New Orleans and came to Manassas ... where it was his fortune to open the last battle.... In the thick of the fight he received a wound which was at the time considered mortal.... A man only 35 years of age of his intelligent courage and energy has vast capacity for public service in these strange wild scenes that surround us. He is a man of fine abilities and good education.... A chance for noticeable service is all that he asks. He has earned promotion by his skill and courage and his blood.... President Davis, General Beauregard, and the Secretary of War know him and can suggest more in his favor than I have said if attention be called to his case. The rank which he now holds is not sufficient to offer him much opportunity for the distinction for which he yearns. Promotion is sought not for the honor which it confers but for what it may enable him to win. I am sure that it cannot be necessary to say more to enlist you in his interest.
> Very Resp[ectfull]y and Truly,
> Jas. Barbour[4]

While the Old Filibuster politicked for a higher position, Beauregard's Army of the Potomac and Johnston's Army of the Shenandoah were merged into one force under the overall command of Johnston. The unified army was subsequently divided into four divisions with at least three generally state-specific brigades each. All of the Louisiana infantry units which had been assigned to the Army of the Potomac, Roberdeau Wheat's Special Battalion and Isaac Seymour's Sixth, Harry Hays's Seventh, Henry Kelly's Eighth, and Richard Taylor's Ninth regiments were assembled into one brigade, the "Louisiana Brigade," and put under the command of Brig. Gen. William H.T. Walker of Georgia, "a man of command military experience." The Louisiana Brigade was then assigned to Maj. Gen. Richard "Old Baldy" Ewell's division along with the brigades of Arnold Elzey and Isaac Ridgeway Trimble.[5]

General Joseph Eggleston Johnston, commander, Confederate Department of Northern Virginia, 1861–62. *USAMHI*

The hard-hitting 6th Louisiana, much like Wheat's Battalion, consisted mostly of Irish or German immigrant dock workers from New Orleans with a sprinkling of up-country farmers and such from Union, Sabine, Tensas or St. Landry parishes. They were "hardy fellows, turbulent in camp and required a strong hand, but responded to kindness and justice and readily followed their officers to the death." The Irish Sixth, as the regiment was popularly known, was commanded by 57-year-old Yale graduate and Seminole and Mexican wars veteran Isaac Seymour, who had been, at the outbreak of this war, the editor of the New Orleans *Commercial Bulletin*.[6]

Maj. Gen. Richard "Old Baldy" Ewell, the Tigers' able division commander during the difficult Valley and Seven Days' campaigns of 1862. *USAMHI*

The 7th Louisiana or "Pelican"

Regiment was commanded by Harry Thompson Hays, a 41-year-old Mexican War veteran and New Orleans attorney. It consisted mostly of *bourgeois* New Orleans Creoles, many of whom belonged to the prestigious Pickwick Club, which helped organize the annual Mardi Gras. The 8th and 9th regiments, commanded by Colonels Henry Kelly and Richard Taylor, respectively, unlike the 6th and 7th regiments, which principally hailed from southern Louisiana, consisted of farmers, laborers, and planters' sons from northern Louisiana.[7]

Many of these men, coming from the more "Suthrun" part of the state, felt especially apprehensive about being brigaded with the lowly "wharf rats, thieves, and outcasts" from the Tiger Battalion. They apparently feared them worse than the Federal army. Richard Taylor, commander of the 9th Louisiana at the time, remembered: "With the army at this time was a battalion ... commanded by Major Wheat.... So villainous was the reputation of the battalion that every commander [in the brigade] desired to be rid of it."[8] Private Henry Handerson, a soldier in Taylor's regiment, echoed his commander's sentiments when he wrote: "Considerably to our horror, in the formation of the brigade encampment, Wheat's battalion, was located immediately next to the 9th Louisiana Regiment, and, indeed, just alongside of my company."[9] Private William Trahern of the 6th Louisiana said of the Tigers: "A greater lot of thieves and cut-throats never trod this hemisphere.... [They had] gorgeous uniforms and fairly good drilling [to fool the people to think that they were] men of great courage and bravery.... [But] they possessed neither of these qualities.... [They were in fact] cowards and wharf rats drawn from the low down population of every human race known."[10] Private Randolph Abbott Shotwell of the 1st North Carolina Battalion, Trimble's brigade, said of them, "Major Bob Wheat's famous battalion of New Orleans 'Tigers' (composed of the dregs of that great city, and certainly not ill-named, for a more fierce, ruffianly, ferocious set of desperadoes are rarely assembled in a civilized country) were encamped near Manassas, and were the terror of the neighborhood; even their own officers could not always restrain them."[11] Captain William Oates of the 15th Alabama, Trimble's brigade, remembered that the Tiger Rifles of Wheat's Battalion, "with their half savage uniform, made the observed of all observers. They were composed mainly of adventurous wharf rats, cut throats, and bad characters generally; and although they fought with reckless bravery ... they were actuated more by a spirit of adventure and love of plunder than by love of country. They had neither respect nor fear of any man, but one, and he was Major Wheat, their commander."[12]

The Tigers' fame and reputation quickly spread throughout the rest of the Confederacy. Mrs. Sallie Putnam of Richmond, for example, wrote: "The battalion of 'Tigers' from New Orleans, commanded by the intrepid Wheat, were, as their name denotes, men of desperate courage but questionable morals. They were well suited to the shock of battle, but wholly unfitted for the more important details of the campaign. Among them were many of lawless character, whose fierce passions were kept in abeyance by the superior discipline of their accomplished commander.... Educated under influences the most pious and refining, he was gentle, easy, grateful and dignified in society; toward men in his command he was kind, but grave and reserved, and exacting in the performance of duty; in battle he was fiery, impetuous and resolute."[13] In short, one Virginian wryly proclaimed, "The wild, looting Tigers of Major Bob Wheat made not a pious crew, but they fought."[14]

In August and September, many of the Tigers, as with others in Johnston's army, stuffed in crowded, muddy, and bug-infested camps around Manassas, came down with the dreaded "camp fever" that always tended to plague armies of the period. In Wheat's Battalion alone, of the 390 soldiers listed as being present in August 1861, a full 239, well more than half, were on the sick rolls. To help alleviate the crisis, in late September, Johnston sent his divisions out to create their own encampments, and Ewell's division was dispatched north to build Camp Beauregard, a new fortified encampment around Centreville.[15]

With the Star Battalion snuggled in with the rest of the Louisiana Brigade, and with Wheat still convalescing in Culpeper, General Walker placed the Tigers, who had been nominally commanded by Captain Harris of the Walker Guards since the battle, under the tutelage of a known disciplinarian, Lt. Col. Charles de Choiseul of the 7th Louisiana. De Choiseul did not relish his new assignment, however, as evidenced in a letter he wrote to Emma Louise Walton on September 5, 1861: "I have become a 'Tiger.' Don't start. I am the victim of circumstance, not of my own will.... Whether [the] Tigers devour me, or whether I will succeed in taming them, remains to be seen. What is more likely, is that they will remain in their high state of undiscipline. For the officers, or at least the majority of them, are worse than the men."[16]

It didn't take long for the raucous Tigers to test out their new commander. "The whole set got royally drunk," de Choiseul remembered, and a nasty brawl ensued soon after he took command. When the colonel sent his staff to quell the disturbance, one of Lieutenant Adrian's fiery Zouaves apparently grabbed his rifle, pointed it at one of de Choiseul's lieutenants, and "snapped the lock at him." This was an act of extreme insubordination and insolence, and the Tiger was quickly arrested and thrown into the brigade stockade. Later that same day, several Zouaves from the same company reportedly beat up and robbed their washerwoman — after she was no doubt paid — and de Choiseul also had them arrested.[17]

In spite of this crackdown, however, the drunken brawls continued. Private Randolph Abbott Shotwell of the 1st North Carolina Battalion, Trimble's brigade, remembered, "[Colonel de Choiseul] was said to have used his pistols now and then to quiet some outbreak. Unfortunately, he left camp on one occasion, and many of the worst characters became so drunk and unruly, that the officer of the guard undertook to maintain order, but was set upon, badly beaten, and forced to fly in peril of his life, pursued by the mutinous 'Tigers.'

So great was the tumult that the 7th Louisiana, the nearest regiment adjacent, was called to overawe the mutineers. Several men were injured more or less in the fray."[18] It was also during this period that eighteen men were listed as deserting from the Special Battalion, and before the year was out, Lieutenant E.B. Sloan of the Walker Guards resigned his commission.[19]

It didn't take a battle to create casualties in the Special Battalion, either. Sergeant Joseph Cooper of the Tiger Rifles, for example, was "killed by accident, September 23, 1861." Private James Purcell, from the same company, was "killed accidentally by Thomas Riggs of Company D on October 4, 1861."[20] On October 20, Private John Travers of the Tiger Rifles reportedly murdered a fellow Irishman, James McCormack of the 6th Louisiana—probably during a drunken brawl—and once members of the 6th hunted him down, he was thrown in the brigade stockade to await trial.[21] Inactivity, the lack of Wheat's towering presence, alcohol, and cultural proclivities, hearkening back to their days along the docks of New Orleans, seemed to be the root causes of the mayhem.[22] Captain James Nisbet of the 21st Georgia, Trimble's brigade, remembered one particular rumble in which alcohol played a pivotal role. He wrote:

> [One day] I was reading by a comfortable fire in my quarters, when I heard a tremendous racket down in the company quarters. On looking out, I saw a fight going on between ten or twelve [Tiger] Zouaves and men of my company. I ran down there and commanded the peace, which the sergeants restored after much difficulty. Several of Wheat's Tiger Rifles were lying on the ground, having been knocked down by my men. They said they had been robbed of their whiskey, by some boys of [my] company, who met them, and asked for a drink, and then ran off with the bottles; that they had followed them to get satisfaction. I said, "You seem to have gotten it, from the looks of your bloody heads." I ordered the sergeant to take them to my quarters and give them water and towels, and after they had washed, I got them a drink all round, and said I was sorry they had been robbed; that if such disorders were reported to men, I would punish the perpetrators, but to come into that company for a row, was a dangerous business. "These men would have killed some of you if I had not stopped em," said I. And they went off, saying: "We are much obliged, sor [sic, sir], but Wheat's battalion kin [sic, can] clean up the whole damned 21st Georgia any time." They were Irish; and of course, loved a scrap.[23]

The in-camp shenanigans, plus the fact that the battalion was not being converted into a full-blown regiment as Wheat had promised, spurred Captain Buhoup—who had originally joined the battalion with the understanding that he would gain a field commission—to petition to have his Catahoula Guerrillas transferred out of the battalion. Without Wheat around to dissuade or stop him, Buhoup's incessant politicking worked, and by October the Guerrillas were assigned to the 7th Louisiana Battalion and later the 15th Louisiana Regiment.[24]

Soon thereafter, Wheat, who was barely fit for service and certainly not well enough to tame his rowdy Tigers, rejoined his now-dishonored battalion, and Colonel de Choiseul was relieved of his burden. One Tiger reported:

Maj. Wheat is with us again, but looking badly. He came back Saturday. It would have done anyone good to have seen the boys on Friday evening. We came in from a hard drill of about three hours and were cooking something to eat when [Lieutenant John Coyle from the Walker Guards] told us that Major Wheat was coming. We fell in ranks, and with the rest of the battalion went to meet him, singing and shouting. We marched about two miles, only to be disappointed, for the Major had stopped on the road, too weak to come farther. There are not many officers who could get a reception as he did on Saturday. We went out again, and escorted him in, and he then made us a speech.[25]

Upon his return to active duty, Wheat undoubtedly replaced the bloodstained blue uniform that he had worn during the late battle with a bluish-gray wool double-breasted frock coat as per Confederate army regulations. His blue collar would have sported a single golden star, denoting the rank of major, and he probably would have had a double braid of Austrian knot running up his sleeve. He reportedly retained his distinctive red kepi.[26]

In early November, Ewell's division was moved to Camp Florida, about a half mile from Centreville, where General Walker was dubiously transferred from the Louisiana Brigade and Colonel Richard Taylor of the 9th Regiment was promoted to take his place. Needless to say, Taylor's promotion to brigadier general was controversial. For one, General Walker was simply brushed aside, and, more importantly, Taylor was the junior-most colonel of the brigade. Colonel Seymour, a veteran of the Seminole and Mexican wars as well as the recent battle of Manassas, was not only the most senior officer in the brigade, but also arguably the most qualified. In fact, of all the colonels in the brigade — Seymour, Hays, and Kelly — Taylor had the least combat experience (none). Many within the brigade therefore felt that Taylor was promoted only because of his famous father, President Zachary Taylor, and his relationship with Confederate President Jefferson Davis, who was once married to his bereaved sister. Colonel Seymour, the man who probably should have gotten the job in the first place, said, "I never stood a ghost of a chance for [brigade command]; I never expected it and of course, I am not disappointed — because — I can not be used as a politician." Private Henry Handerson of the 9th Louisiana, Taylor's old command, felt that the St. Charles Parish sugar planter was promoted because he was a "a regular martinet in the line of discipline ... who cared nothing for the men but for his own advancement."[27]

Whatever the reasons for his promotion, Taylor was challenged by General Johnston to whip his Louisianans, especially Wheat's seemingly out-of-control Tigers, into shape. To do so, Johnston promised to support Taylor "in any measures to enforce discipline." On October 28, just a few days after Taylor's elevation, a gang of drunken Zouaves from the Tiger Rifles, apparently led by Privates Dennis Corcoran and Michael O'Brien, made the terrible mistake of testing Taylor's resolve when they attacked the brigade stockade, knocking the officer on duty to the ground and seizing the guards' weapons. The mob then proceeded to break fellow Tiger John Travers, who was being held on a murder charge, out of the jail. During the scuffle, one of the Zouaves reportedly struck Colonel Harry Hays of the 7th Louisiana. Enraged, several other men of the brigade, who had had it with the Tigers, quickly squashed the riot and Corcoran, O'Brien, and their Tiger brethren were subsequently arrested and thrown into the stockade to await trial.[28]

This little episode led to the first executions in the Confederate Army of the Potomac. In an effort to enforce discipline, the government had given general courts-martial the power to execute soldiers convicted of capital crimes such as murder, treason, or mutiny. General Taylor, as well as most of the other officers of the brigade who were sick and tired of the depraved activities of the Tigers, agreed that Corcoran and O'Brien were among the more caustic men of the battalion (not to mention the army), and decided to make an example of them. Because the riot at the guard house and Hays's subsequent thrashing were considered to be acts of mutiny, the two men were court-martialed the next day, November 29, found guilty, and sentenced to be shot by members of their own company, "for the sake of the example."[29]

The highly publicized execution took place a week later on December 6, 1861, in a "little hollow or depression forming a natural amphitheater, upon the slopes of which a vast multitude of soldiers assembled at 10:00 A.M." It was witnessed by Ewell's entire division, which was drawn up on three sides of a hollow square, facing inward, with Taylor's brigade in the center, Elzey's on the right, and Trimble's on the left. Members of the press and other onlookers watched from vantage points in some trees or surrounding hills. Once the division was formed, a covered wagon, escorted by two companies from Colonel Kelly's 8th Louisiana, slowly drove into the open portion of the square, where it stopped in front of two large stakes "driven into the ground about ten feet apart." Beside the stakes were "two plain wooden coffins and matching grave sites, stark reminders of the business at hand." Soon after the wagon stopped, six men got out, Corcoran and O'Brien, still in their distinctive brown Tiger Zouave uniforms, a Catholic priest, Father Smoulders of the 8th Regiment, who was dressed in a "long black cassock and three-corned cap," and three officers. At the same time, 12 files (24 men) from the Tiger Rifles marched forward toward the stakes which were "awaiting their occupants."[30] Private Randolph Shotwell of the 1st North Carolina Battalion, Trimble's brigade, remembered:

> Bright and beautiful was the morning; the sky unclouded; the air crisp and unbracing, and all nature looking fresh and buoyant as if in contrast with the gloom that rested upon the hearts of the thirty thousand spectators gathered upon the hillsides. The solemnity of feeling became so deepened into intense silence as slowly toward the fatal spot approached the funeral cortege; the brass band mournfully playing the dirge "Death March" from "Saul," the doomed men with a priest, and the guards following the musicians, and being followed in turn by the "firing party" of 24 men of the same company to which the offenders belonged. The procession halted at the graves.[31]

Left: Brig. Gen. Arnold Elzey, commander, 1st Brigade, Ewell's division. *USAMHI.*
Right: Brig. Gen. Richard Taylor, commander, 3rd (Louisiana) Brigade, Ewell's division. Post-war photograph. *Library of Congress*

The condemned men were led forward to the stakes; then Colonel Kelly rode up and read the charges with which they had been found guilty and the accompanying sentence which condemned them to death. Once done, Corcoran and O'Brien's hands were tied behind their backs and they were led backward a short distance where they were "made to kneel with their backs resting against two strong posts driven into the ground, about twenty or thirty yards apart." As this was done, Father Smoulders went back and forth between the condemned men, "comforting them and preparing them for the awful death."[32] Once situated, Kelly read Corcoran and O'Brien's supposed last statement to their comrades:

> We acknowledge the justice of our sentence. May the rendering up of

Brig. Gen. Isaac Trimble, commander, 2nd Brigade, Ewell's division. *USAMHI*

our lives prove a benefit ... and a lesson to all to guard against the vice of drunkenness.... We die a soldier's death [to the] altar of military order and discipline.... Don't grieve for us! We are going to a better world! Do not mangle us; shoot at our hearts if you love us! Boys, God bless you, and good-bye!³³

Kelly next signaled Father Smoulders to move away, to have Corcoran and O'Brien blindfolded, and to have the firing squad prepare to carry out their duty. Little did the Tiger executioners know that a company from the 8th Regiment was not far behind, ready to gun them down if they failed to carry out their assigned mission.³⁴ Major David French Boyd of the 9th Louisiana remembered:

> There had been some reason to suspect that the firing squad of the Tigers, as detailed, would at the critical moment disobey orders and refuse to fire on their comrades. To meet this contingency, firm old Henry Kelly, colonel of the 8th Louisiana Regiment, was relied on, with but few in the secret. He had his men load their guns in camp before marching. Why they never knew, only they thought it was a matter of course somehow at an execution. A trusted company merely happened to take position immediately to the rear of the firing party of Tigers, their captain with the secret orders to fire on them should they prove mutinous and fail to fire.³⁵

All doubts were removed, however, when Lieutenant Adrian, who was wearing a "long scarlet tunic," dryly hammered out the appropriate commands of "Ready," "Aim," and "Fire!" In the subsequent volley, Corcoran and O'Brien were "killed instantaneously, falling forward on their knees, riddled with bullets."³⁶ Overwhelmed with emotion, Private Daniel Corcoran broke from the Tiger Rifles' formation and ran up to his dead brother's body and held it, sobbing.³⁷ A Richmond *Dispatch* correspondent wrote:

> The most affecting part of this scene was immediately following the discharge of musketry. One of the men [who was executed] had a brother in the crowd, who, before the smoke of the volley cleared from the spot, ran to his side and supported him as his life-blood ebbed away, and felt the last quiver of mortality as the soldier's body fell into his arms.... It was heart-rending, to see the poor brother's agony.... The death of the criminal was borne with stolidity, but the simple sight of such heartfelt, brotherly grief moistened every eye.³⁸

Once the bodies were cut away from the posts and loaded into the coffins, they were lowered into their graves and covered up. Afterwards, some curious soldiers combed the execution site for pieces of the stakes or other macabre relics until some men from the Star Battalion, led by Daniel Corcoran himself, angrily dispersed the foragers with fixed bayonets or bowie knives.³⁹ Sergeant Zachary Gilmer of the 18th Virginia, witness to the execution, wrote:

> Today I witnessed the most effecting [sic, affecting] sight and heart rending affair that has transpired during the campaign. It was the public execution of Denis Cochrane [sic, Dennis Corcoran] and Mik O'brian [sic, Mike O'Brien] (two of the New Orleans Tigers).... They met their fate without a sigh, without a murmur. They neither feared God, man nor the Devil.... These two men I think are the first that have been shot and I hope the last. My idea of this decision is that the men are now

5. Dishonored Heroes

Top: The Centreville Church, where Michael O'Brien's and Dennis Corcoran's remains were interred by archaeologists in the early 1980s. Their grave site is under a magnolia tree in the right foreground. *Right:* Grave marker for the two executed Tigers at Centreville.

going into winter quarters and to prevent them slipping off home, for they thought they would have to make an example of some one and they concluded this the best time and it fell to these poor Tigers to share such an unfortunate lot. Yet perhaps they deserved it for they are the lowest scrapings of the Mississippi and New Orleans and fear not death itself. Court Martials are always formed entirely of officers. Never have a single Private.[40]

After the executions, things apparently began to calm down. "Punishment, so closely following

offense," Taylor snidely proclaimed, "it produced a marked effect."[41] Besides, winter was setting in, alcohol was strictly forbidden, and Ewell's division was moved to Camp Carondolet, about three miles east of Manassas atop Willcoxen Hill, to build cabins for the winter.[42] It was also during this time that Wheat's long lost company, the Rough and Ready Rangers from New Orleans, was finally sent up from Camp Moore to join the battalion. Wheat put the company under Robert Atkins, his Irish aide-de-camp who was recently commissioned by the Confederate government for his actions at Manassas. Atkins renamed the company Wheat's Life Guards and it officially became Company E, 2nd Louisiana Battalion.[43]

With the addition of the Life Guards, the Star Battalion took on its permanent organization. The Old Dominion Guards, formerly Company E, became Company D, taking the Catahoula Guerrillas' old slot. Wheat's Life Guards, the new addition, became the new or second Company E. The Walker Guards remained Company A, the Tiger Rifles Company B, the Delta Rangers Company C, and Major Wheat remained the battalion's commander, Captain Harris acting as his second. Lieutenant Charles Pitman of the Delta Rangers replaced Lieutenant Richard Dickinson, who was seriously wounded at Manassas, as the battalion adjutant. Lieutenant Samuel Dushane of the Tiger Rifles remained the battalion quartermaster; Bruce Putnam, the battalion's original sergeant major, was promoted to lieutenant in the Life Guards, and Sergeant John Wrigley of the Walker Guards took his place. Sergeant H.H. Tabor of the Delta Rangers was appointed as Wheat's ordnance specialist; Dr. William Love remained the battalion's surgeon; and Solomon Solomon, a Jewish merchant from New Orleans and Obedia Miller's business associate, remained the battalion's sutler. Lieutenant William Foley, with Obedia Miller's return to New Orleans, became the commander of the Old Dominion Guards until the battalion was disbanded in 1862.[44]

Also around this time, the Louisiana Brigade received a generous uniform issue from its state government. For the first time since the war began, every man in the brigade, except those from Captain White's Tiger Rifles, who apparently elected to retain their signature *Zouav d'Afrique* visage as best they could, gained a uniform appearance. The standard issue consisted of two shirts, one checked and one flannel, two pairs of drawers, two pairs of wool socks, a bluish-gray jean-wool jacket with nine Louisiana State buttons and epaulettes, and trimmed with black cotton tape; a pair of matching trousers, a pair of white canvas leggings, a blue-gray jean-wool kepi with a stiff black leather bill and black

Opposite top: "The Grigsby House, Centreville," was General Johnston's H.Q. during the winter encampment of 1861-62. *USAMHI*. *Opposite bottom:* "Confederate winter quarters at Manassas." After the executions, the Tigers were put to work in building cabins like these at Camp Carondolet, about three miles east of Manassas Junction on Willcoxen Hill. *Library of Congress*

Left: "William and James Martin." James, on the left, is photographed wearing the standard uniform that was issued to all units of the Louisiana Brigade in the fall of 1861. Note the black piping and trim on the kepi and jacket. His father, William, is wearing a Home Guard Militia uniform. This photograph was more than likely taken during the winter of 1861-62 while William was on leave. Both are holding M1842s. The majority of Wheat's Tigers, save Capt. White's company of Zouaves, would have looked much like James Martin. Photographed by Claude Levet. *Confederate Memorial Hall*, New Orleans, LA. *Right:* "Pvt. Thomas Taylor, Co. K, 8th Louisiana Infantry Regiment." Pvt. Taylor was photographed wearing the uniform that the men of Louisiana Brigade were issued by their state government in autumn 1861. He is holding an M1842. *USAMHI.*

wool band, and one jean-wool overcoat of various shades. The men of the Tiger Rifles didn't refuse the general issue, but wished to simply retain their distinctive Zouave trappings as a matter of pride. As such, they most probably looked like an eclectic band of brigands from Barataria — Wheat playing the part of Jean Laffitte — or a drunken group of outlandish hooligans who were celebrating Mardi Gras, as they continued to wear either their original wool Zouave jackets, now faded blue or brown, or the gray jean-wool issue jackets that were modified to more closely match their original uniforms. For trousers, they either continued to wear their durable blue-and-white-striped cottonade pantaloons or replaced them with their newly issued jeans with or without the white canvas leggings. For headgear, they would have donned with pride, if still available, their red fezzes of Manassas fame, broad brimmed felt hats of various earthen tones, or issue kepis. Most men from the other companies seemingly retained their red battle shirts. The battalion colors, which had been soiled by Wheat's blood at the foot of Dogan's Ridge, were replaced by what eventually became known as an Army of Northern Virginia battle flag with yellow edging.[45]

Once the New Orleans Battalion settled into its winter encampment, well under Taylor's heel, Wheat felt comfortable enough to host several "Tiger dinners" to entertain friends and impress dignitaries in order to polish his own and the Tiger Battalion's tarnished reputations. Major David French Boyd of the 9th Louisiana remembered:

> Wheat gave what was known as "The Tiger Dinner" to many of his friends, including the leading officers of the army. Beauregard and Dick Taylor, our brigade commander, suspecting what might occur, prudently excused themselves. A more brilliant set of clever men, military or civilian, perhaps never sat around a board during the war.... Wheat was the prince of hosts and entertained royally. He had a superb dinner for his distinguished guests within his large marquee, and gave a more plebeian feast to his Tigers on the outside. But all were filled with plenty and good cheer. The choicest of liquors and wines were served within the tent; the Tigers stole all they wanted from the outside, and all were happy. A fine band enlivened the occasion with its sweetest strains. And while the Major and his guests within were toasting and responding, reviving old memories and dreaming of glorious careers, the Tigers were having fun, too, on the outside. To the music of the band, mounted on the horses of the generals; two big Tigers on Joe Johnston's big bay; they rode around and around, circus fashion, and ran races up and down the road as long as they were sober enough to stick on.... At about two o'clock in the morning Wheat and his guests were well *hors de combat*, and the commander [Joe Johnston] was hauled to his headquarters in an ambulance; maybe his horse was too tired![46]

Similarly, Wheat and Major Frederick Skinner of the 1st Virginia Regiment were supposedly engaged in a friendly contest to see who was better at creating gourmet meals in the field. Major Skinner wrote:

> [I found it] difficult to compete with Wheat's *cabeza de buey al ranchero*; an ox head, with skin and horns intact, covered in a pit of coals and baked like a potato. To prepare the meal, Wheat decapitated an ox, sewed loose skin over the neck cut,

and buried the head in the coals at tattoo. The next morning, the head was dug up and brought into [a] tent covered with ashes and dirt. [It was] as repulsive an object as my eyes ever beheld, but giving a most appetizing odor. The dirt and ashes were brushed off and the skin and horns [were] speedily and skillfully removed, and lo! A metamorphosis occurred. We had before us a dish as grateful to the eyes as to the nostrils.[47]

The Tiger dinners seem to have eased the trepidations of many at Camp Beauregard and a good relationship was in fact forged between the Special Battalion and the 9th Louisiana, a regiment that was initially horrified by the Tigers' presence. Private Harry Handerson remembered:

> We never had the slightest difficulty with [the Tigers], and in fact the regiment and the battalion got along together so well that they were often jestingly called "the happy family." ... Major Wheat and [Colonel] Stafford [of the 9th Louisiana] became warm friends, and in this way we saw quite a little of the renowned filibuster and free-lance.[48]

6

Tiger Fury

The Battle of Front Royal

> *I for the first time saw some of the much talked about Louisiana Tigers.... They looked courageous and daringly fearless.*
>
> — George Neese

After recuperating from the first winter of the war, in March 1862, Confederate forces in Virginia braced themselves for a renewed Federal push into their proclaimed territory. This time, it would be a four-pronged assault orchestrated by President Lincoln himself. His main effort, the newly created Federal Army of the Potomac, commanded by 35-year-old Maj. Gen. George Brinton McClellan, was to sail down the Chesapeake from Annapolis, Maryland, to Fortress Monroe, Virginia, with some 90,000 men in three corps (later enlarged to five), the II, III, and IV (and later the V and VI), the artillery reserve, and the bulk of the cavalry forces. From there McClellan was to march up the peninsula between the York and James rivers and attack Richmond from the east. While this occurred, McClellan's I Corps, commanded by Maj. Gen. Irvin McDowell (who wasn't relieved of command, but was simply superseded by McClellan), was to advance from Alexandria and fix Joe Johnston's 60,000 or so rebels at Manassas with 45,000 men. This would not only shield the U.S. capital from a feared Southern lunge, but would also give McClellan the time he needed to conduct his elaborate turning movement. Once Johnston moved south to protect Richmond, McDowell was to shadow him and join McClellan in his siege of Richmond.

To support this grand scheme, Maj. Gen. Nathaniel Banks's Army of the Shenandoah, 20,000 strong, was to continue its drive up the Valley of Virginia not only to occupy and pacify the region but also to prevent Confederate forces operating there from reinforcing the Richmond defenses. And on Banks's right, Maj. Gen. John "the Pathfinder" Frémont's Mountain Army, 15,000 strong, was to march across the forested Allegheny Mountains of western Virginia, take

Staunton and cut the main east-west Confederate rail line between Lynchburg and Knoxville. If all went as planned, it was hoped, the Southern Rebellion would be crushed by the end of the year.[1]

To better meet this multiple threat, General Robert E. Lee, commander of all Confederate forces in Virginia, ordered Johnston to fall back behind the Rappahannock River near Fredericksburg.[2] On Sunday, March 9, therefore, in accordance with Lee's order, the rebel encampments around Manassas and Centreville were abandoned. The Louisiana Brigade, being the last unit to leave Camp Carondolet, was tasked with burning the huts and superfluous supplies. Once done, the Tigers and others headed south, bringing up the rear of the column. The subsequent twenty-five-mile march to Orange County was an arduous journey made over roads that were turned into rivulets of mud by incessant spring rains. These ambient factors, coupled with the fact that the men had been cooped up all winter, weighed heavily upon them. "We had," recounted Louisianan W.G. Ogden, "a wet, miserable time of it."[3] On March 11 the Tiger Battalion, which now numbered only 250 men due to combat losses, sickness, and desertion from the previous year, crossed over the Orange and Alexandria Railroad Bridge to the south side of the Rappahannock and helped establish Camps Bellevue and Buchanan. Because of the continuing heavy rains, maneuvering was halted on both sides and the men saw little action along the bloated river.[4]

In early April, as the Federals' intentions became clearer, Lee moved the bulk of Johnston's

Maj. Gen. George Brinton McClellan of Philadelphia, Pennsylvania, commanded the Army of the Potomac during the Peninsula and Seven Days' campaigns. Although a master of positional warfare, "Little Mack" lacked the intestinal fortitude to face the Tigers and others in a stand up fight. *USAMHI*

Maj. Gen. Nathaniel Banks, commander, U.S. Army of the Shenandoah, with wife and family. A self-made man who worked his way up from a Massachusetts mill, Banks rose to become a newspaper editor, an attorney, a U.S. congressman, the Speaker of the House and, from 1858 to 1861, the governor of Massachusetts. Being one of Lincoln's strongest supporters, Banks was given an independent command in Virginia. Once the Tigers and others soundly thrashed him at Front Royal and Winchester, however, Banks was transferred to head up the Department of the Gulf. Strangely enough, his headquarters was located in New Orleans for the rest of the war. His boy is wearing a Zouave jacket. *USAMHI*

forces closer to Richmond, leaving only Ewell's division behind to guard the Rappahannock line. While there, Ewell was probed by McDowell's cavalry from time to time, getting into small unit actions along the river. After several weeks of this, Ewell finally received his much-anticipated marching orders. Instead of joining Johnston down on the peninsula, Ewell was ordered to burn the railroad bridge that he had so carefully guarded and march his division west to the Shenandoah Valley with Thomas Munford's 2nd and Thomas Flournoy's 6th Virginia Cavalry regiments. There he was to reinforce Maj. Gen. Thomas "Stonewall" Jackson's grandly-named Army of the Valley — of one division — which was busily holding off three invading Federal divisions under Generals Banks and Frémont.[5]

Maj. Gen. John Charles "the Pathfinder" Frémont, commander, U.S. Mountain Department, 1862. Perhaps the best-known Union general at the beginning of the war, Frémont, an ardent abolitionist who had unsuccessfully run for president on the Republican ticket in 1856, was easily handled by the Tigers and others at Strasburg and Cross Keys. *USAMHI*

When the Tigers and others marched out of Camp Buchanan on April 18, the weather was reminiscent of their march out of Camp Carondolet. They had to march in a steady, soaking rain, sometimes coupled with sleet or wet snow. The freezing precipitation continued to torture the men of the battalion, one-time residents of the sub-tropical docks of New Orleans, for the next ten days.[6] Although Taylor's marching orders stipulated that each soldier should carry only the "barest of necessities," this was hardly applicable because most of the men possessed very little following the Centreville withdrawal anyway. Taylor's own kit, for example, consisted of a mere "change of underwear and a tent fly." He reasoned that a fly, as opposed to a tent, "could be carried on [a] horse ... [and could] be put up in a moment, and by stopping the weather with boughs a comfortable hut [could be] made." His soldiers were to each carry:

> His blanket, and extra shirt and drawers, two pairs of socks (woolen), and a pair of extra shoes. These, with his arm and ammunition, were a sufficient load for strong marching. Tents, especially in a wooded country [as Virginia is] are not only a nuisance, involving much transportation, the bane of armies, but are detrimental to

health. In cool weather they are certain to be tightly closed, and the rapidity with which men learn to shelter themselves, and their ingenuity in accomplishing it under unfavorable conditions, are surprising. My people grumbled no little at being "stripped," but soon admitted that they were the better for it, and came to despise useless impedimenta.[7]

During this movement, Louisiana Private T.A. Tooke remarked, "We have nothing but march, march, march, and halt and sleep in wet blankets and mud. I thought that I [knew] something [about] soldiering, but I find that I had never soldiered it this way."[8] On Wednesday evening, April 30, Ewell's division crossed over the Blue Ridge Mountains through Swift Run Gap and marched into Jackson's camp at Conrad's Store. While the totally exhausted men established their bivouac sites in the dark, Ewell met with his new commander, "Stonewall" Jackson.[9]

Maj. Gen. Thomas "Stonewall" Jackson, commander, Valley District, 1861-62. Jackson came to depend heavily on Wheat's Tigers and the rest of the Louisiana Brigade during his now-famous Valley Campaign. *USAMHI*

Jackson informed Ewell that he planned to march his own division south and west, through Port Republic and Staunton, to the hamlet of McDowell, at the foot of the Alleghenies, and stop Frémont's drive across the mountains. In the meantime, Ewell's division, reinforced by Munford's and Flournoy's cavalry regiments, was to hold Banks in check—that is, prevent his army from taking Staunton (from either the east or west side of the Massanutten) or, as per Lee's instructions, to discourage him from sending reinforcements east over the Blue Ridge to support McClellan's drive on Richmond.[10]

When Jackson marched his division out of Conrad's Store the next morning, May 1, 1862, Ewell was left to his own devices to deal with Banks. At the time, unbeknownst to "Old Bald Head," Nathaniel Banks's army consisted of only one division, Brig. Gen. Alpheus Williams's, and some assorted cavalry. Banks was so weak because soon after he drove Jackson from the northern reaches of the Valley in March, he was ordered by the War Department to send two of his three divisions, Brig. Gen. John Sedgwick's and Brig. Gen. James Shields's, east by rail to Manassas. From there, they were to march further south to join McDowell's corps, which had pushed down to the north bank of the Rappahannock River near Fredericksburg. Williams's lone division, now Banks's entire army, was therefore spread thin throughout the northern reaches of the Valley, in Winchester to Strasburg on the west side of the Massanutten, and at Front Royal and Columbia Bridge on the east side.[11]

Over the next month, while Jackson marched west to drive Frémont back over the Alleghenies, Ewell established several outposts north of Conrad's Store and sent numerous patrols down both sides of the Massanutten to ascertain the whereabouts, strength, and intentions of Banks's army. On May 7 one of these patrols, led by Major Wheat himself, ran into elements of Banks's force near the hamlet of Somerville. Wheat's command consisted of one company from his battalion, a company from the 9th Louisiana, two companies from Flournoy's 6th Virginia Cavalry, and one cannon. As his column approached the Shenandoah River just north of the town, he was surprised and driven back by Colonel Robert Foster's 13th Indiana Regiment and a company from the 1st Vermont Cavalry. In the early phase of this skirmish, coined the battle of Somerville Heights, the Federals were able to push Wheat back two miles to Dogtown, where he was reinforced by the rest of his battalion and Col. Hays's 7th Louisiana. Once assembled, Hays and Wheat counter-attacked and drove the now-outnumbered Unionists back to Columbia Bridge, their starting point.

Colonel Robert S. Foster, commander, 13th Indiana Volunteers. Foster's regiment drove Wheat's command from Somerville but was defeated later in the day as the rest of his battalion and Colonel Hays's 7th Louisiana Regiment reinforced the Old Filibuster. *USAMHI*

Although the Tiger Battalion surprisingly listed no casualties in this engagement, the Pelican Regiment, "thrown headlong into the Federals," lost two dead, four wounded, and one deserter, a "crazy Greek."[12]

The next day, May 8, Jackson defeated the lead element of Frémont's army, Brig. Gens. Robert Schenck's and Robert Milroy's brigades, at the battle of McDowell and forced them to fall back upon Frémont's headquarters at Franklin, Virginia. Content with Frémont's subsequent inaction, Jackson informed Ewell that he intended to march back into the Valley and drive Banks back beyond the Potomac. On May 18, Stonewall met with Ewell at Mount Salon, about twelve miles southwest of Harrisonburg, to formulate a course of action. It was decided to hit Banks's outpost at Front Royal, on the eastern side of the Massanutten, between the south fork of the Shenandoah River and the Blue Ridge. The Manassas Gap Railroad ran through the place, and it was this line that Banks was using to shift his army, most recently Shields's division, to General McDowell, who was preparing to cross the Rappahannock near Fredericksburg in order to support McClellan down on the peninsula. If Jackson captured Front Royal, the key to the Shenandoah Valley, Banks would not only be cut off from McDowell, but his fortified position at Strasburg would also be turned.[13]

With the general strategy worked out, Jackson cut the orders to unify his army. His own division was to march north along the macadamized Valley Pike through Harrisonburg and along the western side of the Massanutten, to New Market. Ewell's division, on the eastern side of the Massanutten, was to march down to Luray. To help deceive the enemy into thinking that Jackson actually intended to attack Strasburg, on the western side of the Massanutten, Taylor's brigade was detached from Ewell and ordered to march west, around the Massanutten, through Keezletown, and onto Harrisonburg. From there it headed north down the graveled pike, and, after marching twenty-six miles, pulled into New Market, linking up with Jackson on the evening of May 20, 1862.[14]

When the Louisianans marched into the encampment, the men of Jackson's division, although worn out by their recent campaign, stood up alongside the road to catch a glimpse of the famed Louisiana Tigers. They were, one man remembered, "stepping jauntily as if on parade ... not a straggler, but every man in his place, though it had marched twenty miles and more, in open column with arms at right shoulder shift."[15] Private George Neese of Chew's (Virginia) Artillery, Jackson's division, remembered: "I for the first time saw some of the much talked about [Louisiana] Tigers.... They looked courageous and daringly fearless."[16]

Once the Tigers and others marched past Jackson's veterans, Taylor ordered them to halt, stack arms, and break ranks to establish a bivouac. As they did so, he sought out Jackson for further instructions. Finding his new commanding general perched atop a rail fence which overlooked the field the Louisianans were in the process of occupying, Taylor rode up to the Valley commander, crisply saluted, and declared his name and rank. Jackson slowly looked up, peering from beneath his "mangy cap with visor drawn low" and in "a low, gentle voice" asked the Louisiana sugar planter how far his brigade had marched that day.

"Keezletown Road, six and twenty miles," Taylor proudly replied.

"You seem to have no stragglers," Jackson interestingly noted.

"Never allow straggling."

"You must teach my people; they straggle badly," Jackson concluded with a pained grimace.

Just then, the brigade band started to play a gleeful waltz, and some of the Tigers and others began to dance. Watching from his fence post, Jackson, "after a contemplative suck at a lemon," murmured to Taylor, "Thoughtless fellows for such serious work." Taylor assured the no-nonsense Presbyterian that his bayou-bred Louisianans were well up to the task at hand — that looks could be deceiving. He then politely excused himself to rejoin his brigade, more than likely to put a damper on the festivities.[17]

The next day, May 21, Jackson placed the Louisiana Brigade on point to link up with Ewell's division, which was on the east side of the Massanutten. With the colorful Zouaves from the Tiger Rifles in front as skirmishers, setting the pace, Jackson's column marched over the Massanutten toward Luray, the designated assembly point. Jackson adopted, at Taylor's behest, the "old army" technique of marching for fifty minutes and resting for ten.[18] Private George Neese of Chew's battery remembered: "The troops are all in light marching order, having left all their surplus baggage, even their knapsacks at New Market, and as the Romans of old used to say of the gladiators, they are stripped for fight."[19] By evening, Jackson united with Ewell near Luray. The Louisianans impressed Captain Nisbet of the 21st Georgia, Trimble's brigade, Ewell's division, as they marched into the encampment. He remembered:

> Each man [of the Louisiana Brigade], every inch a soldier, was perfectly uniformed, wearing white leggings, marching quick step, with his rifle at "right shoulder shift," while the band at front played "the Girl I Left Behind Me." The blue-gray uniforms of the officers were brilliant with gold lace, their rakish slouch hats adorned with tassels and plumes. Behold a military pageantry, beautiful and memorable. We stood at "present arms" as they passed. It was the most picturesque and inspiring martial sight that came under my eyes during four years of service.[20]

Jackson's army, with Ewell's arrival, would now consist of two full divisions, his own and Ewell's. Jackson's consisted of four brigades of infantry, Brig. Gen. Charles Winder's, Brig. Gen. William Taliaferro's (pronounced TAL-iver), Colonel John Patton's, and Colonel William Scott's, seven batteries of Virginia artillery, and two regiments of Virginia cavalry, the 7th and 11th, under Colonel Turner Ashby. These troops, coupled with Ewell's division and Munford's and Flournoy's cavalry, would give Jackson 16,000 men to take on Banks's 7,500.[21]

On May 22 the Valley Army continued its historic journey north toward Front Royal with the Tigers and others again leading the march. The men trudged for hours through a soaking rain and ankle-deep mud, and their exhaustion grew more acute. "Almost tired to death," one soldier remembered. Jackson encamped that evening within ten miles of Front Royal, the army's first objective. Before the men were allowed to sleep, however, they were ordered to polish their rust-encrusted weapons, which was a sure sign of an up-coming battle.[22]

During the next day's march, Jackson learned that a large portion of the Federal garrison at Front Royal consisted of Colonel John Reese Kenly's 1st Maryland Regiment. He therefore placed his own Marylanders, Colonel Bradley Johnson's 1st Maryland (C.S.), in the van to have a crack at them first. Jackson planned to use Johnson's Marylanders and Taylor's Louisianans to take Front

Royal from the south while Flournoy's 6th Virginia Cavalry, crossing a mile and a half below the town at McCoy's Ford, rode up the west side of the south fork of the Shenandoah and cut the Federals' communication lines to Strasburg.[23]

In order to avoid the Union pickets who were posted on the main road, Jackson chose to march his men up a steep, winding path, called Snake Road, about a mile south of the town, just past McCoy's Ford. Soon after 1:00 P.M., Johnson's Marylanders, somewhat winded by the climb, crested the last wooded rise that led into Front Royal and scattered some Federals from Company H, 1st Maryland, who were resting quietly at the intersection of Snake and Gooney Manor roads. Pushing forward another half mile, flushing out a few more Union pickets, the Confederates were met by the famous Rebel spy Belle Boyd, a "rather well-looking woman ... [and] citizen of the town," who was drawn by the fire. Boyd extolled the approaching Southerners to "charge right down and [you will] catch them all."

Colonel John Reese Kenly, 1st Maryland Regiment (U.S.), Army of the Shenandoah, commanded the Federal forces that were overrun by the Tigers and others at the battle of Front Royal. Kenly himself was captured. This is a post-war photograph. *USAMHI*

Believing young Belle's story, Jackson ordered Johnson, Wheat, and Taylor to do just that—charge right down and catch them all—while he brought up the rest of his army.[24]

Front Royal was about mile to the Tigers' front, down below. Another half mile or so beyond the town, atop a commanding hill, was Kenly's fortified camp. And beyond that was the confluence of the north and south forks of the Shenandoah River. A bridge spanned each fork and a trestle of the Manassas Gap Railroad traversed the south fork and headed west to Strasburg, Banks's headquarters. The Federal garrison at Front Royal consisted of fifteen companies of infantry, nine from the 1st Maryland, three from the 2nd Massachusetts, two from the 29th Pennsylvania, and one each from the 3rd Wisconsin and the 27th Indiana. They were supported by Lieutenant Charles Atwell's section of long-range Parrott Rifles from Captain Joseph Knap's Independent Battery E, Pennsylvania Light Artillery ("the Fort Pitt Artillery"), two companies from Major Philip Vought's 5th New York Cavalry, and a company of Empire State engineers. All told, there were about 1,100 Federal soldiers in and around the town.[25]

As ordered, Johnson's Marylanders and Wheat's Tigers swept down the hill and stormed into Front Royal while Taylor brought up the rest of his brigade. Major Wheat, excited by the order and no doubt wanting to vindicate his name after Somerville, charged down the left side of the road and was the first Confederate to enter the town. He "shot by like a rocket," Johnson remembered, "his red cap gleaming, revolver in hand, and got in first, throwing his shots right and left."[26] General Taylor reported, "Major Wheat's battalion, of five companies, was immediately ordered forward into the town, to assist the Maryland Regiment in dislodging the enemy.... Major Wheat performed his part in gallant style, charging through the town."[27] General Jackson similarly reported:

> The 1st Maryland Regiment, supported by Wheat's battalion of Louisiana Volunteers, and the remainder of Taylor's brigade, acting as a reserve, pushed forward in gallant style, charging the Federals, who made a spirited resistance, driving them through the town and taking some prisoners.[28]

Lucy Rebecca Buck, the daughter of a respected local landowner, remembered the initial clash between Union and Confederate forces at Front Royal:

> Going to the door we saw the Yankees scampering over the meadow below our house.... By this time some scattered parties of Confederate infantry came up and charged their ranks, when firing one volley they wheeled about — every man for

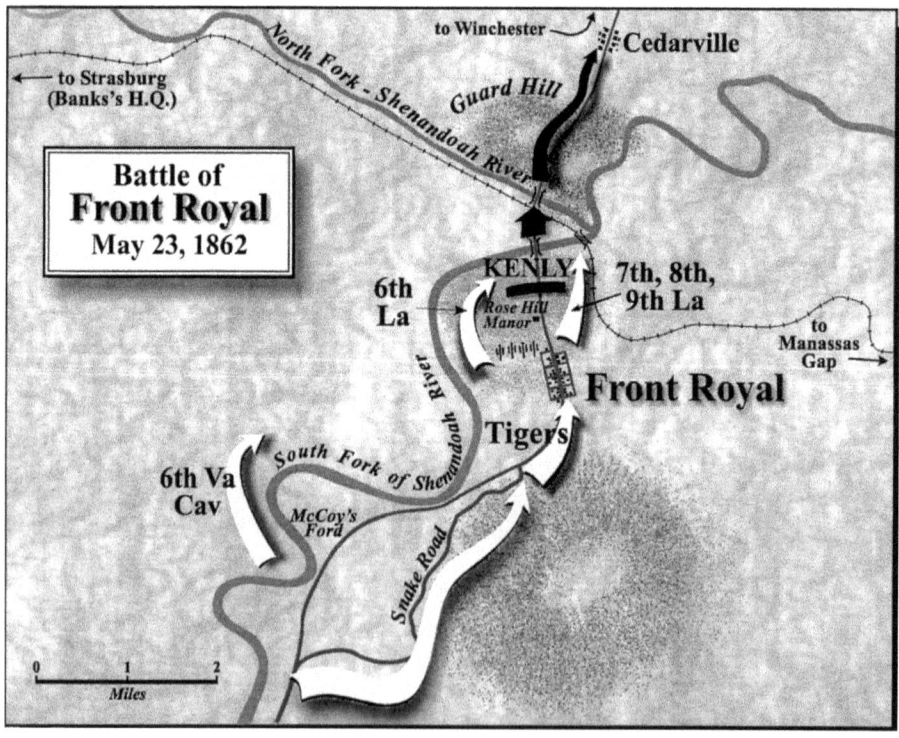

himself they scampered out of town like a flock of sheep — such an undignified exodus was never witnessed before.[29]

Once the Federal provost, Company I, 1st Maryland, was driven from the town, Wheat and Johnson ordered their men to head for the main Federal camp atop the hill. Colonel Kenly, the Union commander, reported: "Two battalions of the enemy's infantry [i.e., Johnson's and Wheat's] pushed rapidly forward on both sides of the road leading from town toward the camp."[30] As the emboldened Tigers approached the ridge that fronted the hill, however, they were forced to the ground by Atwell's Parrott Rifles, firing canister, and nine or so companies of infantry who were firing musketry down from the Federal stronghold. Lieutenant Thompson of the 1st Maryland (U.S.) remembered: "A brisk fire was opened by our men ... doing great damage to the enemy's rank and file, and throwing them into confusion, but they rallied."[31]

Wheat ordered his men to take cover around Rose Hill, a large brick and wood mansion, about 250 yards to the right-front of Kenly's camp, where, according to Lucy Buck, "a good deal of fighting was done."[32] Before long, Jack-

The Tigers charged up this street and past this house, Dr. Garrison's, as they moved through Front Royal to dislodge the main Federal encampment near Rose Hill. Colonel Bradley Johnson of the 1st Maryland remembered that Wheat "shot by like a rocket, his red cap gleaming, revolver in hand, and got in first, throwing his shots right and left."

son himself arrived on the scene with Carrington's, Courtney's, and Brockenbrough's Virginia batteries, armed with 4.62-inch smoothbores of various makes, and ordered them to be posted atop a hill to the Tigers' right-rear. With Wheat's and Johnson's battalions pinned in front of the Federal breastworks, and with the Confederate artillery gaining fire superiority, General Taylor recommended a double envelopment. While Wheat's and Johnson's men would continue to fix Kenly's position in front, with Carrington's, Courtney's, and Brockenbrough's guns offering suppressive fire against Atwell's Parrotts, Taylor could maneuver his 7th, 8th, and 9th regiments to the far right, out past Johnson's Marylanders, and cross the relatively unguarded railroad trestle that spanned the south fork, getting in Kenly's rear. As they did so, Colonel Seymour's Irish Regiment would sweep to the left, making a dash for the South Fork Bridge, immediately behind Kenly's camp, drawing the Federals' fire. Without a second thought, and no doubt impressed by the Louisiana planter's enterprise, Old Jack nodded in approval and Taylor led the first attack of his life.[33]

Kenly watched helplessly as the Pelican Staters worked their way around his flanks and decided to order his men to torch the camp and retreat across both branches of the Shenandoah River before they were completely cut off. Once across the North Fork Bridge, screened by the 5th New York Cavalry, Kenly ordered Vought's troopers to torch the bridge while he established a new line along the riverbank, anchored by a dominating rise called Guard Hill, previously held by two companies of the 29th Pennsylvania. He was determined to hold Jackson's minions back as long as possible to alert Banks of the threat.[34]

On the heels of the rapidly retreating Federals, Johnson's Marylanders charged through the burning camp, snagged a few prisoners, and crossed over the South Fork Bridge — beating the 6th Louisiana — onto a low crop of land between the two forks where Riverside mansion stood. Progressing another 400 or so yards up the road, the Marylanders were stopped cold by Kenly's new line atop Guard Hill and the burning North Fork Bridge. General Taylor soon joined Johnson with some of his Louisianans. With the low-lying bridge on fire, overwatched by a reinforced Federal infantry regiment and two pieces of artillery, and with no sign of reinforcement in sight, Taylor rode back to Riverside for instructions from Jackson, who resolved to continue the attack. Taylor's Louisianans would charge across the North Fork Bridge, burning or not, and drive the enemy into the ground.[35]

At that moment, almost by dumb luck, Wheat was escorting his desperadoes up through the destroyed Federal camp and across the South Fork Bridge. Jackson would use these Tigers to lead the forlorn attack and ordered them to pass through the Marylanders and take the burning bridge. Ewell's assistant adjutant and future son-in-law, Captain G. Campbell Brown, remembered:

> I shall never forget the style in which Wheat's battalion passed us as we stood on the road. [Wheat] was riding full gallop, yelling at the top of his voice; his big

Riverside Manor, which the Tigers blew past on their way to charge across the burning North Fork Bridge. After the battle of Front Royal, Jackson established his headquarters here, planning his next moves to Middletown and Winchester.

> sergeant-major [James Wrigley] running at top speed just after him, calling upon the men to come on; and they strung out according to their speed and "stomach for the fight," following after, all running; all yelling; all looking like fight. Their peculiar Zouave dress, light striped, baggy pants, bronzed and desperate faces and wild excitement made up a glorious picture. Wheat himself looked in a fight as handsome as any man I ever saw.[36]

With Wheat in the lead, the Tigers descended the dirt road toward the river's edge, stormed across the bridge through the flames, and secured the opposite shore in the face of the enemy's galling fire, which was plunging down from their left front atop Guard Hill. Wheat's gutsy filibusters were soon joined by the rest of the Louisiana Brigade, who helped put out the blaze. The span was saved, "but it was rather a near thing," Taylor recalled. "My horse and clothing were scorched, and many men burned their hands severely while throwing brands into the river."[37]

With the North Fork Bridge now in Confederate hands, Jackson ordered Johnson's Marylanders and Taylor's Louisianans to push up the road and through the wooded gap to press the Federals in front while Flournoy's cavalry, just arrived, would exploit the breach. After another hour of fighting, Kenly's position was once again turned and the frantic Yankees were forced to

Present-day site of the low-lying North Fork Bridge, where the Tigers gallantly breached the final Federal protective line at Front Royal. The pilings are still present, as is Guard Hill, to the left. One of General Ewell's aides, Virginia Captain G. Campbell Brown, remembered: "I shall never forget the style in which Wheat's battalion passed us as we stood on the road.... Their peculiar Zouave dress, light striped baggy pants, bronzed and desperate faces and wild excitement made up a glorious picture."

run for their lives toward Winchester. "The pursuit begun was kept up vigorously," remembered Captain Henry Kyd Douglas, Jackson's acting inspector general. "There was much handsome work done by Flournoy's cavalry, with good results." Flournoy's pursuit, like Taylor's double envelopment near the river's edge, was carried out in textbook fashion. By late afternoon, four of his companies had run down what was left of Kenly's command near Cedarville, five miles from Front Royal. Literally cutting the Federals to pieces, Flournoy's troopers captured almost all of Kenly's command, including the colonel himself, Lieutenant Atwell's invaluable rifled guns (which were given to the Rockbridge Artillery), and the once-proud colors of the 1st Maryland (U.S.).[38]

As the Virginia cavaliers pursued Kenly's doomed command, Wheat's exhausted Tigers were recuperating along the shady banks of the north fork of the Shenandoah when they unexpectedly heard a train whistle coming from the direction of Manassas Gap, passing behind their position. Earlier in the day, Ashby's cavalry had cut the telegraph lines between Strasburg and Manassas, and the engineer of the Federal train, which consisted of two locomotives, three passenger cars, and fifty tonnage cars, apparently had no idea that the town had been seized by Jackson's insurgents. No doubt sensing opportunity and more glory for his battalion, Wheat quickly roused his men from their late-afternoon snooze and ordered them to charge the slow-moving train. Swarming up the embankment and across the flat land behind Riverside, the Tigers hopped aboard the locomotive, threw its wholly surprised driver to the ground, and brought the train to a stop. When the filibusters opened the cars, they were pleasantly surprised to find over $300,000 worth of commissary stores packed inside, which were eagerly consumed by the Valley Army over the next few weeks.[39]

With the battle won and the town secured, Jackson encamped the bulk of his army on the north side of Guard Hill, established his headquarters at Riverside, and garrisoned Front Royal with men from each regiment in Ewell's division to care for the wounded. Among those left behind was Captain Henry Gardner of the Delta Rangers, Wheat's Battalion. Lucy Buck remembered:

> [After the battle] Captain Gardner of the N.O. [New Orleans] Battalion came [into our parlor for breakfast]. He wore the badge of the battalion, one of the prettiest imaginable designs—a little silver crescent in a concavity of which revolved a silver star upon a pivot on which was inscribed on one side "The Star Battalion from the Crescent City" in a revolution—on the reverse side "Wheat's New Orleans Battalion." It was a cunning little ornament and I really coveted it.[40]

All told, the battle of Front Royal cost General Banks about 900 men (750 prisoners, 32 killed, and 122 wounded) and Jackson 36 (mostly from Flournoy's cavalry). Of this total, Wheat's Battalion officially listed one man killed and six wounded, including Lieutenant Robert Grinnell of the Life Guards, who was "injured in the hand."[41]

7

Give No Quarter to the Damned Yankees

The Battle of First Winchester

> *The gentle Tigers were looting right merrily, diving in and out of wagons with the activity of rabbits in a warren; but this occupation was abandoned on my approach, and in a moment they were in line, looking as solemn and virtuous as deacons at a funeral.*
>
> — Richard Taylor

In the wake of the crucial victory at Front Royal, Jackson's scouts reported that General Banks was evacuating his forces from Strasburg and was retreating down two parallel roads, the Valley and Cedar Creek pikes, and back to Winchester, his entrepôt. In response, Jackson resolved to cross over the northern spur of the Massanutten and intercept the part of Banks's army that was strung out along the Valley Pike near the hamlet of Middletown with his main force while Ewell, with Trimble's and Scott's brigades, continued the march up to Winchester direct.[1]

Jackson created a "flying column" to reach the enemy first. It consisted of Colonel Ashby's 7th and 11th Virginia Cavalry regiments, Captain Robert Chew's battery of horse artillery, one section (two guns) of newly-acquired Parrott rifles from the Fort Pitt Artillery that were now being utilized by Lieutenant William Poague's Rockbridge (Virginia) Artillery, and, to support Poague's guns, Wheat's battalion of infantry which was required to trot not far behind. Following the Tigers, at some distance, marched the rest of Taylor's brigade, then Jackson's division, now commanded by its senior-most brigadier, Charles Winder. Elzey's brigade from Ewell's division brought up the rear.[2]

About four miles up the serpentine, hilly, and muddy road, surrounded on both sides by trees, Ashby's horsemen ran into Lt. Col. Calvin Douty's 1st Maine Cavalry Regiment. For the next several hours, the two mounted forces jockeyed for position in the woods and scattered fields that lined the road. Occasionally, the fighting grew severe enough that Poague's section, supported by Wheat's Battalion, had to be brought up to help Ashby and Chew blast away the Federal troopers. At around 3:30 P.M., the Confederate cavalrymen finally topped the ridge that overlooked Middletown, where they were surprisingly greeted, in light of the day-long skirmish, by the coveted sight of Federal supply wagons "of all kinds, miles of them," stacked up on the enclosed pike.[3]

Riding forward to the low ridge, Jackson, surveying the scene with an artillerist's eye, ordered Chew's and Poague's guns to go into battery astride the road and rake the clogged pike with shot and shell.[4] He remembered:

> Upon arriving there [I] found the Valley Turnpike crowded with the retreating Federal cavalry, upon which the batteries of Poague and Chew, with [Wheat's] infantry, promptly opened, and in a few moments the turnpike, which had just before teemed with life, presented a most appalling spectacle of carnage and destruction. The road was literally obstructed with the mingled and confused mass of struggling and dying horses and riders. The Federal column was pierced, but what proportion of its strength had passed north toward Winchester I had then no means of knowing. Among the surviving cavalry the wildest confusion ensued, and they scattered in disorder in various directions.[5]

As the terrified Federals tried to jump the wall that lined the pike, Major Wheat ordered Captain White's Tiger Rifles to open fire on them with their long-range Mississippi rifles. Private George Neese of Chew's battery remembered:

> When we opened fire a Yankee captain of cavalry left the fleeing fugitives, jumped his horse across a fence, flourished his saber, and beckoned his comrades to follow him, but his mixed-up troop kept on down the pike as if they were deeply impressed with the ideas that the safest and surest way to save their country's flag was to run away with it. The Tigers saw the Yankee captain when he jumped into the field. They opened fire on him with their long-ranged rifles. I saw him fall soon after, and heard some of the Tigers say: "That will do him. Fire at the others in the road." It was fun for the Tigers to fight cavalry, but it looked a shame to shoot down the lone Yankee captain as he was vainly trying to rally his men, to defend the running remnant of Banks's Army, but alas! Such is war.[6]

When the rebel artillerists could no longer see a target through the smoky haze, Jackson ordered Ashby's cavaliers to charge down the slope and sweep through the trapped wagons. To protect their vulnerable left flank, Stonewall directed Wheat and a couple of Chew's guns to advance and block any Federal sortie from Middletown. As the Tigers approached to within eighty yards of the pike, however, they were intercepted by a company from Douty's command, barely discernible through the haze, which was charging up from the town and seemingly intent on stampeding the renegade Louisianans into the ground. The stalwart Tigers didn't panic, didn't run, but instead took a knee and fired a "deadly volley" into the Federal horsemen at close range. Their musketry was apparently so effective that it caused a chain reaction, toppling the rear rank of the unfortunate Yankee troopers into the collapsing front rank.

They "went down in a tangled heap," remembered Captain Henry Kyd Douglas. "The rear, unable to check themselves, plunged on, in, over, upon the bleeding pile, a roaring, shrieking, struggling mass of men and horses, crushed and dying. It was a sickening sight, the worst I have ever seen then, and for a moment I felt a twinge of regret [for the Tigers who were ordered to carry out] that bloody work."[7]

Once the Yankee cavalrymen were dispatched, Wheat's intrepid Tigers leapt over the wall and secured sixty or so wagons with most of their teams intact and 200 dazed Union soldiers. Just then, General Taylor arrived with the rest of the brigade, the 7th Louisiana on point, and Jackson sent them down to the pike to assist the Special Battalion. When Taylor reached the road, however, he noticed that the only help the Tigers needed was to get more haversacks to accommodate their plunder. "The gentle Tigers were looting right merrily," Taylor recalled, "diving in and out of wagons with the activity of rabbits in a warren; but this occupation was abandoned on my approach, and in a moment they were in line, looking as solemn and virtuous as deacons at a funeral."[8]

As Wheat's booty-laden filibusters straightened up to the officer who had executed two of their comrades a few months before, several rifled shells came flying into their position from Captain Robert Hampton's Independent Battery F, Pennsylvania Light Artillery, which had just set up on a hill to the southwest, on the other side of the road. One of the battery's accurately fired shells exploded above the Pelican Regiment and wounded several of its soldiers. Another exploded near Taylor, tearing his saddlecloth and smothering him with dirt. It was now feared that the Federals were planning to make a strong drive up the pike from Middletown—that a larger battle loomed. Jackson therefore ordered Ashby's cavalry, Chew's artillery, and Wheat's infantry to continue their pursuit of the fleeing Yankees who had escaped the ambush north down the pike while Taylor's Louisiana Brigade turned south toward Middletown to meet the new threat.[9]

Pressing southward, through the town and toward Strasburg, Taylor's stalwart brigade, which reportedly stretched a mile-and-a-half astride the pike with colors flying, easily drove the Federals before them. Included in this force was Banks's personal bodyguard, Captain Charles Collis's exotic company of Philadelphia Zouaves, who were courageously covering what was left of Banks's wagon train that was now frantically heading for Cedar Creek Pike. Once Jackson realized that he was engaged in a mere rearguard action, he recalled Taylor, turned the whole column around, placing the Stonewall Brigade on point, and headed north to Newtown to link up with Ashby, Wheat, and Chew.[10]

The march north, although on the smooth pike, was not easy. All along the way, "the road was encumbered with evidence of the hurry of flight. Wagons broken down, overturned, some with their contents scattered, some sound and untouched, some with good teams, some horseless, sutlers' stores, officers' luggage, knapsacks, Bibles, cards, photographs, song books, and cooking utensils; and general wreck of military matter."[11] Private George Neese remembered seeing "abandoned baggage wagons, commissary wagons, wagons laden with medical stores, sutler goods, and all sorts of army equipments strewn along the track of the hastily retiring enemy."[12] When Jackson marched his column into Newtown, four miles up ahead, he was "pained to see that so many of Ashby's command, both cavalry and infantry [i.e., Wheat's Battalion], forgetful of their high trust as the advance of a pursuing army, deserted their colors, and abandoned themselves to pillage to such an extent as to make it necessary for [Ashby] to discontinue further pursuit."[13] The cavalry, instead of running down the enemy as ordered, had apparently stopped to plunder Federal wagons that had been abandoned along the pike. And Wheat's Tigers, tired out, fell far behind Chew's battery and seemingly joined Ashby's troopers in pillaging the captured wagons.[14]

In spite of this serious breach of discipline, Jackson ordered his men to continue the march. They would travel those last nine miles to Winchester if it was the last thing they did. Not only was Ewell marching up a parallel road to Winchester, but it was also imperative, in Jackson's mind, to run down Banks's disorganized army before it was able to fortify the hills that surrounded the town.[15] Captain Douglas remembered:

> [Jackson] had no thought of going into camp. True, the army had been marching almost daily for weeks, had been up nearly all night before, had been living for some time on much excitement and very small rations; it was exhausted, broken down, and apparently unfit for battle; but [Jackson] was determined to push on that night. Of course no one was surprised for that was already Stonewall's Way. The soldiers were tired and weary and grumbled a bit as usual, but they had faith and plodded on, not cheerfully but resignedly. By the sweat of their brow, he was saving their blood.[16]

The night march from Newtown to Winchester was, to say the least, torturous and surreal. Private Harry Handerson of the 9th Louisiana remembered, "Our orders were to press forward to Winchester ... and foot-sore and faint, we struggled forward until late in the night."[17] Another Confederate recalled: "We moved at a snail's pace and [halted repeatedly], falling asleep at the halts and being suddenly wakened up when the motion was resumed, we fairly staggered on, worn almost to exhaustion by the weariness of such march."[18] Burning wagons and the white gravel of the pike marked the way north. And behind every fence and wood lot, it seemed, the desperate Federals had set up ambushes against the punchy Confederates. This occurred all night long, slowing the column appreciably.[19] Sometime after 2:00 A.M., Sunday, May 25, Colonel Sam Fulkerson, temporarily in charge of Taliaferro's brigade, pleaded with Jackson to let the men rest lest they get slaughtered in the up-and-coming fight. Jackson listened patiently to his trusted lieutenant and then replied: "Colonel, I do not believe you can feel more for your men than I do. This is very hard on them, but by night march I hope to save many valuable lives. I want to get possession of the hills of Winchester before daylight." Then after a moment's reflection, Jackson seemed to have a sympathetic change of heart and said, "Colonel, you may rest your command for two hours."[20] This order applied to the rest of the column as well, and for the next two hours, from 2:00 to 4:00 in the morning, most of the men were allowed to sleep, Jackson himself standing guard at the head of the column with Colonel Ashby.[21]

The quaint town of Winchester, Jackson's next target, was the veritable northern gateway of the Shenandoah Valley. Located in its lower reaches, just thirty miles from the Potomac River and Harpers Ferry, it had, by 1862, grown to become the region's largest settlement, with tidy, well-laid streets, several taverns, a courthouse, a central market, a railroad stop, and some 2,000 souls. Jackson's troops had garrisoned the borough during the early months of the war with Joe Johnston and "Jeb" Stuart when he and his brigade were dispatched east by rail to fight at Manassas. After the battle, in which he had gained notoriety for his actions on Henry Hill, Jackson was promoted to major general and put in command of the Valley District, Department of Northern Virginia, with headquarters in Winchester. In March 1862, on the heels of the abortive Romney Campaign, Jackson's army was driven from Winchester by Nathaniel Banks's advancing army and was forced to retreat to the southern end of the Valley, near Staunton, yielding most of the strategic region to the Federals. If Old Stonewall could recapture Winchester from Banks, it would not only free his adopted home of Yankee interlopers and return some luster to his tarnished reputation, but could also change the course of war.[22]

The hills around Winchester that Jackson feared the most were west of the Valley Pike, just south of the town. The southernmost eminence, Parkin's Hill, was the most dominant. A broad valley, about a thousand yards wide, separated it from a parallel ridge called the Central Heights by the Federals or Bower's Hill by the locals, which ran perpendicular to the pike and abutted the southern end of the town. And unfortunately for the men of the Valley Army, what remained of Banks's army was indeed able to deploy along both hills and await Jackson's attack from the direction of Newtown and Ewell's from the direction of Front Royal. If Winchester was to be had, these hills would have to be taken first.[23]

At 4:00 A.M., Stonewall's appointed "early dawn," Jackson led General Winder down the pike and across Abraham Creek on a leader's reconnaissance. Stopping near Hollingsworth's Mill, the Valley commander pointed through the early morning fog to his left front, toward Parkin's Hill, and laconically instructed his protégé to "occupy that hill." Winder subsequently grabbed the celebrated Stonewall Brigade and led it across the creek and up the wooded slope of Parkin's Hill, easily driving the thin Federal picket line before it. Once the Virginians gained the hill's crest, however, crossing over to the cleared northern slope, all hell broke loose when a storm of Union artillery poured in from the central heights and drove them back into the wood line. Winder imme-

7. Give No Quarter to the Damned Yankees

Present-day view of the "Central Heights" at Winchester. The Louisiana Brigade charged across this valley to get at Colonel George Gordon's Federal brigade.

diately ordered up his own artillery—Poague's, Carpenter's, and Cutshaw's batteries—and directed the rest of his division, Patton's and Taliaferro's brigades, to deploy to the left of the Stonewall Brigade.[24]

Manning the heights opposite Winder were twelve 3-inch rifles from Captains James Thompson's, Joseph Knap's, and Robert Hampton's independent batteries C, E, and F, Pennsylvania Light Artillery, and Captain G.W. Cothran's Battery M, 1st New York Light Artillery. About seventy-five yards below the guns were six regiments of supporting infantry: the 5th Connecticut, 2nd Massachusetts, 3rd Wisconsin, 27th Indiana, 29th Pennsylvania, and the 28th New York. And hidden from Confederate view, behind the guns, awaited five companies from Colonel Thornton Broadhead's 4th Michigan Cavalry. The entire force, about 3,000 strong, was commanded by Colonel George Gordon of the 2nd Massachusetts.[25]

Pinned down by these Federals, whose fire "was decidedly more effective, both in rapidity and precision of fire," Jackson sent back for the Louisiana Brigade, the next unit in his line of march.[26] Riding up to Parkin's Hill ahead of his command, Taylor met with Jackson, who pointed across the valley and impassively said to the Louisiana brigadier: "General, can your brigade charge a battery?"

"It can try," Taylor responded.

"Very good; it must do it then. Move it forward."[27]

Taylor quickly rode back down the hill and directed his brigade, the colorful Star Battalion in front, off the road, to the left, and along the southern base of Parkin's Hill that was "steep, though nowhere abrupt." As the Tigers and others ascended the ridge toward the Confederate left, just beyond Taliaferro's brigade, they entered a shallow depression where enemy shells began to rain down upon them. "Many men fell," Taylor recalled, "and the whistling of shot and shell occasioned much ducking of heads in the column. This annoyed me no little, as it was but child's play to the work immediately at hand." To rally his men, Taylor screamed: "What the hell are you dodging for? If there is any more of it, you will be halted under this fire for an hour!" The men quickly straightened up "as if they had swallowed ramrods" and continued their steady march toward the far left.[28]

Once Taylor reached the proper spot, a little after seven o'clock, he judiciously ordered Wheat to refuse the brigade's vulnerable left by fanning his battalion out in skirmish formation while he deployed the bulk of the brigade along the reverse slope of Parkin's Hill, facing north. Once all were in position, Taylor ordered his regiments up and over the crest and into the dismal valley, which was "densely and obscurely filled with smoke and fog ... so dense as to make it impossible to see over a few rods."[29]

Taylor knew that if his men were to accomplish their mission and not get slaughtered in the process, they had to get at the Union line as soon as possible. As such, the brigade was ordered to move at the quick time, without stopping to fire. "The enemy poured grape [i.e., artillery canister] and musketry into Taylor's line as soon as it came in sight," Jackson's chief of staff Major Robert Dabney recalled. "General Taylor rode in front of his brigade, drawn sword in hand, occasionally turning his horse, at other times merely turning in his saddle to see that his line was up. They marched up that hill in perfect order, not firing a shot!" Private William Goldsborough from the 1st Maryland (C.S.) remembered that the Louisianans "moved with the most beautiful precision, although their trail was marked by dead and wounded men at every step." Colonel Seymour of the 6th Louisiana was, according to General Taylor, "on foot, with sword and cap in hand, his gray locks streaming, turning to his sturdy Irishmen with 'Steady, men! Dress to the right!'"[30] The subsequent highly disciplined charge of the Louisiana Brigade at the battle of First Winchester became legendary. Henry Kyd Douglas remembered:

> General Taylor threw his brigade into line where directed, and it moved forward in gallant style. I have rarely seen a more beautiful charge. This full brigade, with a line of glistening bayonets bright in that morning sun, its formation straight and compact, its tread quick and easy as it pushed on through the clover and up the hill, was a sight to delight a veteran.[31]

As Taylor's men began their vulnerable ascent up the Central Heights, the five cavalry companies from the 4th Michigan were ordered to swoop down and

7. Give No Quarter to the Damned Yankees

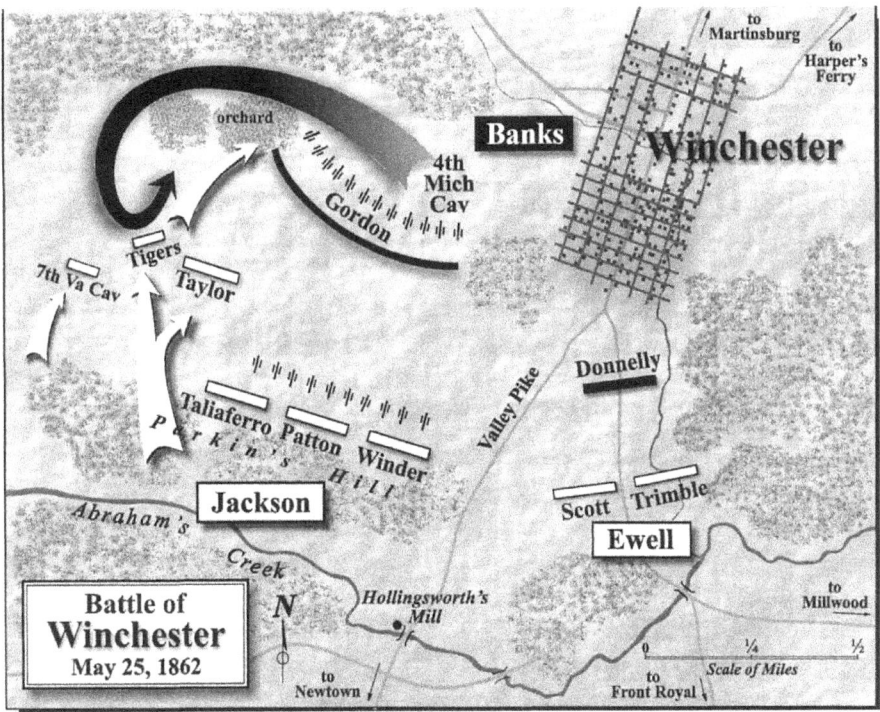

charge through the valley and smash their left and rear. But the Tigers, now joined by some of Ashby's cavalry, had refused Taylor's flank and were therefore directly facing the advancing Yankee horsemen. Firing almost point blank into their ranks, the Tigers killed several of Brodhead's surprised troopers and Ashby's belligerent cavaliers, bearing down on their flank with saber, pistol, or shotgun, forced the Michiganders to retreat up the hill. Pressing his advantage, Wheat led his crafty filibusters up the hill and into an orchard, not 150 yards from the extreme right of the Federal line, which was held by Lt. Col. Edwin Brown's 28th New York and Hampton's Independent Battery F. The dispersed Tigers were soon joined by the 10th and 23rd Virginia regiments of Taliaferro's brigade, who helped pour a "murderous fire" into the Yankee line.[32]

Seeing Taylor's regiments bearing down on his front and Taliaferro's, Ashby's, and Wheat's valiant troops swinging around his right, Colonel Gordon ordered his brigade, starting with its artillery support, to pull out. Noticing this movement through the haze on the hill below, Taylor rose in his stirrups and in a "commanding voice" that even the Yankees were apparently startled to hear, ordered his Louisianans to charge up the last 300 steep yards and take the crest. Private John Worsham of the 21st Virginia, Campbell's brigade, Winder's division, remembered: "That charge of Taylor's was the grandest charge I saw during the war. Every man was in his proper place. There was all

Colonel Thornton Brodhead, commander, 4th Michigan Cavalry. *USAMHI*

the pomp and circumstance of war about it that was always lacking in our charges."[33]

The Pelican Staters swept "grandly over the ledge and fence to crown the heights" and drove the retreating Federals before them. Seeing Banks's defensive line crumble under the weight of Taylor's charge, Jackson yelled, "Order

Right: Colonel George Gordon of the 2nd Massachusetts commanded the Federal brigade at Winchester that the Tigers and others soundly defeated. *USAMHI*

the whole line forward, the battle's won!" All units in Jackson's army now converged upon Winchester on the heels of the retreating Unionists: Taylor's, Winder's, Patton's, Taliaferro's, and Elzey's brigades from the southwest, and Trimble's and Scott's brigades from the southeast, attacking up the Front Royal Road with Ewell.[34]

To add to the confusion, the Federals had torched their warehouses in Winchester, setting part of the town on fire. The townsfolk, "who for more than two months had been suffering under the hateful surveillance and rigors of military despotism," came out of their dwellings not only to put out the flames and cheer Ashby's advancing cavalry, but also to join the Southern horsemen in assaulting the departing Federals.[35] Union Colonel George Gordon reported with disdain:

> My retreating column suffered serious loss in the streets of Winchester. Males and females vied with each other in increasing the number of their victims, by firing from the houses, throwing hand grenades, hot water, and missiles of every description. The hellish spirit of murder was carried on by the enemy's cavalry, who followed to butcher, and who struck down with saber and pistol the hapless soldier, sinking from fatigue, unheeding his cries for

Right: Present-day view of Winchester, looking up its main street.

mercy, indifferent to his claims as a prisoner of war.... The Rebel cavalry, it would appear, give no quarter. It cannot be doubted that they butchered our stragglers; that they fight under a black flag; that they cried as they slew the wearied and jaded, "Give no quarter to the damned Yankees."[36]

When Jackson entered the town, he rode up to Taylor, grasped his hand, and quietly congratulated him for the hard-won victory. Once again, the little battalion from New Orleans played a significant role in bringing about a Southern success. By securing the Confederate left flank — stopping an enemy cavalry charge and turning the Federal right — the Tigers enabled the rest of the Louisiana Brigade to storm the Central Heights almost single-handedly.[37]

8

Retreat to the Upper Valley

There we lay in deathly silence, like a Bengal Tiger when he crouches down ready to spring upon his unsuspected prey.
— George Nisbet

After Banks was defeated at Winchester he ordered what was left of his army north, out of the Valley and down the pike through Martinsburg and Falling Waters to Williamsport, Maryland, on the north bank of the Potomac River. Jackson, of course, pursued, and ordered Ashby to send his cavalry as far north as Falling Waters, astride the Baltimore and Ohio Railroad and just eight miles from Williamsport. While these movements occurred, the trusted Stonewall Brigade was dispatched to occupy Bolivar Heights, which overlooked Brig. Gen. Robert Saxton's paltry command of 2,000 Federals posted in Harpers Ferry. And the Louisiana Brigade, coupled with Munford's and Flournoy's cavalry regiments, was sent east to guard Jackson's right at Berryville, which was twenty miles south of Harpers Ferry and eight miles west of Snicker's Gap.[1]

It was Jackson's intention to recapture Harpers Ferry at the head of the valley, cross the Potomac River into Maryland and Pennsylvania, and burn the important railroad bridges that traversed the Susquehanna near Harrisburg, Pennsylvania. This, according to the victor of McDowell, Front Royal, and Winchester, would not only raise McClellan's siege of Richmond (as he would no doubt be ordered by President Lincoln to return to defend the Keystone State), but would also change the course of the war. "If my command can be gotten up to 40,000 men," Jackson promised Lee, "a movement may be made beyond the Potomac, which will soon raise the siege of Richmond and transfer this campaign from the banks of the Potomac to those of the Susquehanna."[2]

That same day, May 28, General Banks reported to Edwin Stanton, President Lincoln's secretary of war, that the Valley Army was in fact arrayed to deliver such a blow. He wrote:

> A merchant from Martinsburg, well known, came to inform me that in a confidential conversation with a very prominent secessionist, also merchant of that town,

[he] was informed that the policy of the South was changed; that they would abandon Richmond, Va., everything south, and invade Maryland and Washington; that every Union soldier would be driven out of the Valley immediately. This was on Friday evening, the night of attack on Front Royal.... He told the truth, I am satisfied so far as he pretended to know.... He says the Rebel force [is] very large; not less than 25,000 at Winchester and 6,000 or 7,000 at Front Royal; that the idea was general among the men that they were to invade Maryland.... I received General Saxton's dispatch and the statement from my own officer that 4,000 Rebels were near Falling Waters, in my front.[3]

In reaction to the unexpected and serious threat posed by Jackson's army, President Lincoln made the controversial decision of detaching Irvin McDowell's large 1st Corps from George McClellan's Army of the Potomac and designating it the "Army of the Rappahannock," answerable only to the War Department. McDowell was not only to halt his southward movement across the Rappahannock River and cease to support McClellan's all-important campaign against Richmond, depriving the latter of valuable troops, but was also ordered to march the bulk of his army—James Shields's, Edward Ord's, and Rufus King's divisions—into the northern reaches of the Valley via Front Royal. McDowell's remaining division, George McCall's, would remain behind to hold the Rappahannock line. And while the Army of the Rappahannock entered the Valley from the east, John Frémont's Mountain Army was to enter it from the west, establishing a blocking position somewhere near Strasburg, trapping Jackson's petulant army once and for all.[4]

On May 30 Jackson received word from Ashby's trusted scouts that Shields's division was indeed returning to the Valley and was heading straight for Front Royal and the army's rear. He also learned that Frémont's divisions were marching north and east out of Franklin via Moorefield to Strasburg. The Valley Army was between them all, seemingly trapped. But the icy Stonewall didn't panic. Instead, he recalled his scattered forces and marched them south, back up the pike, toward Strasburg. It seemed as though his proposed offensive north of the Potomac would have to be postponed, at least for now.

First went the captured U.S. supply wagons, then 2,000 Federal prisoners, then Winder's division (minus the Stonewall Brigade, which was still marching back from Bolivar Heights), then Ewell's. The cavalry brought up the rear, along with scores of stragglers who were separated from the ranks. "Hundreds of our best infantry fell by the wayside," remembered Colonel Thomas Munford of the 2nd Virginia Cavalry.[5]

Later in the day, as the Tigers marched the twenty or so miles south up the pike toward Strasburg, Shields's fast-marching division punched through Manassas Gap and captured Front Royal. The Confederate garrison that was left behind there after the May 23 battle, under the command of a noted hero of the battle of McDowell, Colonel Zachariah Connor of the 18th Georgia Regiment, was subsequently surprised and overwhelmed. Over 150 soldiers were captured, some of whom had been wounded in the previous battle and could not be evacuated in time. From Wheat's Battalion alone, seventeen are listed as being captured during this period.[6]

Soon after nightfall, just north of Strasburg, Jackson decided to inform his principal lieutenants of the situation. He told them that Frémont's army was closing in from the west, that Shields's division was closing in from the east, and that what was left of Banks's hapless army was no doubt closing in from the north. The only way to safety, Jackson averred, was to out-march Shields, hold Frémont at bay, and maneuver into a better position farther south, smashing Shields and Frémont in detail before they united. To facilitate this, Ewell was tasked with holding Frémont at Strasburg long enough to allow the Stonewall Brigade to pass through and grant the rest of the army time to march up the Valley Pike to Harrisonburg before Shields beat them to it.

Thus apprised, the men of the Valley Army moved out the next morning, June 1, 1862, with supreme confidence in their bold but mysterious commander. One soldier said, "Old Jack got us into a fix, and with the blessing of God he will get us out." While Jackson marched south up the macadamized pike toward Harrisonburg with the wagons and three brigades, Ewell deployed four brigades, Elzey's, Trimble's, Taylor's, and Scott's, along the hills northwest of Strasburg to meet Frémont's seven.[7]

Pushing his skirmishers up the Capon Road, Ewell soon came under "desultory cannonading from Frémont's line" about four miles north of the town. As he surveyed the scene, Taylor rode up to join him. For some odd reason, the Louisiana sugar planter was especially on edge. "Whether from fatigue, loss of sleep, or what, there I was," Taylor recalled. "Nervous as a lady, ducking like a mandarin. It was disgusting." When he mentioned his nervousness, Ewell laughed, "cocked his head to the left in his peculiar way," and replied with a gentle lisp: "Nonsense! 'Tis Tom's [Taylor's slave's] strong coffee. Better give it up. Remain here in charge while I go out to the skirmishers. I can't make out what these people are about, for my skirmish line has stopped them."[8]

While Ewell rode on ahead, Taylor noticed that several of his brigade's "camp servants" (slaves) were distressed by the Federal artillery barrage. He later remembered:

> My brigade was in reserve a short distance to the rear and out of the line of fire. Many slaves from Louisiana had accompanied their masters to the war, and were a great nuisance on a march, foraging far and wide for "prog" [victuals] for their owners' messes. To abate this, they had been put under discipline and made to march in rear of the regiments to which they pertained. They were now, some scores, assembled under a large tree, laughing, chattering, and cooking breakfast. All of a sudden, a shell burst in the tree-top, rattling down leaves and branches in fine style, and the rapid decampment of the servitors was most amusing.[9]

The slavery question is often brought up as the main cause of the war. Taylor, as well as many other Southern men writing after the war, saw the slavery issue merely as a symptom of the conflict, but not necessarily the cause of the conflict. He wrote:

The history of the United States will show the causes of the "Civil War" to have been in existence since the Colonial era, and to have cropped out into full view in the debates of the several state assemblies on the adoption of the federal constitution, in which instrument Luther Martin, Patrick Henry, and others, insisted that they were implanted. African slavery at the time was universal, and its extinction in the North, as well as its extension in the South, was due to economic reasons alone.

The first serious difficulty of the Federal government arose from the attempt to lay an excise on distilled spirits. The second arose from the hostility of New England traders to the policy of the government in the war of 1812, by which their special interests were menaced; and there is now evidence to prove that, but for the unexpected peace, an attempt to disrupt the Union would then have been made.

The "Missouri Compromise" of 1820 was in reality a truce between antagonistic revenue systems, each seeking to gain the balance of power. For many years subsequently, slaves, as domestic servants, were taken into the territories without exciting remark, and the "Nullification" movement in South Carolina was entirely directed against the tariff.

Anti-slavery was agitated from an early period, but failed to attract public attention for many years. At length, by unwearied industry, by ingeniously attaching itself to exciting questions of the day, with which it had no natural connection, it succeeded in making a lodgment in the public mind, which, like a subject exhausted by long effort, is exposed to the attack of some malignant fever, that in a normal condition of vigor would have been resisted. The common belief [i.e., majority Northern] that slavery was the cause of civil war is incorrect, and abolitionists are not justified in claiming the glory and spoils of the conflict and in pluming themselves as "choosers of the slain."

The vast immigration that poured into the country between the years 1840 and 1860 had a very important influence in directing the events of the latter year. The numbers were too great to be absorbed and assimilated into the native population. States in the West were controlled by German and Scandinavian voters, while the Irish took possession of the seaboard towns. Although the balance of party strength was not much affected by these naturalized voters, the modes of political thought were seriously disturbed, and a tendency was manifested to transfer existing topics from the domain of argument to that of violence.[10]

Writing in the 1870s, Taylor said, "During all these years the conduct of the Southern people has been admirable. Submitting to the inevitable, they have shown fortitude and dignity.... Accepting the harshest conditions and faithfully observing them, they have struggled in all honorable ways, and for what? For their slaves? Regret for their loss has neither been felt nor expressed. But they have striven for that which brought our forefathers to Runnymede [to create the Magna Carta in 1215], the privilege of exercising some influence in their own government. Yet we fought for nothing but slavery, says the world."[11] On a similar note, General P.G.T. Beauregard, the highest-ranking Louisianan in Confederate military service, said: "It was in no sense a civil war, but a war between two countries; for conquest on the one side, for self-preservation on the other."[12]

Ohio-born Private Harry Handerson of the 9th Louisiana, a man who had tutored the children of a Louisiana planter, had this to say about the South's "peculiar institution":

> As an example of a form of civilization which has now [c. 1880s] largely disappeared from our country, it may be well to say a few words about slavery as it

appeared to my observation. Most of the Negroes were fat, lazy fellows, indisposed to do anything more than was absolutely required of them, but rarely giving serious trouble. Often, as their day's labor was completed, the sound of the violin and the shuffle of the merry dancers at the "quarters" bore witness to the lightness of their hearts and the elasticity of their muscles. Men and women labored together in the fields, clad in coarse gray home-spun cloth, and with their heads protected by an old straw or felt hat, or a red bandana handkerchief. Every morning the daily ration of cornmeal and bacon was served out by the master or mistress at the house and convoyed these in a cart or upon the shoulders to the "quarters," where it was prepared by the old women for the meals of the laborers. The Negroes also kept their own poultry, and often made considerable pocket-money by selling eggs and chickens to the mistress of the house. In sickness they were attended by the family physician and nursed by one of the old women or other person detailed for that purpose. As a rule their treatment was humane, nor were they by any means overworked.

The great curse of the system was the management by overseers [on large plantations], usually ignorant and unprincipled whites, to whose carelessness and brutality the indolent masters consigned their slaves. The smaller planters like Mr. Compton [the man whose children Handerson tutored], however, usually managed their own plantations and treated their Negroes well. Even Mr. Compton, however, employed for a time an ignorant Kentuckian as overseer and I suspect that he was occasionally harsh and tyrannical, though no direct evidence to this effect ever came to my observation. Indeed, I never saw a slave whipped, though on one occasion I heard Mr. Compton himself whipping his house-servant Jeff, an intelligent, but rather morose Negro of perhaps thirty-five years. Mr. Compton was a man of violent temper when aroused, and looked a very devil on these occasions, but this particular whipping at least was neither long nor severe. Jeff was a good-looking Negro and very popular among the girls of the neighboring plantations, and I suspect that some escapade in this line was the occasion of the castigation which I overheard.[13]

As for the men of Wheat's Battalion, coming in large part from the bustling docks of New Orleans, they were almost certainly fighting to preserve the institution of slavery. Not only had their livelihood depended upon it, but many of them had also fought for its expansion into Latin America during the 1850s. And some of them, men like Obedia Miller, actually owned slave property. Furthermore, if the slaves were ever freed, many of the Tigers' already precarious positions in Southern society would be even more threatened, as they either would have to compete with cheap, free-black labor or, if Lincoln followed through with his ambitious African colonization scheme, would simply sink further to the bottom to replace the expatriated slaves. On top of that, the charismatic Wheat no doubt filled his men's heads with visions of grandeur if the South won its independence: that the Caribbean would essentially become a Confederate lake and the victorious Tigers would become the new plantation owners — the *nouveaux riches* of the emerging Golden Circle.[14]

Soon after Taylor watched the Louisiana slaves reassemble under the tree to finish cooking their hasty meals, General Ewell returned from his reconnaissance. He said to Taylor: "I am completely puzzled. We have driven everything back to the main body, which is large. Dense woods everywhere. Jackson told me not to commit myself too far." Taylor suggested that he could maneuver his brigade to the right and develop the situation. Ewell concurred, saying, "Do so; that may stir them up, and I am sick of this fiddling about."[15]

When Taylor marched the Louisiana Brigade around the Union left and deployed it perpendicular to Frémont's line, the Federals, surprisingly, broke and ran. Sensing easy victory, the Tigers and others pressed them and scooped up prisoners by the score. "It was a walk over," Taylor proudly proclaimed. "Sheep would have made as much resistance as we met. Men decamped without firing, or threw down their arms and surrendered." As the Pelican Staters continued their hasty attack, a move that Taylor later conceded as being "rash," they were fired at by elements of the rest of the division. To stop the fratricidal combat, Taylor quickly halted the advance, consolidated his brigade, and sought out Ewell for instructions. Although both officers instinctively wanted to press the attack, they coolly reminded themselves of Jackson's intent. And with the exhausted Stonewall Brigade now in hand, just up from Bolivar Heights, they decided to pull the men back and march up the pike to join the main body.[16]

When Ewell's division reached Jackson by dusk, Taylor was ordered by the commanding general himself to pull the Louisiana Brigade off the pike and establish a rear guard against Frémont's pursuing cavalry. At one point, well after midnight, the Federal horsemen broke through the 6th and 7th Virginia Cavalry regiments—Flournoy's and Ashby's commands—and drove them into Colonel Munford's 2nd Virginia Cavalry, which then tumbled into the 6th Louisiana, on guard astride the pike. In the confusion that followed, the dazed Irishmen fired into the cavalrymen's intermixed ranks, bringing the rest of the Louisiana Brigade to its feet. Sensing disaster, Taylor ordered his men, after "some stumbling, swearing, and much confusion," to continue their march up the pike while he detached two companies from the Irish Regiment, already engaged, to cover their hasty withdrawal.[17]

The rain-soaked night was so dark, Taylor remembered, "owls could not have found their way across those fields.... [Only] the white of the pike guided us." Out of this blackness came an occasional enemy cavalry probe, but little damage was inflicted. "From time to time the enemy would charge," Taylor remembered. "But we could hear him coming and be ready. The [rear] guard would halt, about face, front rank with fixed bayonets kneel, rear rank fire, when, by the light of the flash, we could see empty saddles. Our pursuers' fire was wild, passing over head; so we had few casualties, and these slight; but the [Federals] were bold and enterprising, and well led, often charging close to the bayonets." And as for the Irish dock workers from the 6th Louisiana, much like the men from Wheat's Battalion, they remained cheerful despite the rigors of the miserable, rainy night and passed the time, to Taylor's pleasant surprise, joking about their predicament. "It was a fine night entirely for diversion [sic]," they said.[18]

Soon after dawn, the Stonewall Brigade relieved the Louisianans of enervating rearguard duty, and the march continued on through the next day, June 2, with Federal corsairs continually harassing the Confederate column. Conditions were apparently so desperate during Jackson's "repositioning" that his men were on the verge of collapse. General Taylor remembered: "The day was uncommonly hot, the sun like fire, the water scarce along the road; and our men suffered greatly." Captain Joseph Edmonson of the Stonewall Brigade recalled: "I never saw a brigade so completely broken down and unfitted for service as our brigade.... I am satisfied that my brigade has lost at least a thousand men broken down, left on the way and captured." Lieutenant George Ring of the 6th Louisiana wrote: "I have passed through some exciting times.... [I] have marched over 200 miles, been in three battles and through the mercy of God still unharmed and well, only a good deal fagged out on the hard marches and bad weather.... We have not three consecutive days in one camp for the last four weeks, sometimes not getting more than four hours sleeping after marching from twenty to twenty-five miles a day."[19]

The Tigers and others marched and fought their way all day until they reached their immediate march objective, Rude's Hill, on the eastern bank of the north fork of the Shenandoah River. There, Jackson ordered the bridge to be burned behind his retreating army, foiling Frémont's pursuit. As such, for the next thirty-six hours or so, from the evening of June 2 until the morning of June 4, Wheat's volunteers remained in camp, sleeping, eating, and cleaning themselves and their clothes the best they could. And because Frémont was unable to run down the Valley Army before it crossed over to the eastern side of the north fork, his already-weary men were forced to retrace their steps down the Valley Pike, back to Strasburg, and take the parallel Cedar Creek Pike to continue the pursuit.[20]

On June 4, the Tigers' march was resumed southward. Jackson decided to push through Harrisonburg and on into Port Republic. From there, the Valley Army could deal with Frémont's divisions, which were coming up along the western side of the Massanutten, and with Shields's division, which was coming up its eastern side, up the Luray Valley. When the Valley Army passed through Harrisonburg and turned off the macadamized pike onto a muddy road that led down to Port Republic, however, it became "quickly mired down [and] progress was slow." The condition of the roads probably surprised Jackson, as the spring of 1862 was the wettest, coldest season that anyone could remember. The Shenandoah River, for example, was at its highest level in at least twenty years. George Ring of the 6th Louisiana wrote to his wife: "You can not think darling how much we have suffered.... Two thirds of the time it rained every night. When it did not, it was very cold and our sleep did us little good. Were it not for the oil cloths we captured from the enemy, I do not know what we would have done as a good many times our wagons did not catch us in time to get our blankets."[21]

On June 6, still a full day's march ahead of Frémont and McDowell, Jackson deployed his men to meet them. To prevent the two Federal forces from uniting and to keep his own retreat route through Brown's or Rockfish gaps in the Blue Ridge open, Jackson split his army into two parts. Surmising that the Mountain Army was the greater threat, Jackson deployed Ewell's division and the 2nd and 6th Virginia Cavalry regiments four miles northwest of Port Republic near the village of Cross Keys along a wooded ridge that commanded an open valley. "The ground," according to Taylor, "was undulating, with much wood, and no extended view could be had." Ewell deployed Scott's brigade on the left and Trimble's brigade on the right. In the center, astride the Port Republic–Harrisonburg Road, he placed his six batteries of artillery with Elzey's brigade in support, followed by the Louisiana Brigade, which was held in reserve. The 15th Alabama from Trimble's brigade and Munford's and Flournoy's cavalry regiments were sent one mile forward to serve as the division's picket post.[22]

To watch Shields, Jackson deployed Winder's division along the bluffs that overlooked Port Republic and the North River Bridge, which connected Harrisonburg with Waynesboro, as Shields was marching up the Luray Valley, on the east side of the Massanutten. Locating his headquarters in the low-lying town itself, Jackson was guarded by only one section of artillery and one company each of cavalry and infantry. Across the South River, about two miles northeast of the town, Jackson instructed the 7th and 11th Virginia Cavalry, now commanded by Brigadier General George "Maryland" Steuart (Colonel Ashby was killed while fighting a rearguard action near Harrisonburg), to post themselves at the Lewiston plantation to watch out for Shields. And south of the town, along the Waynesboro Road, Stonewall positioned his cumbersome but invaluable trains. He did this so that if either Frémont or Shields attacked Port Republic, they could get a head start toward Rockfish Gap and safety.[23]

In positioning his army at Cross Keys and Port Republic Jackson purposely placed himself between two enemy forces. It was his apparent intention, using interior lines, to hold Frémont's larger army with Ewell's division while he smashed Shields's division with Winder's. He could then turn about with his entire force and drive Frémont back across the Alleghenies, pursue what was left of Shields's forces down the valley, or abandon the valley altogether and reinforce Johnston's army near Richmond. From Frémont's and Shields's perspective, however, it looked as though Stonewall had foolishly boxed himself in and moved accordingly. General Shields, for example, extorted Frémont to drive rebels into the Shenandoah River from the west while he closed the trap from the east with his division. The next battle, he thought, should prove to be Jackson's Waterloo—Shields playing the part of Blücher.[24]

So while Jackson positioned his forces around Cross Keys and Port Republic, the enterprising Shields ordered Colonel Samuel Carroll's brigade, reinforced by some cavalry and artillery units, to lurch forward from Conrad's Store and burn the North River Bridge at Port Republic in order to trap the Valley Army on the west side of the river for Frémont. Jackson had ordered "Maryland" Steuart to guard the same road upon which Carroll was advancing with his command, but the fiercely independent volunteers from the 7th and 11th Virginia Cavalry regiments, actually a collection of various companies, refused to respect Steuart's imposed authority and thus the road was left wide open. Sam Carroll therefore had a rare easy jab at Stonewall Jackson.[25]

The morning that Carroll's brigade surprised Jackson's paltry Port Republic garrison was, according to Captain Douglas, "bright, warm, calm, and peaceful. The absolute quiet of it, after so much noisy activity, was unnatural but it was most welcome. Orders were sent out that the troops would spend the day in camp and their chaplains hold services." Jackson was about ready to ride up from his headquarters at the Kemper Estate to inspect his forces on the heights that overlooked the town when Carroll's Federal cavalry unexpectedly invested the borough at around 7:30 A.M. Once recovered from the initial shock — barely escaping capture from the onrushing Yankee cavalry — Jackson crossed the bridge and mustered up a few of Winder's regiments to drive them out. The situation seemed critical enough that he went so far as to send a courier to Ewell, four miles away at Cross Keys, to specifically send Taylor's brigade, Ewell's only reserve, to march on Port Republic and help evict Carroll's interlopers.[26]

The Federals held the town for about twenty minutes until Colonel Fulkerson's 37th Virginia Regiment of Taliaferro's brigade, supported by three batteries, charged across the bridge and drove them out. Seemingly overwhelmed, Carroll ordered his men to fall back to Lewiston, a local plantation, where he intended to retreat all the way back to Conrad's Store, his starting point. But as he withdrew, he was met by Brigadier General Erastus Tyler, Shields's second-in-command, who resolved to hold Lewiston with his own and Carroll's brigades and sent a message back to General Shields to come forward and support them with the rest of the division.[27]

Concurrently, almost by chance, Frémont began to engage Ewell's command at Cross Keys as Jackson had expected. With Taylor's brigade marching off toward Port Republic, Ewell was left with only 6,000 men to face Frémont's 10,000. After bombarding Ewell's relatively masked line for an hour, Frémont ordered his infantry to attack with Brigadier Generals Robert Schenk's and Henry Bohlen's brigades on the right, facing Scott's brigade, and Brigadier Generals Robert Milroy's and Julius Stahel's brigades on the left, facing Elzey's and Trimble's troops. Colonel John Koltes's brigade was held in reserve. The Federal line "was probably a mile and a half in length," one Pennsylvania soldier remembered, "with the old flag floating from every regiment.... [It] was a spectacle too grand for description."[28]

After a sharp fight in the valley, Schenk's, Bohlen's, and Milroy's brigades, on Frémont's right, were driven back by Scott's and Elzey's brigades and Ewell's massed artillery. On the Federal left, Julius Stahel's Federal brigade, principally consisting of German immigrants from New York and Pennsylvania, continued its now-unsupported advance against Trimble's line, which, unbeknownst to them, was deployed in a declivity behind a fence that faced a 200-yard-wide field. As the lead regiment of Stahel's brigade, Francis Wutschel's 8th New York, moved up the clear slope that fronted Trimble's brigade, Trimble's Confederates "waited in deathly silence, like a Bengal Tiger when he crouches down ready to spring upon his unsuspected prey."[29]

Once the New Yorkers approached to within thirty or so yards of Trimble's hidden line, the crusty rebel brigadier ordered his men to rise and open fire, ripping the unsuspecting 8th New York into shreds. After but a few minutes, the mauled New Yorkers retreated across the field and into the woods, throwing the rest of their brigade into confusion. Sensing victory, Trimble quickly ordered his men to vault the fence and drive into the Yankee-held woods with fixed bayonets. They did so, advancing almost 500 yards before Trimble judiciously ordered them to pull back.[30]

As Trimble's troops reassembled behind the fence, at about 3:00 P.M., Ewell received reinforcements from Jackson in the form of Taylor's and Campbell's brigades. Thus strengthened, he sent the 13th and 25th Virginia regiments from Elzey's brigade and the 6th and 9th Louisiana regiments and Wheat's Battalion from Taylor's brigade to support Trimble, keeping Campbell's brigade and the 7th and 8th Louisiana in the center, behind the guns with the rest of Elzey's brigade. The Tigers and others marched over to Trimble's position "in quick time, by the flank, each four in perfect line. Arms at right shoulder shift." Captain James Nisbet of the 21st Georgia Regiment, Trimble's brigade, noticed that once the Louisianans situated themselves—stacking arms and breaking ranks—many of them, especially the Irishmen from the 6th Louisiana who were posted closest to his position, walked between the lines to pillage the Federal dead. This marked the end of the battle of Cross Keys, a conflict in which the Louisiana Brigade, for once, played no active part. In all, the fight cost Frémont's army 684 men and Ewell 287 (including General Elzey and Colonel Scott, who were wounded).[31] Captain Henry Kyd Douglas remembered:

> General Frémont did not fight [the battle of Cross Keys] so well, or his troops were not equal to it. It was a conflict which never received the attention it deserved in the series of engagements which made up that Valley Campaign. It was another Sunday fight, which ended with the day, and the moon that shone over the valley that night threw her rays upon the wounded soldiers and not far off upon their mothers and sisters going to church to pray for them. The result of the battle confirmed the wholesome belief of the old soldiers that the side that inaugurated a battle on Sunday, lost it.[32]

On a similar note, the Irishmen of the 6th Louisiana, as they plundered the dead from Frémont's army, prophesied events to come when they said, "These German bounty-men are poor creatures, but Shields's boys [supposed fellow Irishmen] will be after fighting."[33]

9

The Very Devil in Them

The Battle of Port Republic

It was the best charge of the war! There was only one more as desperate: that of Pickett's ... on the last day of Gettysburg. [The Louisianans'] ranks were torn asunder, and where a line [once] advanced were seen only bodies, without legs, without arms, without heads, with breast[s] torn open; the whole lying still, or weltering in pools of blood.

— Staunton *Vindicator*, February 15, 1867

While the Tigers and others faced the Mountain Army at Cross Keys, Jackson decided to hold Frémont at bay with only two brigades, Trimble's and Campbell's, while he smashed half of Shields's command, Carroll's and Tyler's brigades, encamped near Lewiston, with five: Winder's, Taylor's, Steuart's (formerly Scott's), Taliaferro's, and Walker's (formerly Elzey's). Once done, these brigades would then reinforce Trimble and Campbell at Cross Keys and the entire Valley Army would drive Frémont's army back across the Alleghenies.[1]

In order to better strike the Federals at Lewiston, Jackson ordered his 62-year-old engineer officer, Captain Claiborne Mason, and his corps of "African Pioneers"—free blacks and slaves who had been mustered into Confederate service—to bridge the swollen Northern Ford of the South River with sunken wagons and wooden planking. By 4:00 A.M., June 9, 1862, with the bridge complete, Stonewall ordered General Winder to march the Stonewall Brigade through Port Republic and cross Mason's bridge to begin the attack against Tyler's forces. Taylor's and Scott's brigades were to follow.[2]

Winder crossed the bridge with a thousand infantry and eight guns. William Allen's 2nd Virginia led the way, followed by Captain Joseph Carpenter's Alleghany Artillery, the 4th, 5th and 27th Virginia regiments, and then Poague's Rockbridge Artillery. At about 7:00 A.M., Winder's troops passed through Colonel Munford's 2nd Virginia Cavalry, posted just south of the Lewis mansion, and opened the battle.[3]

Winder's Virginians easily drove the Federal pickets up the foggy bottomlands until they reached Baugher Farm Lane. There they were stopped cold by a massive enemy artillery barrage that rained in from their right front, from a clear undulating spur just south of Lewiston, known locally as the Coal Hearth or the Coaling. All who fought in the up-and-coming battle knew that this hill would be the key to victory.[4]

The six Federal cannon that were posted on the Coaling were from three different batteries. On the right (west) were two guns from Battery H, 1st Ohio, commanded by Captain James F. Huntington; in the center was one twelve-pounder howitzer from Battery L, 1st Ohio; and on the left (east) were three rifles from Captain Joseph Clark's Battery E, 4th U.S. Artillery. The Coaling, on which these guns were positioned, was about twenty-five yards higher than other points on the field. And because the hill was undulating, the six guns were not simply arrayed in a single line, but were staggered on multiple elevations. Although dominating, the position did have its faults, the worst of which was that it was fronted by a ravine — dead space into which the guns couldn't fire — and it was flanked on the east by the heavily wooded foothills of the Blue Ridge, leaving it vulnerable to a determined infantry attack.[5]

While the Coaling guns hammered away at the Stonewall Brigade, which was seeking shelter along Baugher Farm Lane, General Tyler, the Federal commander, ordered his infantry and what was left of his artillery to move out from their bivouac sites along the wooded mountainside and to deploy along Lewiston Lane. From the Federal right to left was the 7th Indiana; the remaining section of Clark's Battery E, 4th U.S.; the 29th, 7th, and 5th Ohio regiments; a section of Battery H, 1st Ohio; and the 1st Virginia Regiment (U.S.). The 69th Ohio and one company from the 5th Ohio were sent to support the Coaling guns, and the 84th and 110th Pennsylvania regiments were held in reserve.[6]

Brig. Gen. Erastus Tyler of Maj. Gen. James Shields's division, U.S. Army of the Rappahannock, commanded the Federal forces that were defeated by the Tigers and others at Port Republic. *USAMHI*

Jackson ordered Winder and his Stonewall Brigade to attack this strong line while he brought up Taylor's and Steuart's brigades. Winder sent his 5th and 27th regiments to charge through a peach orchard and across a wheat field to attack the Federals frontally, the Rockbridge Artillery offering support, while the 2nd and 4th Virginia were to swing to the right, up the mountain, and take the Coaling guns in flank. Carpenter's Alleghany Artillery would support this movement.[7]

The suicide attack progressed as expected. The 5th and 27th Virginia were cut to pieces in the face of four Federal guns and a reinforced brigade of infantry, and fell back after about an hour of fighting. Off to the far right, up near the Coaling guns, the 2nd and 4th regiments fared no better. These regiments had worked their way up through the rugged woods and dense stands of mountain laurel, exhausting themselves in the process. They eventually reached the bluff that overlooked the open ravine that separated them from the Coaling by about a hundred yards. The six enemy guns were directly in front of them, firing

Captain James F. Huntington, commander, Company H, 1st Ohio Artillery at the battle of Port Republic. Huntington's battery bore the brunt of the Tigers' charge across the Coaling. *USAMHI*

obliquely to the left at the 5th and 27th Virginia. Colonel William Allen, commander of the Old Dominion's 2nd Regiment, apparently hoped to drive off the Federal artillerymen with musketry and then charge the guns. His plan was foiled, however, when skirmishers from the 4th Virginia were forced to engage some pickets from the 5th and 69th Ohio on the mountainside. Quickly alerted to the threat, the Federal cannoneers swung their tubes around to the left, loaded canister, and fired across the ravine into the gathering ranks of the 2nd and the 4th Virginia, forcing them to retire. With Colonel Allen repulsed on the right, the Stonewall Brigade, for all intents and purposes, was neutralized, and its constituent parts began to reassemble near the Baugher Farm to await reinforcement.[8]

Luckily for them, the next unit in Jackson's line of march happened to be the Louisiana Brigade. By the time Taylor's men began to cross Mason's bridge, however, it had become so rickety that the Louisianans were forced to cross it in single file, appreciably slowing the crossing. Colonel Kelly's 8th Regiment crossed first, followed by Stafford's 9th Regiment, Wheat's Tiger Battalion, and Seymour's 6th Regiment. Harry Hays's 7th Regiment crossed last. Because of the length of time in negotiating the obstacle, and the fact that the battle had not yet started, Taylor allowed the men who had crossed the river to stack their arms, eat from their haversacks, and brew coffee. After about an hour of this, Taylor heard the battle heat up near Lewiston, and, although his 7th Regiment wasn't totally across, he ordered the bulk of his brigade forward.[9]

Riding ahead to find Jackson, who was "a little advance of his line, where the fire was the hottest, with his reins on his horse's neck, seemingly in prayer," Taylor begged for orders.[10] Enlivened by the Louisianan's approach, Jackson summoned over Captain Jedediah Hotchkiss, his expert topographical engineer, and pointed toward the Coaling, saying: "Take General Taylor around and take those guns!" While Taylor and Hotchkiss surveyed the Coaling, Colonel Kelly marched the Louisiana Brigade past the Morris House, near Jackson's and Taylor's position, where it came under artillery fire from the Federal line. Kelly remembered that the enemy shells passed "low along and just above the ranks."[11]

Immediately ordering the column off the road and into a field on the right, Kelly deployed his regiment, the 8th Louisiana, from column into line. Seymour's 9th Regiment and Wheat's Battalion followed suit from right to left (the Tigers being closest to the road). While the front of the brigade deployed in the field to the right, the rear of the brigade, some members from the 6th and 7th regiments, still stacked up on the road, observed Jackson's and Taylor's meeting. Captain Daniel Wilson of the 7th Louisiana remembered that Jackson "looked for a while thoughtfully on the scene, and then turning to Taylor, inquired, 'Can you take that battery? It must be taken or the day will be lost.' Taylor replied, 'We can,' and pointing his sword to the battery, called out to his men, 'Louisianans, can you take that battery?' With one universal shout that made the mountains to echo, they declared they could; whereupon, he gave the order."[12]

Before General Taylor and his guide Hotchkiss had a chance to catch up with the front of the brigade, however, Colonel Kelly had already moved out to attack the Coaling. Major Wheat apparently told Kelly that he had just seen Jackson and that his orders were to take the Federal guns. To make matters even worse for the Louisiana brigadier, Jackson, without informing Taylor, detached the 7th Louisiana, at the rear of the column, to reinforce Winder in his fight against the Federal right. Taylor's brigade, therefore, went forward into three generally disparate groupings: Kelly's 8th Regiment, Stafford's 9th Regiment, and Wheat's Special Battalion on the right; Taylor, Hotchkiss and Seymour's 6th Regiment in the center; and Hays's 7th Louisiana on the left, with the Stonewall Brigade.[13]

Kelly led the 8th and 9th Louisiana and Wheat's Battalion up the moun-

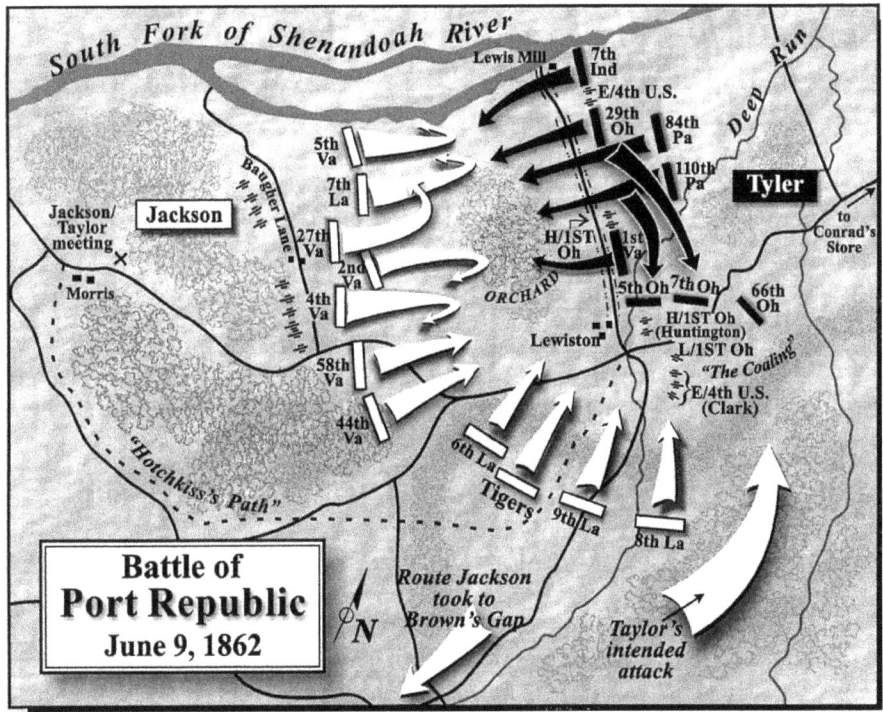

tain at "a run ... with guns at [the] trail," where they, like the 2nd and the 4th Virginia before them, had to chop their way through the thick patches of laurel. Kelly threw out two companies as skirmishers and advanced the battle line forward as best he could. It was reported that Wheat, mounted on a sturdy horse (to carry its massive rider) made such a swath through the laurel in leading his men forward that General Jackson was able to discern Wheat's "trail" and used it to ride atop the Coaling at the battle's successful conclusion. Colonel Seymour's Irish 6th, nearest the road, didn't have to deal with the thick laurel, however, because it was guided by Hotchkiss, who led it along a trail of sorts that wove its way through the tangled undergrowth.[14]

As the determined Louisianans moved toward the Coal Hearth, Jackson ordered Winder's five regiments, the 2nd, 4th, 5th, and 27th Virginia and the 7th Louisiana, supported by three batteries, Poague's, Carpenter's, and Chew's, to attack the Federal right to support Taylor's movement. "The air trembled with a continual roll of musketry and the thunder of the artillery shook the ground," remembered George Neese of Chew's battery. "The ground opened all around us, and the air was full of screaming fragments of exploding shell, and I thought I was a goner." In this attack, the Stonewall Brigade and the 7th Louisiana were able to drive the Federal right back a few hundred yards. But Tyler, committing his reserves, the 84th and 110th Pennsylvania, counter-attacked and forced Winder to retreat to his starting point near the Baugher farm.[15]

Here, the battle reached its crescendo. If the Federals were able to drive Winder back any further, Taylor's Louisianans would be cut off and decimated. And although Taylor had not yet finished his deployment, he resolved to attack the Coaling before it was too late.[16] The New Orleans *Daily Picayune* (June 10, 1866) reported:

> The formation of [Taylor's] line had scarcely been completed when loud and prolonged cheers [from the Federals] ... announced [their] success, while the hoarse thunder of artillery, mingled with the sharp rattle of musketry, heralded the bloody work being there enacted. [Taylor's men] waited with breathless anxiety: not a man in the line but understood the import of that measured cheer.... They stood transfixed, hoping to hear the defiant yell of the Confederates, but the only sound that greeted them was the renewed cheer of the enemy. Even the cannoneers working the enemy's guns ... took up the shout and tauntingly reechoed it.... It was evident to all that the left of the Confederate line had been repulsed.[17]

So instead of turning the strongly held Coaling as originally intended, Taylor directed his brigade to conduct a hasty attack into the left flank of the Federal cannon. "I ordered the attack," he remembered, "though the deployment was not completed, and our rapid march by a narrow path had occasioned some disorder." Jed Hotchkiss of Jackson's staff recalled: "After a consultation, it was agreed, in view of the present emergency, that the flank movement should be abandoned and an immediate attack, obliqued to the left, should be made upon the Federal position and the battery across the ravine."[18]

The ravine that Hotchkiss noted was the same open vale that had stopped the 2nd and 4th Virginia an hour before. Its one-hundred-yard stretch was divided in two by Deep Run and Lewiston Lane. To take the Coaling from their present position, the 2,000 or so men of the Louisiana Brigade would have to charge out of the wood line, down into the ravine, across the creek and the road, then up the hill, and into the left or left front of the Federal cannon. If done rapidly, the Federal guns would only get off one salvo at the Louisianans before they were in the battery; speed and audacity, like at Front Royal and Winchester, would be the keys to victory.

Once the brigade was formed in the wood line, General Taylor, in a "sonorous voice," yelled: "Forward, charge the battery and take it!" With that, the Louisianans surged forward into the ravine with an "unearthly scream" that was described as "the regular old Tiger yell." As was hoped, the Federal cannon to their immediate front, closest to the mountain, were unable to fire into the Pelican Staters before they reached them. The three guns facing Taylor's left front, however, from Batteries H and L, 1st Ohio, which were lower to the valley floor and farther away, were able to fire one good salvo of canister into the faces of the 6th Louisiana and the Tiger Battalion, hitting, among others, Wheat's mammoth horse in the head. The Old Filibuster quickly recovered, however, and was "the first field officer" on Taylor's left to reach the guns. In

Wheat's wake, his Tigers quickly swept through the coveted multiple-layered Coaling and linked up with the elements of the 8th and 9th Louisiana regiments, who had swept in from the right.[19]

General Taylor, personally leading the 6th Louisiana, which was horribly cut up by the canister shot, remembered: "The fighting in and around the battery was hand to hand, and many fell with bayonet wounds. Even the artillerymen used their rammers in a way not laid down in the manual, and died at their guns." Captain James Huntington of Battery H, 1st Ohio, whose guns faced Wheat's Battalion and the 6th Louisiana, recalled that his gunners "made a stout but short resistance, as pistols and sponge staffs do not count for much against muskets and bayonets. My guns were taken, so was [the] howitzer."[20] The *Staunton Vindicator* (February 15, 1867) later reported:

> It was the best charge of the war! There was only one more as desperate: that of Pickett's ... on the last day of Gettysburg. [The Louisianans'] ranks were torn asunder, and where a line [once] advanced were seen only bodies, without legs, without arms, without heads, with breast[s] torn open; the whole lying still, or weltering in pools of blood.[21]

The initial fight for the Federal cannon was therefore brief but brutal. Colonel Henry Kelly remembered: "All formation was lost, and officers and men were all thrown into one unorganized mass around ... the guns." The Federal commander, General Tyler, said that the Louisianans' charge was "so rapid ... so sudden and unexpected as to compel the cannoneers to abandon their pieces." As the exhausted and disorganized Pelican Staters milled about the captured guns, Tyler ordered the 5th, 7th, and 69th Ohio regiments to counterattack the scattered Louisianans before they could form to resist. The last section of Captain Joe Clark's Battery E, 4th U.S., was also brought up from the Federal right to support the counter-attack, firing canister at a distance of about 250 yards.[22]

Seeing the massing Federals and fearing to lose the captured guns, Lieutenant Colonel William Peck of the 9th Louisiana hollered to his soldiers to kill the few surviving artillery horses to prevent the cannon from being recovered by the attacking Buckeyes. While most of the Louisiana men simply placed their muskets against the horses' heads and blew their brains out, several Zouaves from the Tiger Rifles, inspired by the Old Filibuster himself, reportedly drew their sturdy bowies knives and slashed the horses' throats, spurting blood all over themselves, looking much like "maddened butchers."[23] Just then, while the horses were still shrieking and kicking, the Ohioans charged up onto the Coaling and engaged the Louisianans in desperate hand-to-hand combat. Sergeant Edmund Stevens of the 9th Louisiana remembered: "It was a sickening sight. Men in gray and blue piled up in front of and around the guns and with the horses dying and the blood of men and beasts flowing almost in a stream."[24] A soldier from the 66th Ohio remembered: "Imagine this terrific collision, then imagine volleys of ... many muskets, the clashing and plunging of ... bayonets. Mingle with these sounds and sights, the yells, hurrahs, screams, and dying groans and gasps of fierce, bleeding, victorious and dying combatants, and [you] will have the mental picture of the fight."[25]

Unable to check the Federal tide, the Tigers and others were driven back into the wooded ravine. In the process, the victorious Ohio volunteers scooped up a few of Taylor's boys. Among these were Privates James Shields, John Switzer, John Eckler, John Murphy, Thomas Rocks, and G. Woods from the Special Battalion, who were later described as being a "rough-looking set." In momentary possession of the Coaling, the Unionists also attempted to remove the guns, "but, the horses having been killed or disabled, found it impossible." They were able to "reclaim only one gun, which [they] carried off, leaving both caisson and limber."[26]

Taylor quickly reorganized his men and ordered them to once again charge the Coaling, an attack that would be even more frenzied than the first. "The hand-to-hand conflict raged frightfully," remembered Sergeant Edmund Stevens of the 9th Louisiana, "resembling more the onslaught of maddened savages than the fighting of civilized men."[27] Confederate artillerist George Neese remembered:

> The fighting grew dogged and stubborn. The opposing forces fired in each others' faces. Bayonets gleamed in the morning sunshine one moment and the next they were plunged into living human flesh and dripping with reeking blood.... The Federals held to the Coaling with bulldog tenacity, fighting like fiends, recognizing the fact that the point they were so gallantly defending was an all-important one, as it was the citadel of strength in [Tyler's] line and the key to his position. But the firm and unwavering courage and invincible prowess of Taylor's Louisianans made them as persistent and obdurate in gaining and demanding, at the point of the bayonet, full possession and control of the death shelf as the Federals were in their inflexible stubbornness to hold it.[28]

In spite of this blitz, Tyler's Ohioans were able to hold on to the Coaling, and the Louisianans were once again thrown back into the ravine. But they were far from being beaten. Colonel Kelly remembered that his men, "disorganized as they were, held their ground with unyielding tenacity." General Taylor, however, for at least a moment, thought that his brigade was doomed. He remembered: "There seemed nothing left but to set our backs to the mountain and die hard." Then, at that instant, Ewell came up from the direction of the Baugher farm with the 44th and 58th Virginia regiments. He aligned his Virginians to Taylor's left rear, down near Lewiston, and ordered them to charge diagonally across the field, slamming into the Ohioans' right and rear. While Ewell plowed into the Buckeyes' flank, Taylor ordered his men to charge a third and final time, hitting the Ohioans in front. Before long, "Northern valor began to succumb to Southern courage. The Federals wavered, sullenly gave back, and finally broke and retreated hastily, abandoning the [guns] for which they had fought so valiantly, and left them in full and undisputed possession of the Confederates."[29]

All around the Coaling, strewn across the ground, were bloody piles of mangled men and horses. "I have never seen so many dead and wounded in the same limited space," General Taylor later recalled. With the Coaling finally in Confederate hands, Jackson rode up "with intense light in his eyes," shook Taylor's begrimed hand and congratulated his men for the victory.[30] The Richmond *Whig* (June 18, 1862) echoed Jackson's sentiments when it proclaimed: "[The Louisiana Brigade] virtually won the battle at Lewiston.... The world produces no better fighters than the Louisianans; few, very few so good.... There is a little touch of the very devil in the Louisianans."[31]

All told, the Louisiana Brigade lost 288 men in the fight (23 killed and 255 wounded), the highest casualty rate of Jackson's army at the battle of Port Republic. Of this, Wheat's Battalion took a horrible blow, especially in officers, as it listed one killed, Lieutenant Frank McCarthy from the Old Dominion Guards; six wounded, Lieutenant John Coyle and Lieutenant E.V. Cockcroft from the Walker Guards, Captain Alexander White, Lieutenants Thaddeus Ripley and Edward Hewitt from the Tiger Rifles, and Lieutenant Bruce Putnam from Wheat's Life Guards; and seven captured: Privates James Shields and John Switzer from the Walker Guards, Private John Eckler from the Delta Rangers, Privates John Murphy and Thomas Rocks from the Old Dominion Guards, and Privates Andrew Murphy and G. Woods from the Life Guards (a total of thirteen casualties).[32]

As the Tigers and others cared for the many wounded, Trimble and Campbell arrived with their brigades from Cross Keys and, as instructed by Jackson, burned the North Fork Bridge behind them. (Because of his mishandling of the battle, Jackson would have to abandon his dream of a double victory as his men were in no position to deal with the Mountain Army.) This left Frémont, who was in guarded pursuit, to simply bombard Jackson's forces from the heights, including the ambulances that were removing the wounded from the field.[33] "If baffled and made ridiculous," Captain Douglas remembered, "General Frémont was at least in a position where he could give vent to his rage. He threw shells among [Jackson's] ambulance corps while they were relieving the suffering of the wounded from both armies, and killed some men and horses. In one instance a piece of shell tore through an ambulance in which a wounded Confederate soldier and a wounded Union soldier were riding side by side; the Union soldier was killed, the Confederate escaped."[34]

No doubt enraged that he could not strike back against his contemptible foe, Jackson was forced to simply scoff at Frémont's cannonade and marched his army eastward toward Rockfish Gap and the Blue Ridge. It was during this march that the weakly constituted (but surprisingly daring) commander of the Louisiana Brigade finally began to unravel due to acute fatigue. He later related: "We passed the night high up the mountain, where we moved to reach our supply wagons. A cold rain was falling, and before we found them everyone was tired and famished. I rather took it out of the train-master for pushing so far up, although I had lunched comfortably from the haversack of a dead Federal. It is not pleasant to think of now, but it was a little hardening." The brigade commissary, Major Boyd, remembered that although Taylor was a "superb soldier and able general," he often suffered from "rheumatism and nervous headaches," which "made him cross and irritable.... When he was sick he was ugly and we had to keep away from him." Also on this march, Lieutenant Samuel Dushane, Wheat's quartermaster, found an abandoned field howitzer in the woods along the road and proudly presented it to Jackson's artillery chief, Colonel Stapleton Crutchfield.[35]

On June 12, on the heels of Frémont's and Shields's retreat toward Strasburg, meeting up with McDowell's main body, Jackson returned to the Valley, crossed the South River below Port Republic, and marched his weary army down the North River to Weyer's Cave. There, for the next five days, from June 12 to 17, he rested his infantry and artillery forces while he sent his cavalry, now commanded by Colonel Munford of the 2nd Virginia, back to Cross Keys and Conrad's Store to monitor Federal activity in the area.[36]

Summing up Jackson's Valley Campaign of 1862 for the Tigers and others, Taylor said: "The Louisiana Brigade marched, in twenty days [May 21–June 12], over two hundred miles, fought in five actions, of which three were severe, and several skirmishes, and, though it had suffered heavy loss in officers and men, was yet strong, hard as nails, and full of confidence. I have felt it a duty to set forth the achievements of the brigade, than which no man ever led braver into action, in their proper light, because such reputation as I guided in this campaign is to be ascribed in excellence."[37]

10

To the Peninsula

> *At the beginning of operations in this Richmond campaign.... A high opinion has been expressed of the strategy of Lee, by which Jackson's forces from the Valley were suddenly thrust between McDowell and McClellan, and it deserves all praise; but the tactics on the field were vastly inferior to the strategy. Indeed, it may be confidently asserted that from Mechanicsville to Malvern Hill, inclusive, there was nothing but a series of blunders, one after another, and all huge.... Time, when he renders his verdict, will declare the gallant dead who fell at Gaines Mill and Malvern Hill, to have been sacrificed on the altar of the bloodiest of all Molochs: Ignorance.*
> — Richard Taylor

The value of Jackson's 1862 Valley Campaign cannot be overestimated. His two scant divisions had immobilized either directly or indirectly seven Federal divisions, markedly impeding their all-important drive toward Richmond. But the rebels were not out of the woods yet; as a matter of fact, they were far from it. In the west, Missouri, Kentucky, most of Tennessee, the northern half of Mississippi and the southern half of Louisiana (including New Orleans) had been over-run by Union forces. In the east, the Federals had taken much of the Carolina coastline, had captured western Virginia, and General George McClellan's Army of the Potomac was still at the very gates of the Confederate capital, preparing to deliver the *coup de grace*.[1]

The Southern high command—President Jefferson Davis and Generals Robert E. Lee and Joseph E. Johnston—realized time was not on their side; that if they allowed McClellan, with superior numbers and equipment, to inch his way slowly toward Richmond, the war would be as good as over. Therefore, on May 31, 1862, while Jackson was retreating up the valley toward Port Republic, Johnston attacked McClellan's isolated left wing at Seven Pines, just a few miles east of Richmond. It was a bloody affair, and in an attempt to rally his faltering forces late in the day, Johnston was horribly wounded near Fair Oaks Station. The next day, the Federals counter-attacked and drove the Confederates back, thus regaining the initiative. Faced with impending doom, Confederate President Davis placed General Lee in *direct* command of all Confederate forces that were operating throughout Virginia.[2]

Lee's assignment was not an enviable one. His primary field armies, the Armies of the Potomac, the Peninsula, and Norfolk, were pinned down by McClellan just east of Richmond. And his only maneuverable element, Jackson's Army of the Valley, still faced the combined strength of Frémont, McDowell, and Banks in the Shenandoah Valley. After some consultation with Davis, Lee whittled his workable options down to two. His first option was to abandon the valley altogether and transfer Jackson's command east by rail to launch another, but bolder, counter-offensive to drive McClellan back from Richmond. His second option was to hold Richmond against McClellan's siege for as long as possible while two divisions were withdrawn from the city's defenses and sent west by rail to Jackson (i.e., the 40,000). Thus reinforced, Jackson could drive north down the Valley, defeat the Federals there, invade Pennsylvania, and "transfer this campaign from the banks of the James to those of the Susquehanna."[3]

Jackson had lobbied hard for the latter since the campaign season began. On June 8, for example, less than a week after Lee took command of the enlarged department, Jackson once again suggested that launching an offensive down the Valley was the best way to stop McClellan. After much tortured contemplation, however, Lee decided to embark upon the more conservative course and instructed Stonewall to discreetly move his vaunted army east and help him drive McClellan away from Richmond directly.[4]

On June 18 Jackson began his secretive withdrawal from the Valley. He marched his men south to Waynesboro and then east through Rockfish Gap to Meacham's Station, Charlottesville, and Gordonsville, where, on June 21, they were loaded aboard some 200 railroad cars. From Gordonsville, the Valley Army proceeded in a southeasterly direction, passing through Louisa Court House and Frederick's Hall, just twenty miles northwest of Richmond, on June 23.[5]

As the men bedded down for the night, Jackson rode ahead to meet with General Lee and three of his most-trusted division commanders: Maj. Gens. James "Dutch" Longstreet, Ambrose Powell (A.P.) Hill, and

General Robert Edward Lee, commander, Army of Northern Virginia, after Joe Johnston was wounded near Fair Oaks Station. Although later revered by friend and foe alike, when the Tigers were assigned to his command in the early summer of 1862, Lee was still derisively known as "Granny Lee" or "Evacuating Lee" for his poor performance in western Virginia. Once the Seven Days were over, however, Lee's reputation soared, and he, like Jackson, was vindicated. *USAMHI*

Daniel Harvey (D.H.) Hill just north of Richmond. In the subsequent meeting — one of the most important of the war — it was decided that Jackson would play the pivotal role in the new counter-offensive against McClellan. Lee planned to turn McClellan's vulnerable right flank, Brigadier General Fitz-John Porter's newly-constituted V Corps, which was deployed north of the Chickahominy River, from its entrenched position just east of Mechanicsville at Ellison's (or Ellerson's) Mill. Once this occurred, the attacking Confederates would move to unhinge the rest of McClellan's army by cutting its supply line that ran back to White House, one of Lee's own estates, on the Pamunkey-York River.[6] With the details hammered out, Lee issued General Order no. 75 on June 24, 1862:

> General Jackson's command will proceed tomorrow from Ashland toward [Hanover Court House] and encamp at some convenient point west of the Central Railroad [i.e., Hundley's Corner]. At 3:00 Thursday morning, 26th instant, General Jackson will advance on the road leading to [Walnut Grove] Church, communicate his march with General Branch [of A.P. Hill's division], who will immediately cross the Chickahominy River [seven miles above Meadow Bridge] and take the road leading to Mechanicsville. As soon as the movements of these columns are discovered, General A.P. Hill, with the rest of his division, will cross the Chickahominy [at] Meadow Bridge.... The enemy being driven from Mechanicsville [by A.P. Hill], and the passage across the bridge open, General Longstreet, with his division and that of D.H. Hill, will cross the Chickahominy at or near that point; General D.H. Hill moving to the support of General Jackson, and General Longstreet's [division directly] supporting General A.P. Hill; the [six] divisions keeping in communication with each other, and moving en echelon on separate roads, if [possible]; the left division [one of Jackson's] in advance, with skirmishers extending their front, will sweep down the Chickahominy and endeavor to drive the enemy from his position above New Bridge [i.e., Ellison's Mill], General Jackson bearing well to his left, turning Beaver Dam Creek and taking the direction toward Cold Harbor. He will then press forward toward the York River Railroad [at Dispatch Station], closing upon the enemy's rear and forcing him down the Chickahominy River. Any advance of the enemy toward Richmond will be prevented by vigorously following his rear and crippling and arresting his progress.[7]

As stated above, Lee intended to turn Porter's corps from its positions at Mechanicsville and Ellison's Mill and then move to cut the Army of the Potomac's main supply line, which ran along the Richmond and York River Railroad from Fair Oaks Station to White House Landing. The Valley Army was to turn the Federal position at Ellison's Mill by sweeping behind it at Walnut Grove via Hundley's Corner. Once done, Jackson was to continue his move, getting further into Porter's rear, and take Dispatch Station. To aid the Valley commander, Lee assigned to him Brig. Gen. William Whiting's division and Brig. Gen. A.R. Lawton's brigade of Georgians, thus giving Jackson a total of three divisions: Winder's (reinforced by Lawton's brigade), Ewell's, and Whiting's.[8]

While Jackson worked his way into Porter's rear, three other divisions, Longstreet's and the Hills,' were to cross over to the north bank of the Chickahominy River at Meadow and Mechanicsville bridges and drive Porter's turned forces across Beaver Dam and Powhite creeks and into Jackson somewhere near Cold Harbor. In this maneuver, Jackson was to be the anvil and Longstreet and the Hills were to be the hammer. Altogether, six Confederates divisions were to unhinge three Federal divisions and, more importantly, cut McClellan's main supply line running back to the York River.

While Jackson and the others conducted offensive operations north of the Chickahominy, the divisions of Maj. Gens. John Bankhead Magruder, Benjamin Huger (pronounced who-ZHAY), Lafayette McLaws, and David Jones were to defend the Richmond approaches south of the Chickahominy. And just to be safe, Lee ordered Maj. Gen. Theophilus Holmes's division-sized Army of Norfolk to move from the south side of the James River and help Magruder and the others defend the Southern capital.[9]

That gave Lee a total of eleven divisions—some 90,000 men, the most he would ever command—to McClellan's 100,000. Concerned that eleven divisions were too many to command separately, Lee dissolved the old Armies of the Potomac, Peninsula, Norfolk, and the Valley and unified them into one army: the Army of Northern Virginia. He then divided his eleven divisions into three wings. Jackson's approaching Valley Army became Jackson's wing, Longstreet's and D.H. and A.P. Hill's divisions became Longstreet's wing, and Magruder's, Huger's, Holmes's, McLaws's, and Jones's divisions became Magruder's wing.[10]

As the paper reorganization was going on, Jackson continued his move around Porter's right flank, passing through Beaver Dam Station on June 24 and down to Ashland on June 25. All seemed well except for the fact that "Old Jack," the normally fastidious Valley commander, was already a day behind schedule. By June 25, for example, he was supposed to be as far east as Hundley's Corner and not still encamped at Ashland. This in and of itself wasn't bad—the day of the attack could have easily been bumped back—but he never informed Lee about the delay. The lack of coordination of the Army of Northern Virginia, just recently slapped together under the most unfavorable of circumstances, would prove disastrous, especially for the men of A.P. Hill's division and Roberdeau Wheat's battalion of Louisiana Tigers.[11]

To add even more difficulty, on the night of June 25-26, just hours before the proposed assault, "a fearfully hard rain came up" and deluged the Tigers and others who were encamped at Ashland. The storm especially affected General Taylor who, already worn by the Valley Campaign, suffered from such "paralyzing pain and numbness" in his limbs that he excused himself from duty and turned command of the Louisiana Brigade over to Colonel Isaac Seymour of the 6th Regiment.[12]

The next morning, June 26, Jackson resumed the march to Hundley's Corner. To better facilitate his movement through the "Slashes of Hanover," an area that "was swampy [and] dense ... with no extended views, almost no population," Jackson split his forces at Hanover Courthouse. While Whiting's and Winder's divisions were to march down Pole Green Church Road, Ewell's division was to traverse Shady Grove Church Road. "The day," according to Captain G. Campbell Brown, Ewell's adjutant, "was very hot and dusty; the men quite tired and of course dirty." As the division approached Shady Grove from the northwest, the 1st Maryland and 13th Virginia regiments, deployed as skirmishers, flushed out a Federal cavalry patrol that was posted around the church, and a running skirmish ensued all the way down to Hundley's Corner. Once the lightly armed Yankee horsemen were driven back, Ewell secured the corners, and Jackson, marching down from the northeast, gave his now infamous order to post pickets and to bed down for the night. The problem was that his wing was supposed to be down at Walnut Grove (i.e., behind Porter's V Corps) this day as A.P. Hill's, D.H. Hill's, and James Longstreet's divisions were preparing to attack Mechanicsville and Ellison's Mill frontally.[13]

While the men of the Valley Army began to construct a bivouac around Hundley's Corner, A.P. Hill crossed his division at Meadow Bridge "expecting," as he later declared, "that General Jackson would be in the position assigned him [i.e., in Porter's rear at Walnut Grove] by early dawn." By 3:00 P.M., Hill's men had driven the Federal pickets out of Mechanicsville and opened the way for Longstreet and D.H. Hill to cross over to the north side of the Chickahominy. Powell Hill then progressed to the next step when he attacked

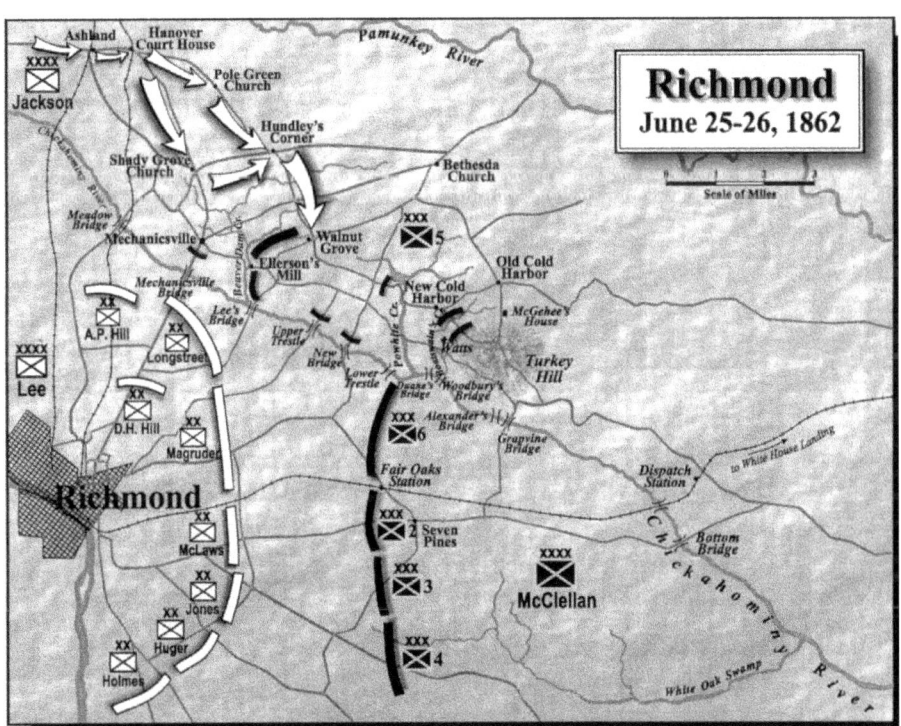

Maj. Gen. George McCall's division, which had recently been sent down from the Rappahannock army to reinforce McClellan, and was strongly entrenched behind Beaver Dam Creek at Ellison's Mill. As Hill assumed that Jackson was already in their rear, the fight was to be a relatively short and bloodless one.[14]

Three miles away, at Hundley's Corner, however, the Valley men, just arrived, heard the yonder battle rage. But Jackson refused to move to Hill's support as he was seemingly content with staying put for the night. As he most probably understood the operation, he was not to march to the sound of the guns, but was to instead make his way around the Federal lines. If there was a fight at or near Mechanicsville, it was because the Confederates on that side of the field saw an opportunity and tried to exploit it. Besides, Longstreet and the two Hills were supposed to support him, follow his lead, and not the other way around. This unfortunate (but understandable) lack of coordination would prove to be ruinous for the men of A.P. Hill's gallant division as the Keystone Staters from McCall's division ripped them to shreds. Unless Lee and his high command, including Jackson, got their act together, and quickly, even more men, including Wheat's cantankerous Tigers, would needlessly be sacrificed at the alter of Southern independence.[15]

11

That's Hell in There!

The Battle of Gaines' Mill

Bury me on the field, boys! Bury me on the field!
— Roberdeau Wheat

As A.P. Hill's bloodied division remained at the foot of Beaver Dam Creek under Porter's guns, General McClellan, now well aware of Jackson's arrival, knew that the wily Valley commander was slowly inching his way down from the north, slipping around his right flank, and making McCall's battle-tested position at Ellison's Mill untenable. He therefore ordered Porter and McCall to move their forces back to an even stronger position, one that could not be turned, would still cover the important bridges that traversed the swollen Chickahominy, and would make the rebels pay dearly for their brazen counter-offensive. This position, surveyed by McClellan's chief engineer, Brig. Gen. John Barnard, was atop Turkey Hill, just south and east of Cold Harbor and Boatswain's Creek, along the north bank of the Chickahominy River.[1]

McCall's victorious 3rd Division therefore pulled back from Beaver Dam Creek and crossed Powhite Creek at Gaines' Mill to join the rest of the V Corps, which was now gathering on the southeast side of Boatswain's Creek atop Turkey Hill. To cover their withdrawal, Porter ordered Colonel Thomas Cass's 9th Massachusetts Regiment of Brig. Gen. George Sykes's 1st Division to establish a rear guard at Gaines' Mill.[2]

As the Pennsylvanians skillfully executed their retrograde, Major Wheat, at dawn, woke his two comrades, Colonel Leroy Stafford of the 9th Louisiana and Major David French Boyd, head quartermaster of the brigade. He wanted to share with them his "daily ration" of a dose of whiskey and a prayer. "Wake up, and listen to the ration for the day!" Wheat playfully exclaimed. Once they tossed down their remedy, the Old Filibuster pulled out a little Episcopal prayer book called *Morning and Night Watches,* which his mother had given to him. He read the citation titled "Joyful Resurrection." As he finished the closing passage, however, "Lord, I commend myself to Thee. Prepare me for living, prepare me for dying...," he began to well up with emotion, predicting that he'd be dead by the end of the day. Boyd and Stafford, taken aback by Wheat's tender attitude, said, "Nonsense." But Wheat was insistent, and made them promise to bury him on the field of battle. To this, they reluctantly agreed.[3]

Soon after this ominous incident, Jackson resumed the march to Walnut Grove, where, to his surprise, he was met by General Lee, who had crossed Beaver Dam Creek with A.P. Hill's division soon after the Federal withdrawal. The general commanding, although still smarting from the Mechanicsville fiasco, apparently did not direct any personal criticism at Jackson, but simply reiterated to the Valley commander the need to swing his wing to the far left, getting in Porter's supposed rear near New Cold Harbor. That maneuver, it was hoped, would turn the Federals from their strong position along Powhite Creek at Gaines' Mill and allow A.P. Hill and Longstreet to advance their divisions down to Dispatch Station, thus unhinging McClellan's critical Richmond-York River Railroad supply line. To further support Jackson, Lee ordered D.H. Hill to march his division behind the Valley Army along the parallel Bethesda Church Road and follow Stonewall's lead.[4]

The complicated advance along parallel roads made it imperative that each command stick to its assigned route and not be late. But unlike during his brilliantly executed Valley Campaign of which he was in overall command, Jackson, now a subordinate of Lee's, incredibly became lost during the march. Instead of turning right on the second road out of Walnut Grove to Old Cold Harbor, he was erroneously instructed by his assigned guide to turn down the first road. The mistake became brutally clear when his advance element, Elzey's brigade, stumbled into the rear of A.P. Hill's division, just north of Gaines' Mill. A large part of the problem stemmed from the simple fact that, unlike during the Valley Campaign, the Confederates did not have proper maps of the area. And as for the local guide, Jackson simply instructed him to march his wing to Cold Harbor, which he did, in the most direct fashion.[5] Richard Taylor summed up this problem after the war by saying:

Brig. Gen. Fitz-John Porter, commander, Fifth Corps, U.S. Army of the Potomac during the Seven Days. *USAMHI*

> A high opinion has been expressed by the strategy of Lee, by which Jackson's forces from the Valley were suddenly

thrust between McDowell and McClellan, and it deserves all praise; but the tactics on the field were vastly inferior to the strategy. Indeed, it may be confidently asserted that from [Mechanicsville] to Malvern Hill, inclusive, there were nothing but a series of blunders, one after another, and all huge. The Confederate commanders knew no more about the topography of the country than they did about Central Africa. Here was a limited district, the whole of it within a day's march of the City of Richmond, capital of Virginia and the Confederacy, almost the first spot on the continent occupied by the British race, the Chickahominy itself is classic by legends of Captain John Smith and Pocahontas; and yet we were profoundly ignorant of the country, were without maps, sketches, or proper guides and nearly as helpless as if we had been suddenly transferred to the banks of the Lualaba.[6]

Realizing his blunder, Jackson, instead of simply about-facing his troops, ordered them to counter-march back to Walnut Grove Road. That maneuver, while allowing Stonewall to retain Ewell's tested division in the van, took a long time to complete. The problems caused by Jackson's misdirection were compounded, for by the time his column was on the correct road, D.H. Hill had advanced his division ahead of the Valley Army as it had marched to Old Cold Harbor the right way. Lee's ambitious plan, it seemed, was once again doomed to failure.[7]

During the time-consuming counter-march, in which the Tigers and others noticed the remnants of several abandoned Federal camps, Wheat openly talked about his mother and early acquaintances and liberally spoke of his death in the upcoming battle. More than once he turned in his saddle to his red-shirted filibusters and proclaimed: "Bury me on the field boys! Bury me on the field!"[8]

Meanwhile, on the right, A.P. Hill had carefully plucked his way to Gaines' Mill, the place where Porter was expected to make a stand. But, surprisingly, Hill found only a few Federals on the south side of Powhite Creek, Cass's Bay Staters, and determined to once again attack without allowing Jackson's turning movement to culminate. When he pushed into the sleepy hamlet of New Cold Harbor, however, he was fired upon by Porter's main line, which was situated behind Boatswain's Creek, atop Turkey Hill, about 2,000 yards farther back than Lee had anticipated. Jackson's grand turning movement was therefore a bust, as his men would now come out in front of the Federals and not behind them. Nevertheless, Lee decided to make the best of a bad situation, however, and ordered Hill's and Longstreet's divisions to find and fix the enemy as best they could while Jackson and D.H. Hill, coming up from the left, would deliver the knockout blow.[9]

The position which Hill's and Longstreet's men were attacking was indeed formidable. It was essentially an elongated plateau with its right terminating in the vicinity of the McGehee house, on a wooded bluff, and its left upon the swollen bottomlands of the Chickahominy River. At the foot of the hill ran Boatswain's Creek, with steep and sandy banks. The creek was encased by a belt of trees, tangled undergrowth, and felled timber that were manned by skirmishers from Colonel Hiram Berdan's green-clad 1st U.S. Sharpshooters. As the ground steadily rose south and east, about a hundred yards behind the creek, a line of Federal infantry was stationed behind a breastwork of dirt, branches, logs, and fence rails, followed by a second, farther up the hill, which was crowned by artillery and another line of infantry. In all, about 30,000 men and 80 cannon defended Turkey Hill and its approaches. In order to take this position, Lee's attacking Confederates had to cross a large field, which was over-watched by artillery, make their way through a line of felled trees infested with skirmishers, cross a steeply-banked creek which was defended by two lines of entrenched infantry and supporting artillery, and then storm those positions uphill at close range. If any position could be deemed to be impregnable, this was it.[10]

Hearing the sounds of battle to their right front, sounds that should not have been heard, the men of D.H. Hill's division picked up their pace and headed for the front. Being the first unit to arrive on the Confederate left and unsure of the situation, Hill deployed his division parallel to the Unionists, facing their batteries posted on the clear eastern slope of Turkey Hill near the McGehee house. Jackson arrived soon after with Elzey's brigade of Ewell's division in front. Because he too was confused by the situation — his wing was supposed to turn the enemy from Gaines' Mill — he ordered Ewell to steer the rest of his division to the right and skirt the tree line that paralleled the interconnecting Cold Harbor Road while he got his bearings.[11]

As the Louisiana Brigade pulled off to the right toward New Cold Harbor, passing behind Elzey's and Trimble's brigades, Jackson rode by and uncharacteristically stopped to talk with Major Wheat. Henry Kyd Douglas, of Jackson's staff, remembered:

> While [Jackson] was directing the movements of his divisions and personally seeing the formation of his line, he passed the battalion known as the "Louisiana Tigers" commanded by Major Bob Wheat. By his brave, reckless, and generally loose men and their gallant, big-hearted commander, General Jackson was regarded with superstitious reverence. No two men could be more unlike than "Old Jack" and Bob Wheat, but the latter's affection for [Jackson] was akin to adoration. I never passed by [Wheat's] command that [Wheat] did not stop and ask me how "the Old General" was, sometimes half a dozen times a day, and generally adding, "God bless him."
>
> This day Major Wheat, looking like a mounted Falstaff, was on horseback as [Jackson] passed his battalion. When the General approached [Wheat] rode up to [Jackson], with uncovered head, and almost bluntly said, "General, we are about to get into a hot fight and it is likely that many of us may be killed. I want to ask you for myself and my Louisianans not to expose yourself so unnecessarily as you often do. What will become of us, down here in these swamps, if anything happens to you, and what will become of the country! General, let us do the fighting. Just let me tell them that you promised me not to expose yourself and then they'll fight like, er, tigers!" As he spoke he looked up frankly in Jackson's face, who was listening attentively.
>
> Then suddenly, taking Wheat's hand and shaking it, Jackson said, "Much obliged to you, Major. I will try not to go into danger, unnecessarily. But Major, you will be in greater danger than I, and I hope you will not get hurt. Each of us has his duty to

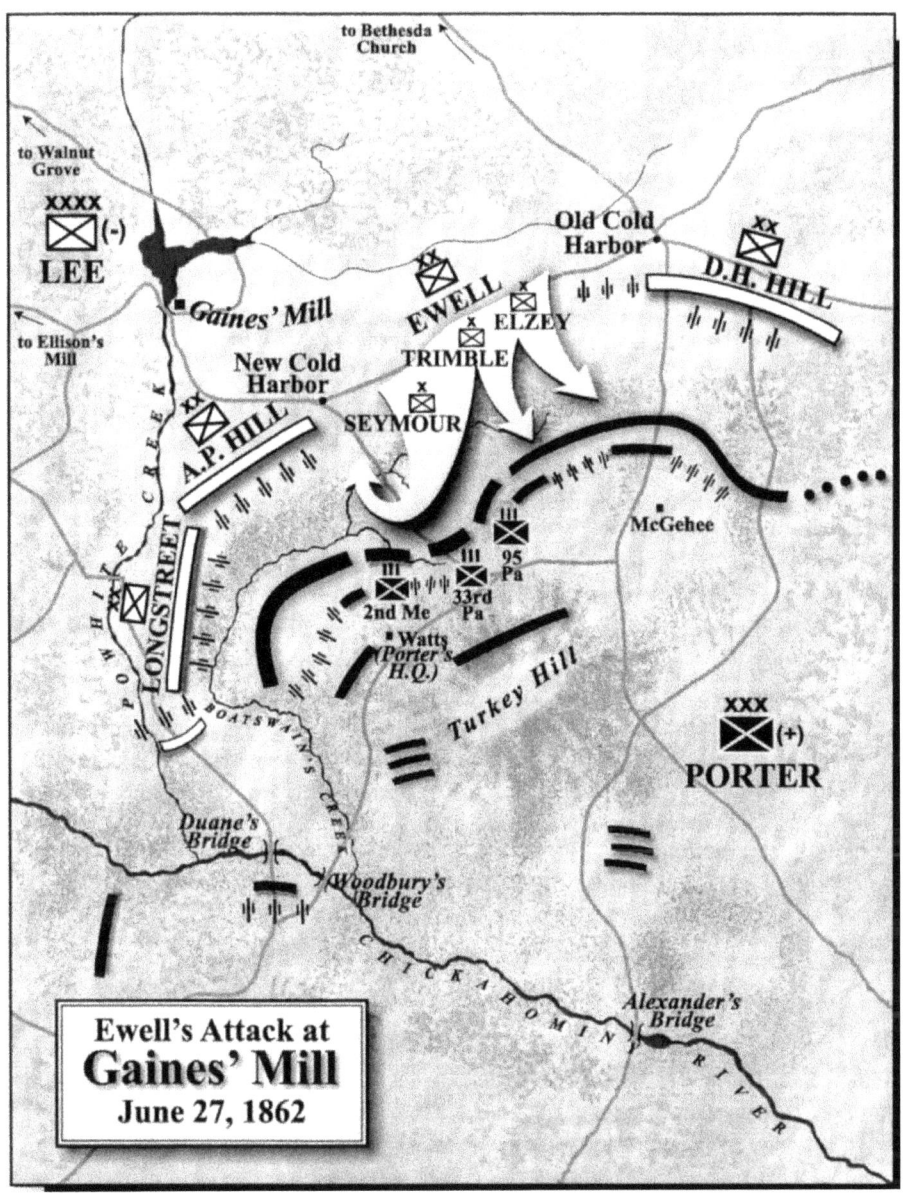

Ewell's Attack at
Gaines' Mill
June 27, 1862

perform, without regard to consequences; we must perform it and trust in Providence." They separated and as [Jackson] rode away he said, "Just like Major Wheat. He thinks of the safety of others, too brave ever to think of himself."[12]

Soon after his surprisingly cordial meeting with Jackson, Wheat, "superbly uniformed, as he usually was, his large handsome figure the better set off for the splendid clay-bank horse he was riding," rode up to his friend, Major Boyd, and said: "Major, just look at my Louisiana planters! I'd like to see any 5,000 button makers stand before them this day!"[13]

A little after 4:30 P.M., as the one hundred or so ragged men of Wheat's Battalion waited in the wood line, Colonel Walter Taylor, Lee's adjutant, galloped up to Ewell and implored him to throw his division into battle to prevent the Federals from launching a counter-attack on the heels of the Hills' failed assaults. Ewell quickly obliged and sent the Louisiana Brigade in first, angling toward the right, heading toward A.P. Hill's pressed division; Trimble's brigade went in second, on Seymour's left, and Elzey's brigade went in third, angling to the left and toward D.H. Hill's division.[14]

Seymour led his Pelican Staters across the dusty road and into a large field that used to be the site of one of Porter's encampments. Once they crossed a dirt track that ran straight to the top of Turkey Hill, the Tigers and others passed through the shattered elements of Brig. Gen. Richard Anderson's Georgia brigade of A.P. Hill's division, which was pulling back from the battle area. Advancing a little farther, the Louisianans began to take horrific artillery fire from Federal guns posted atop Turkey Hill, killing or maiming several. Unbeknownst to the men of the Special Battalion — who were most probably on the extreme left of Seymour's line, adjoined with the 9th Louisiana — they were being thrown into the worst part of the line, as they were headed straight for a precipitous bend in the creek where the sturdy 2nd Maine and the 33rd and 95th Pennsylvania (Gosline's Zouaves) had the area in a complete crossfire. To make matters even worse for Seymour's doomed brigade, the aforementioned Federal units were supported by the 32nd and 33rd New York regiments and Battery L/M, 3rd U.S., deployed fifty yards further up the hill near the Watt house, General Porter's headquarters.[15]

Once the Louisianans crossed the field, stepping over the dead and wounded of Anderson's shattered brigade, they entered the woods and began a quick descent toward the creek. For a while, all was quiet. The Yankee artillery couldn't reach them any longer, and the Federal infantry could not yet be seen. Descending the wooded slope, passing through the felled timber, the Tigers plunged into the cool knee-deep waters of Boatswain's Creek, shrouded by the thick smoke left from the previous battle and shielded by its steep, three- to four-foot-high sandy banks. About fifty yards above them, however, on the clear ridge opposite, sat the first line of Federal breastworks, manned by the 33rd and 95th Pennsylvania and the 2nd Maine regiments. From their dominant positions, the Federal volunteers, who could just barely see the Pelican Staters milling about in the creek bed below, opened a withering fire. At that moment, Colonel Seymour plunged into the creek, horse in tow, and ordered his men forward. "To halt before such a volcano was madness," remembered Harry Handerson of the 9th Louisiana. "The only hope was to storm it rapidly."[16]

Present-day view of Boatswain's Creek looking toward the Federal positions. The Tigers and others advanced across this gully and attempted to charge the Yankees at close range. Wheat was killed, buried, and disinterred somewhere in this area. In 1862, there would not have been trees twenty yards past the brook.

As the Louisianans vaulted over the embankment, however, they were blasted by another volley of Federal musketry, instantly killing, among others, Colonel Seymour, who was hit several times in his head and body. The entire brigade quickly became pinned down as it was caught in a cross fire of epic proportions: Gosline's Zouaves were firing into their left, the 33rd Pennsylvania was firing into their front, and the 2nd Maine was firing into their right. Private Handerson later commented, "Now was the critical moment when a voice of authority to guide our uncertain steps and a bold officer to lead us forward would have been worth to us a victory."[17]

That man was none other than Roberdeau Wheat. Knowing that it would be suicide to stay put or to retreat back into the creek, Wheat determined to once again lead his intrepid filibusters in a bold uphill assault against an entrenched enemy. He turned around, looked through the smoke, found a few of his Tigers, and ordered another one of his brazen charges. But this time, there was apparently too much confusion, too much enemy fire. Wheat gallantly charged up the hill, daring others to follow him. He had got to within twenty-five yards of the Federal breastworks, manned by Philadelphia Zouaves from Colonel John M. Gosline's 95th Pennsylvania, when he was hit by a Yankee

An unidentified officer from the 95th Pennsylvania, "Gosline's Zouaves." It was more than likely a soldier from the 95th who killed Wheat at Gaines' Mill. *USAMHI*

bullet, which passed through one eye and out the back of his head, killing him instantly.[18] Henry Handerson remembered:

> Just then, a little to my left and perhaps ten paces in advance of our line, I noticed Major Wheat picking his way slowly and carefully through the dense underbrush, quiet and determined apparently, but uttering no word and followed by none of his own, or, indeed any other command. A moment later he fell motionless, seemingly without a groan or a struggle, and I knew his restless career was ended. At the same time a comrade just to my left fell with a groan and turned upon me a beseeching look which I could not resist.[19]

All hell was breaking loose. Command was broken to pieces. Men went down by the score. Unable to withstand it any longer, the soldiers of the once stalwart Louisiana Brigade, like Anderson's before it, retreated across the creek, hauling away as many of the wounded with them as possible.[20]

As the beaten Tigers spilled out of the wood line and headed back toward Old Cold Harbor, they ran into some of Trimble's men, who were marching toward the front. The heroes of Manassas, Front Royal, Winchester, and Port Republic tried to warn their Valley brethren of the futility of attacking such position frontally. "You need not go in," one Tiger declared; "we are whipped; you can't do anything!" Another reportedly said: "Boys, you are mighty good, but that's hell in there!" And one teary-eyed Zouave proclaimed: "They have killed the Old Major and I am going home. I wouldn't fight for Jesus Christ now!"[21]

Trimble heeded the Louisianans' warning and attacked a little more to the left, more toward Elzey's brigade. He also seemed to have rallied some companies of the scattered Louisiana Brigade for a brief time and continued his advance. Trimble wrote:

> I formed my force, increased on our left by the fragments of the [Louisiana] regiments which had been rallied, as nearly as parallel with the line opposed to us as I could judge by their fire through the woods, and then rode along the line, distinctly telling the men, in the hearing of all, that they were now to make a charge with the bayonet and not stop one moment to fire or reload ... under the enemy's fire [who had] the advantage over us, posted as he was in a good position, and strengthened by fallen timber, to obstruct our advance, and that the quicker the charge was made the less would be our loss. Leading them on with perfect confidence in their pluck the regiments advanced firmly and gallantly, receiving heavy volleys of the enemy's fire from the opposite height without returning it.[22]

As the battle once again became heated, however, Trimble ordered the Louisianans to "withdraw out of fire because they were still somewhat confused."[23] With Taylor still in an ambulance in the rear and Seymour dead, Colonel Leroy Stafford of the 9th Regiment took charge of what was left of the Louisiana Brigade. He reported simply, "I took command of the [Louisiana] Brigade and was ordered by General Trimble to form the troops in line of battle near the edge of the wood; this was done."[24]

Once Ewell's division was fully committed, Captain Brown rode up from Old Baldy's headquarters to help rally the bushwhacked Louisiana Brigade and two companies from the 15th Alabama of Trimble's brigade who were moving to the rear. He wrote:

> As I went down the road from [New Cold Harbor] towards the swamp, men came rushing out of the bushes on the right. I had seen troops of other commands coming out of these as we came up, but these I knew to be [the] Louisianans and to leave a gap in our line. Colonel Cantey of the 15th Alabama with two of his companies also came out; but they as well as Colonel Stafford's 9th Louisiana and parts of the 8th Louisiana and 7th Louisiana were in some sort of order and soon came under the control of their officers. I concluded that my first duty was to rally these men as Seymour had been killed, to get someone to take command of the brigade. It took three quarters of an hour of hard work. We formed just behind a little crest; on the flank of Trimble's two regiments and when the line was in some sort of order. I reported to [Trimble] the condition of affairs and set off to find General Ewell. Trimble ordered the officer in command (Stafford, I believe, Hays being wounded at Port Republic) to go back out of fire across the road, as he found his men somewhat nervous where they were and let them be [quiet] till needed.[25]

As the shattered Louisiana Brigade continued to pull back toward Old Cold Harbor, General Taylor was brought forward in an ambulance. He remembered:

> It was a wild scene. Battle was raging furiously. Shot, shell and ball exploded and whistled. Hundreds of wounded were being carried off, while the ground was strewn with dead. Dense thickets of small pines covered much of the field, further obscured by clouds of smoke.... The loss of my command was distressing. Wheat was gone, and Seymour, and many others. I had a wretched feeling of guilt, especially about Seymour, who led the brigade and died in my place. Brave old Seymour! I can see him now, mounting the hill at Winchester, on foot, with sword and cap in hand.[26]

It was now past 5:30 P.M. and Lee's attack was completely stalled. In all, he had elements of five divisions on the battle line, all of D.H. Hill's, most of Ewell's, Winder's, and Longstreet's, some of A.P. Hill's, and one two-brigade division, Whiting's, in reserve. The Federal line, it seemed, was impregnable. Lee resolved to break through, however, committed all of his forces, and sent them on a headlong charge against Porter's line. Sixteen brigades of infantry, a full 32,000 men, were meant to smash Porter's remaining 25,000 if it were the last thing they did. At 7:00 P.M., an hour before dark, the attack was ordered.[27] Private McClendon remembered: "All being ready, the command 'charge' was given, we raised a yell and dashed down the slant pell mell ... yelling all the time, expecting a hand-to-hand encounter when we reached their line."[28]

The Special Battalion, as with the rest of the Louisiana Brigade, did not participate in the final and decisive assault against Porter's V Corps, an attack that went down in history as one of the most desperate and extraordinary assaults of the war. Before long, with the seemingly insurmountable Federal line breached in multiple points, McClellan ordered Porter to retreat to the south side of the Chickahominy using Woodbury's, Alexander's, and Grapevine bridges before he and his heroic men were totally cut off. And although his important York River supply line was effectively severed by Lee's advance and his men were pushed back from the very gates of Richmond, McClellan did not publicly admit defeat and instead deployed his army along the southern bank of the Chickahominy — another strong position — hoping to once again bludgeon "the Rebel Secesh" and blast them into oblivion in their own back yard.[29]

All told, the battles at Mechanicsville and Gaines' Mill, days one and two of what later became known as the Seven Days' Battles, cost Lee 8,751 men (8 percent of his command) and McClellan 6,837 (7 percent of his command). Of this, the Louisiana Brigade lost 174 (29 dead and 142 wounded) and the Tiger Battalion, suffering the most in the brigade, lost 22 soldiers (about 11 percent), including its gallant commander, Major Roberdeau Wheat, Lieutenant William Foley of the Old Dominion Guards and Lieutenant Charles Pitman of the Delta Rangers, who were killed; and Privates Mark Jordan, Thomas Maloney, and Dennis Ryan from the Delta Rangers, who were wounded. Three other men, not specified in the records, were also killed, and sixteen others were wounded.[30]

This left Captain Robert Harris, who was now in charge of the Special Battalion after Wheat's gruesome death, with about sixty men and four officers— barely a company. With Harris's unsolicited elevation, Lieutenant W.V. Kinnan commanded what was left of the Walker Guards as Lieutenant John Coyle and Lieutenant Edward Cockroft had been wounded at Port Republic and Lieutenant E.B. Sloan had resigned his commission in December 1861. Lieutenant Thomas Adrian, the brave warrior from Manassas who "loved war," still commanded the remaining Zouaves of the Tiger Rifles after Captain White was wounded at Port Republic. Captain Henry Gardner of the Delta Rangers, one of the founders of the battalion, resigned his commission immediately after the Gaines' Mill debacle (he probably feared for his life), and his tiny company was more than likely commanded by Sergeant Michael Horan as Lieutenant Frank McCarthy was killed and Thaddeus Ripley was wounded, like many other officers, at Port Republic. Lieutenant John Keenan, originally a drummer, now commanded the Old Dominion Guards, Wheat's old company, as Captain Obedia Miller had been sent home after his Manassas wounding and Lieutenant William Foley was killed in the most recent battle. Captain Robert Going Atkins, the Irish soldier of fortune and Wheat's associate, still commanded the Life Guards, and was now second only to Harris in the battalion command structure. If this war were to go on much longer — and it would — the battalion would be left with nothing.[31]

12

Egyptian Darkness:
The Battle for Malvern Hill

Night, dark and dismal, settled upon the battlefield of Malvern Hill, its thousands of dead and wounded. The rain began to fall on the cruel scene and beat out the torches of brave fellows hunting their wounded companions in the dark. The howling of the storm, the cry of the wounded and groans of the dying, the glare of the torch upon the faces of the dead or into the shining eyes of the speechless wounded, looking up in hope of relief, the ground slippery with a mixture of mud and blood, all in the dark, hopeless, starless night; surely it was a gruesome picture of war in its most horrid shape.

— Henry Kyd Douglas

As the Tigers and others licked their wounds in the aftermath of the devastating battle of Gaines' Mill, Major Boyd returned to the spot where Wheat's corpse lay to fulfill his promise to bury his friend on the field of battle. About seventy-five yards from the creek, on a gentle rise near a stand of pines, Boyd and a detail from the Special Battalion buried the mythical filibuster, Lieutenants Foley and Pitman, and three unidentified Tigers.[1] In 1957 historian Charles Dufour, drawing exclusively from Boyd's August 25, 1896, account in the New Orleans *Daily Delta*, described Wheat's burial in this way:

> When [Boyd] arrived, he found Wheat's adjutant, [Lieutenant] Sam Dushane and three or four Tigers ahead of him, preparing the burial of their beloved major. They were working hurriedly.... "It was no time for ceremony or delay ... and we had no business away from our commands ... even to bury the dead" [recalled Boyd].
> When the last shovel of earth was scattered over the grave, and a stone placed to mark it, Dushane turned to Boyd, saying, "Major, please pray."
> "No [lieutenant]," replied Boyd, "you can do that better than I can."
> "Well, if I must, here goes it," exclaimed Dushane, dropping to his knees. "Kneel down boys."
> They knelt down: Major Boyd, Dushane and four of Rob Wheat's tough Tigers.
> "And never before or since," declared Boyd, "have I heard such a prayer; so short, so telling; coming straight out from the big, warm heart of a soldier commending the spirit of his beloved commander and friend to the earlier mercies of God."[2]

Wheat's death ripped the heart out of the battalion. Although Bob Harris and the other Irish officers, Bob Atkins, Thomas Adrian, Bill Kinnan, and John Keenan, attempted to reconsolidate the broken Special Battalion, it would never be the same. If any man had engendered the *esprit* of a unit, it was Roberdeau Wheat and his beloved Tigers.

As what was left of the Star Battalion consolidated, the aggressive Lee pondered his next move. Because Porter's Federals, in their orderly withdrawal from Gaines' Mill, were able to burn the bridges behind them, Lee was unable to immediately follow up his costly victory across the Chickahominy. To add insult to injury, the Confederate commander was unsure exactly where Porter's troops had gone. Had some of them retreated east, down the northern bank of the Chickahominy, to cover White House Landing, or had they all withdrawn to the south side of the Chickahominy? To find out, Lee sent Brig. Gen. "Jeb" Stuart and his cavalry, coupled with Ewell's division, down the north bank of the river to have a look. While Ewell was to secure Dispatch Station, Stuart was to ride all the way out to White House on the York-Pamunkey River.[3]

Once Stuart and Ewell reported that there was no Federal activity on the north side of the Chickahominy, securing the railroad line and the Confederate left flank, Lee put his army to work in rebuilding the Chickahominy bridges so he could press the attack, retaining the initiative that was hard-won at Gaines' Mill. For the next two days therefore, on June 28 and 29, while Ewell's division was sent further down the river to guard the ford near the burned-out remains of Bottom's Bridge, the rest of Jackson's wing was put to work repairing Grapevine Bridge.[4]

Despite his blustering, McClellan apparently became unglued by the fact that Lee's troops had actually broken through his strong lines at Gaines' Mill. Nobody, not even the celebrated French Zouaves of Sebastopol, Inkerman, or Magenta, should have been able to take that position. This, coupled with the presence of Magruder's forces just east of Richmond, spurred McClellan to issue his now-infamous order to give up his siege of Richmond and to "reposition" the Army of the Potomac along the James River at Harrison's and Westover landings. While most of the IV and V corps would be sent ahead to secure the landings, the II, III, and VI corps would act as a rear guard to burn the army's vast supply depot at Savage's (or Savage) Station on the Richmond and York River Railroad and slow Lee's pursuit. Perhaps Wheat's gallant sacrifice at Gaines' Mill would not be in vain after all.[5]

On the north side of the Chickahominy, the Confederates noticed not only the dust kicked up by McClellan's "repositioning" but also the copious clouds of smoke which were produced by his burning stores.[6] Some men, old soldiers like General Whiting, thought that the commotion across the river was merely a *ruse de guerre* and that McClellan was actually trying to lure Lee across the river so that he could maul his army in a well-laid ambush. But Whiting's associate, General D.H. Hill, disagreed. McClellan was running, he averred. Hill remembered:

While [Jackson was] lying all day idle on the 28th, unable to cross the Chickahominy, the clouds of smoke from the burning plunder in the Federal camps and the frequent explosions of magazines indicated a retreat; but Whiting kept insisting upon it that all this was but a *ruse de guerre* of McClellan preparatory to a march upon Richmond. I made him such reply as that once made to General Longstreet, when a cadet at West Point, by Professor Kendrick. The professor asked Longstreet, who never looked at his chemistry, how the carbonic acid of commence was made. Longstreet replied, "By burning diamonds in oxygen gas." "Yes," said Professor Kendrick, "that will do it; but don't you think it would be a leetle expensive?" The old West Point yarn had a very quieting effect upon his apprehensions.[7]

That same day, as Jackson's engineers were stuck rebuilding Grapevine Bridge, Lee ordered Magruder's, Huger's, and McLaws's divisions to move forward from their entrenchments around Richmond and clear the south bank of the Chickahominy down to Savage Station, allowing Longstreet's and Jackson's wings to cross over to the south side once the bridges were completed. When Magruder's wing approached the railroad depot later that afternoon, however, just across the river from Jackson's, it was met by two divisions from "Bull" Sumner's II Corps and a division from William Franklin's VI Corps who held, according to Magruder, "well-manned works." The subsequent battle of Savage Station was a guarded fight, Sumner being tasked with simply holding the place only long enough to burn what was left of McClellan's supplies and Magruder, outnumbered, waiting for Lee's promised reinforcements that never arrived.[8] General Taylor, a mere observer across the Chickahominy at Bottom's Bridge, remembered:

> In the afternoon [of June 29], a great noise of battle came; artillery, small arms, shouts. This, as we afterward learned, was Magruder's engagement at Savage's Station, but this din of combat was silenced to our ears by the following incident: A [Federal] train was heard approaching from Savage's. Gathering speed, it came rushing on toward Bottom's Bridge, and quickly emerged from the forest, two engines drawing a long string of carriages. Reaching the bridge, the engines exploded with a terrific noise, followed in succession by explosions of the carriages, laden with ammunition. Shells burst in all directions, the river was lashed into foam, trees were torn for acres around, and several of my men were wounded. The enemy had taken this means of destroying surplus ammunition.[9]

Private Handerson of the 9th Louisiana, on patrol between Bottom's and Grapevine bridges, heard the same train explosion and later remembered:

> [At] about two P.M. ... A crash as if the very heavens had opened brought me suddenly to my feet, while the dry limbs of the tree beneath which I was sitting rattled about me like drops of rain in a heavy shower.... I looked down towards the river ... and beheld a column of dark smoke rising from the ruins of a bridge over the Chickahominy, while bright flashes of fire and the article of exploding shells told the story of the destruction of the enemy's ammunition train. General McClellan, unable to carry off his reserve ammunition on his retreat, had placed it in cars, applied a slow match and started the train for the bridge, where its explosion had overwhelmed everything in one column destruction. The force of the explosion may be judged from the fact that the house whose windows were all shattered was situated at least three-quarters of a mile from the bridge over the river.[10]

12. Egyptian Darkness

That night, the Federals at Savage Station, incredibly, were directed by McClellan to give up the field, march down to Glendale, burning the bridge over White Oak Swamp behind them, and link up with the main body near the Charles City crossroad. With the Chickahominy crossings now clear, Lee ordered Ewell to march his division back up to the now-rebuilt Grapevine Bridge and cross over to the south side of the river, linking up with the rest of Jackson's wing and the divisions of Longstreet, Huger, Magruder, McLaws, and A.P. Hill at Savage Station. Once the move was completed by 3:30 in the morning of June 30, Lee's entire army, minus Holmes's and Jones's divisions, which were still manning the Richmond defenses, was united.[11]

The Yankees who had abandoned Savage Station left some important clues as to their predicament. A large field hospital, for example, filled with over 3,000 vanquished patients, was capriciously left behind and tons of supplies that had not been burned were left to be ensnared by Lee's advancing legions. "The whole country was full of deserted plunder," remembered Major Robert Dabney, Jackson's chief of staff. "Army wagons, and pontoon trains partially burned or crippled. Mounds of grain and rice and hillocks of mess beef smoldering; tens of thousands of axes, picks, and shovels; camp kettles gashed with hatchets; medicine chests with their drugs stirred into a foul medley, and all the apparatus of a vast and lavish host."[12] General Jackson similarly remembered:

> Many other evidences of the hurried and disordered flight of the enemy were now visible; blankets, clothing, and other supplies had been recklessly abandoned. D.H. Hill, who had the advance, gathered up probably a thousand stragglers and so many small arms that it became necessary to detach two regiments to take charge of them and to see to the security of the prisoners.[13]

With his entire army now on the south side of the Chickahominy and with strong evidence that McClellan was not laying a deadly trap, but was in fact retreating rapidly, Lee resolved to destroy the bulk of the Potomac army that was strung out along the Quaker Road between White Oak Bridge and Glendale. One more good pounding, Lee thought, and McClellan would be finished. He therefore ordered Jackson to march down to White Oak Swamp Bridge and fall upon McClellan's rear guard from the north with four divisions while Lee slammed into McClellan's main body from the west via Darbytown and Charles City roads with five divisions. The next day, Sunday, June 30, 1862, was to be the decisive day of the war.[14]

But things again went awry for Lee. Of the nine divisions that were supposed to engage the enemy at Glendale, only two, Longstreet's and A.P. Hill's, attacked as ordered, and when Huger, Magruder, and McLaws finally did enter the fray, late in the day, they did so without effect. As for Jackson, up at White Oak Bridge, he minimally did his job. That is, he fixed Israel Richardson's and "Baldy" Smith's divisions from the II and VI corps and Henry Naglee's brigade from the IV Corps by threatening them with "a terrific cannonade" and occasional infantry probes across the almost impenetrable swamp.[15]

By dusk, Lee had lost 3,673 and McClellan 3,797 at the battle of Glendale. And although the Federals still held the field in the face of Lee's superior but mishandled forces, McClellan, back at Harrison's Landing, once again ordered his victorious forces to break contact under the cover of darkness and withdraw. Richardson's and Smith's divisions, up at White Oak Swamp, pulled out first, followed by Sumner's, Heintzelman's, Porter's, and Franklin's commands, which reluctantly yielded the field to the hated rebels and marched further south, closer to the James River. On the heels of this fortuitous Federal withdrawal, Jackson crossed White Oak Bridge and joined the rest of Lee's army, which was bedded down around Glendale.[16]

Despite the fact that he and his ranking lieutenants had once again performed miserably, Lee, inspired by the innate bravery and fighting abilities exhibited by the men of his army—men such as the Louisiana Tigers—he resolved to continue the attack. Stuart's scouts had reported that most of McClellan's army had fallen back to Harrison's and Westover landings, leaving behind a strong rear guard atop Malvern Hill, which was but three miles south of Glendale. It was Lee's intention to attack up Malvern Hill, drive off McClellan's covering force, take the landings, and destroy the Army of the Potomac once and for all.[17]

This time, the plan would be simple. There would be no fancy turning movements; these had all failed him before. This time, it would be a frontal assault straight up Malvern Hill. Brute force, like at Gaines' Mill, Lee thought, would win the day. And because Jackson's and Magruder's wings had sat out the battle of Glendale, they would go in first. Longstreet and A.P. Hill's men, now much reduced, would be held in reserve.[18]

Most of the division commanders of Lee's army, especially James Longstreet, agreed with Lee's plan of attack. But D.H. Hill, who was rare to back away from a fight, dissented. He remembered:

> General Lee ... bore grandly his terrible disappointment of the day before, and made no allusion to it. I gave him [a] description of Malvern Hill [a series of rolling hills near the James River], and presumed to say, "If General McClellan is there in force, we had better let him alone." Longstreet laughed and said, "Don't get scared, now that we have got him whipped." It was this belief in the demoralization of [McClellan's] army that made [Lee] risk the attack.[19]

In spite of D.H. Hill's misgivings, Lee ordered Magruder and Jackson to storm Malvern Hill as directed. Jackson's wing, led by Whiting's division, therefore marched down the Quaker Road and reached Willis Church's parsonage and a smithy, just north of Malvern Hill, a little after 11:00 A.M. There, Whiting's skirmishers engaged McClellan's outposts that were deployed along the south bank of Western Run. Once the Federals were driven from the area, Jackson surveyed the scene through his field glasses (binoculars). The Union position, it seemed, was even more formidable than the one at Gaines' Mill. Like Turkey Hill, Malvern Hill was actually an undulating plateau, but bigger. Its western face, fronted by Low Meadow Creek, was extremely precipitous and was called Malvern Cliff by the locals. Its eastern face, closer to Jackson, was also flanked by a creek and it was almost as steep. The center of the hill, bisected by the Quaker Road, was a gentle, rolling slope that was flanked by two structures: the Crew House, on Jackson's far right, and the West House, to Jackson's near right. It seemed as though the Federals were aptly deployed, with entrenched infantry and artillery arrayed throughout the position.[20]

Confronted with this challenging situation, Jackson reluctantly positioned Whiting's division on the left side of Quaker Road, out near the Poindexter Farm. He then posted D.H. Hill's on the right side of the road, linking up with Magruder's division that was due to arrive once Jackson completed his deployment. Winder's division was held in reserve near the parsonage, supporting the artillery, and Ewell's division was split up to support the others: Stafford's Louisiana Brigade was positioned on the right rear of Whiting's division, Brig. Gen. Jubal Early's brigade (formerly Elzey's, who was grievously wounded at Gaines' Mill) was attached to Winder's division, and Trimble's brigade was sent out to the far left of the Confederate line, to buffer General Whiting's flank and rear.[21]

Like most other battles, it was Federal artillery that was the Louisiana Brigade's primary antagonist. The Pelican Staters simply waited in their reserve position near the creek, defenseless, and got pounded by Federal case shot and shell for several hours.[22] Henry Handerson of the 9th Louisiana remembered:

> The rattle of musketry and boom of cannon in close proximity to our line of march informed us that we had at last overtaken our retreating foe. Filing into an open field in our front, we had for a few moments a good view of the heights of Malvern Hill: a view too which earned for us a few shots well-aimed, though fortunately at such a distance as to prove ineffective. Yet one shell struck the ground just under the horse of General Jackson, who with his staff had ridden into the fields to reconnoiter, but fortunately the missile failed to explode. Here too for the first time I saw a shell in its course from the mouth of the cannon until its explosion. Coming directly towards me, it appeared as a small black object apparently changing its position very little from moment to moment, but gradually enlarging as it approached, until it burst perhaps a hundred yards in my front. Withdrawing speedily from this field where the enemy would have soon found our range, we formed in line of battle in the adjacent woods and advanced down a wooded slope to a swampy bottom where we were ordered to lie down while the shells and cannon balls whistled furiously through the tree-tops, doing us, however, no harm.[23]

McClellan's "rear guard" atop Malvern Hill in fact consisted of 17,000 infantrymen from every corps of the army and over 250 pieces of artillery, including 14 mammoth siege guns that were deployed along the northern bank of James River, on the reverse slope of Malvern Hill. Lee intended to open the attack with Holmes's unbloodied division on the far right, conducting a feint at Malvern Cliff, followed by an *en echelon* assault, passing through Huger's and Magruder's divisions, on the right, and then cascading through D.H. Hill's and Whiting's divisions, on the left. Longstreet, A.P. Hill, and Winder, held in reserve, would be thrown in to exploit any breakthrough.[24]

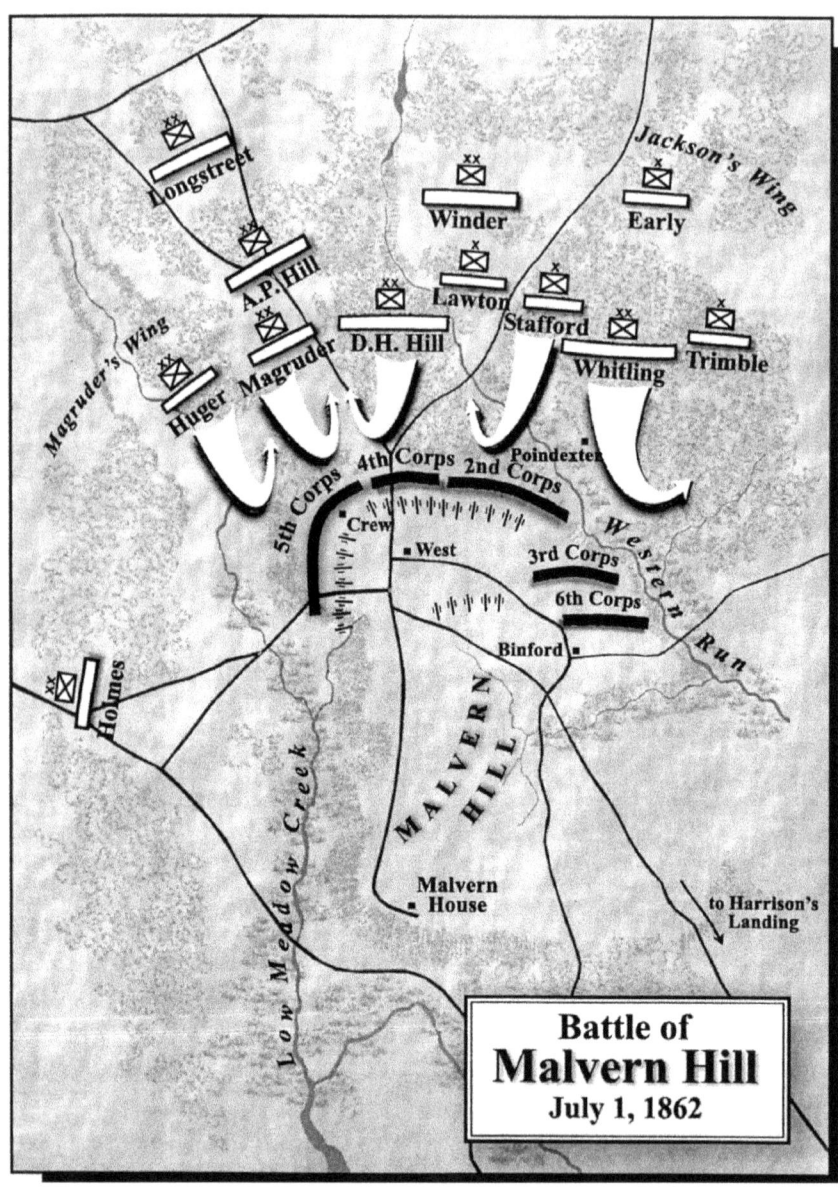

Because of Lee's reliance on the ineffectual Holmes, the Tigers and others were forced to wait five key hours in tactical reserve under a Federal artillery barrage until that commander finally got situated. It wasn't until 5:00 P.M., therefore, that Lee finally issued the attack order.[25] But even this attack degenerated into piecemeal jabs as miscommunication and a general lack of leadership continued to haunt Lee and his command. Holmes's division, for example, never attacked (even though everyone else had waited upon it). Huger's and Magruder's divisions, deployed on the western side of the Quaker Road, attacked *en echelon* by brigade as ordered but charged straight into the mouths of awaiting Federal guns, centered around the Crew House, and were "dreadfully slaughtered" by elements of Fitz-John Porter's tenacious V Corps. D.H. Hill's division, the next in line, attacked elements of Darius Couch's 2nd Division from the IV Corps almost an hour after Magruder's assault, and, being the only Confederate unit attacking on the field at the time, was also repulsed with heavy losses.[26]

In the wake of these uncoordinated and disastrous attacks, just before dark, the Louisiana Brigade, still in its reserve position on the northern bank of Western Run, was mistakenly ordered to attack across the creek and take a Federal battery to support General Whiting's assault against the Federal right. But like the rest of the Confederate forces that day, not only did the Louisiana Brigade go in piecemeal (the 9th Louisiana and the Tiger Battalion, on the brigade's left, apparently did not get the order to advance), but Whiting's division, the unit it was supposed to support, never attacked. So it was that three lonely Louisiana regiments charged across Poindexter's wheat fields, overwatched by two score pieces of Federal artillery and three brigades of infantry from the 2nd Corps, and were massacred.[27] Colonel Leroy Stafford, *de facto* commander of the Louisiana Brigade, reported:

> At dusk, an order was brought (we were under orders of General Whiting and supporting his division) to charge forward on the battery. This order was given by an officer unknown to myself or any officers of my command. Three of the regiments, the Sixth, Seventh, and Eighth Louisiana, advanced as ordered. It now being night, this order was not heard or properly understood by the 9th Louisiana [and what was left of Wheat's battalion, which was probably attached to it], and no advance was made by that command. This charge resulted in the loss of some valuable men.[28]

After this unnecessary and tragic charge was repulsed, the once-proud Louisiana Brigade, now eviscerated by Federal artillery, was withdrawn back into the woods on the north side of Western Run to reconsolidate. Companies were reformed, then battalions, then regiments. The 9th Regiment and what was left of the Special Battalion were rejoined with the rest of the brigade. Leave was even obtained by General Ewell for some of the men to get water back at Willis Church. A little later, after dark, "a portion of the brigade," most likely the 9th Louisiana and the pitiful remains of Harris's Tiger Battalion, was sent back into the field from which the infamous charge was made and there stayed for the rest of the night on picket duty.[29]

All told, Lee's army suffered 5,355 casualties at Malvern Hill, the last major altercation of the Seven Days' Battles. Of this, the Louisiana Brigade lost 24 dead and 92 wounded, almost exclusively from the day-long artillery attack and the twilight assault. The Star Battalion listed only two men wounded, one of which was Private Joe Perkins from the Tiger Rifles, who was probably clipped by a piece of shrapnel during the artillery barrage.[30]

As darkness descended upon the battlefield, McClellan once again ordered his men to withdraw from a field that they had bravely defended. The Tigers and others stayed in their forward position for most of the night, however, and helplessly listened to the tormenting screams of the wounded. Captain Douglas remembered:

> Night, dark and dismal, settled upon the battlefield of Malvern Hill, its thousands of dead and wounded. The rain began to fall on the cruel scene and beat out the torches of brave fellows hunting their wounded companions in the dark. The howling of the storm, the cry of the wounded and groans of the dying, the glare of the torch upon the faces of the dead or into the shining eyes of the speechless wounded, looking up in hope of relief, the ground slippery with a mixture of mud and blood, all in the dark, hopeless, starless night; surely it was a gruesome picture of war in its most horrid shape.[31]

The darkness, enhanced by rain, wreaked havoc on Confederate reorganization. During its eventual movement to the rear, for example, the 9th Louisiana and the Tiger Battalion left behind several of its soldiers, men who had fallen asleep. This included men such as Private Handerson of the 9th and Corporal Stephen Jenny of the Walker Guards, Wheat's Battalion, who was listed as deserting that night.[32] Handerson remembered:

> It was now nearly sun down and, as no order to move reached us, worn out and hungry, I fell fast asleep. I do not know at what hour I awoke, but the rain was falling upon my face and Egyptian darkness surrounded me. For a moment I failed to recall where I was. Then, reaching out on either side I touched my adjacent comrades, arousing them too from sleep. In whispers we exchanged ideas as to where we were and after a few moments I rose from the ground and groped my way to the point where I supposed Capt. Cummings to be. To my surprise I not only failed to find him, but after proceeding a few steps to my right all trace of my regiment was lost. Only some ten or a dozen of us were left together, all on the extreme left of the line. Puzzled at the state of affairs and anxious we held a sort of council of war in the rain and darkness. I remembered having seen a line of battle in front of us when I lay down and volunteered to go forward and see if it was still there. Groping my way cautiously to the front, I stumbled over the prostrate form of a man, and asking in a low tone what regiment he belonged to, received the non-committal answer: "What regiment do you belong to?" Replying that I was a member of the 9th Louisiana Regiment, he said he belonged to the ["up-teenth"] Virginia. I then inquired if he knew what had become of the regiment in his rear. He said he did not, he had heard the noise of some troops moving there some little time before. Returning to my companions we discussed anxiously our position and our most judicious course of action, and finally decided, in the absolute uncertainty of all our surroundings, to remain quietly where we were until daylight should at least enable us to see what we were doing. Accordingly we again lay down and listen with anxious ears at the distant rumbling of artillery which alone disturbed the silence of the night. Finally however, we all once more fell asleep and rested quietly until aroused by the advent of daylight.[33]

Although the Federals abandoned their position at Malvern Hill and had retreated to Harrison's and Westover landings during the night, most on the

Confederate side rated the battle as a ruinous defeat, Lee deservedly shouldering much of the blame. Private Handerson wrote: "The battle of Malvern Hill seems to have been conducted on the part of the Confederates without system or mutual cooperation and with the natural result a complete defeat. Fortunately the Federal Army was equally disorganized as and still more dispirited than our own, and retreated after the battle to the protection of the gunboats on the river."[34] General Taylor shared Private Handerson's sentiments when he proclaimed,

> At the beginning of operations in this Richmond campaign ... a high opinion has been expressed of the strategy of Lee, by which Jackson's forces from the Valley were suddenly thrust between McDowell and McClellan, and it deserves all praise; but the tactics on the field were vastly inferior to the strategy. Indeed, it may be confidently asserted that from Mechanicsville to Malvern Hill, inclusive, there was nothing but a series of blunders, one after another, and all huge.... Time, when he renders his verdict, will declare the gallant dead who fell at Gaines' Mill and Malvern Hill, to have been sacrificed on the altar of the bloodiest of all Molochs: Ignorance.[35]

The next day, as rain continued to drench the battlefield, Harris's sixty-three stalwart Tigers remained in bivouac, resting, getting rations, and trying to stay as dry as possible under their gum blankets, ponchos, or canvas shelter halves. The dead from both armies were also buried in the mud, and the wounded were transported back to Richmond. While this macabre work was done, Confederate President Davis and General Lee held a council of war a few miles back from Malvern Hill with Generals Jackson, Longstreet, Magruder, and Stuart. After some debate, it was decided to press the attack, if not cautiously. Jackson and Longstreet would march their wings down to Westover Landing and probe McClellan's defenses there, hoping to launch a general attack if conditions permitted.[36]

When General Taylor discovered that Jackson was ordered to pursue McClellan down to the James, he asked for and received official leave from his duties as commander of the Louisiana Brigade to convalesce in Richmond. "The crisis of my illness now came in a paralysis of the lower limbs," he remembered with some regret, "and I was taken to Richmond." Colonel Leroy Stafford of the 9th Louisiana thus became the *de jure* commander of the Louisiana Brigade for the remainder of the campaign.[37]

The next day, July 3, 1862, Jackson began his less-than-enthusiastic movement toward Westover Landing, following Stuart's cavalry. But owing to the condition of the roads and his men, Jackson didn't get very far. When his veterans went into camp at sunset, Stonewall "was not in a very good humor" and, in an attempt to inspire the boys who had pulled off miracles in the Valley, directed that "the Army" would move at "early dawn." When the designated time came on July 4, however, Jackson could not get his men moving again. They had, after two straight months of heroic campaigning, finally broken down. General Ewell himself had to be awakened by Jackson's staff and his division, which had counted 8,500 at the beginning of the campaign season, now numbered less than 3,000.[38]

Not surprisingly, when Jackson's broken-down forces finally reached McClellan's defenses along Evelington Heights, just north of Westover, they were stopped cold by Federal artillery. When Lee arrived, he found Longstreet and Jackson arguing about the probability of an attack against the well-fortified Federal position, supported by gunboats in the James. While Longstreet favored assaulting the heights, making Westover Landing untenable, Jackson, remembering the slaughter at Malvern Hill and Gaines' Mill and knowing the condition of his men, was against it. After some more discussion, Lee acquiesced to the Valley commander and called off the attack.[39]

The Tigers and others stayed in front of McClellan's army at the foot of Evelington Heights until July 8, when they were ordered, with the rest of Ewell's division, to withdraw to Strawberry Hill, a shady, half-civilized place about two and a half miles south of Mechanicsville, near Richmond. "And so ended for us the Seven Days Battle," recounted Captain G. Campbell Brown. "The loss of [Ewell's] division in killed and wounded was 985, mostly at [Gaines' Mill]. But the seeds of disease sown by the malaria of the swamps carried off a good many more."[40]

13

A Tiger's Death

> *[The Tigers] were brave, desperate fighters, and on account of their bravery, and daring, their organization was destroyed [after Gaines' Mill].... They would fight in any other command to which they might be assigned, but as Wheat's battalion, never again would they fire a gun.*
> — David French Boyd and William McClendon

The Seven Days' Battles (as Mechanicsville, Gaines' Mill, Savage Station, Glendale, and Malvern Hill collectively came to be called) were a mixture of triumph and tragedy for the Southern Confederacy. On the one hand, the Rebels had driven the Federals back from the very gates of their capital and had seized the initiative. On the other was the sacrifice. Robert E. Lee's education in field command cost the Army of Northern Virginia a little over 20,000 men, or 22 percent of its strength (and McClellan 16,000, about 16 percent of his strength).[1] But the big question, in spite of the atonement, was what to do next. General Jackson, of course, once again suggested a thrust across the Potomac with 40,000 men. General Taylor remembered:

> While at Harrison's Landing, General Jackson suggested both to General Lee and the administration at Richmond that 40,000 troops should be sent to the Shenandoah Valley to clear it of the enemy, move toward Maryland and threaten Washington, and that this force should move as lightly as possible. He wished General Lee to take command of the expedition, but said he was willing to serve in it under Longstreet or Ewell or one of the Hills, if the government preferred any one of them to himself. At the time, Richmond declined to adopt the suggestion, and until finding out more certainly what McClellan intended to do, it would have been extremely hazardous to weaken the forces defending the Confederate capital.[2]

Lee could have also laid siege to McClellan's army at Westover as Washington did to Cornwallis at Yorktown in 1781. But unlike Cornwallis, McClellan ruled the seas, and Lee would have had little hope of conducting a successful siege operation. Besides, a new threat was entering the fray from the north and west in the form of Major General John Pope. After the recent and disastrous Valley and Seven Days' campaigns, U.S. president Lincoln reduced McDowell's, Frémont's, and Banks's armies to corps status and put them under the Army of Virginia, commanded by General Pope, the victor of Island Number Ten in the Western Theater.[3]

Pope was to assemble his new army along the Rappahannock River between Culpeper and Fredericksburg and await the arrival of McClellan's army, which was to be evacuated from the peninsula. Once assembled, McClellan, unbeknownst to him, would be relieved of command and Pope was to march south to Richmond with 150,000 men. This mammoth army, it was hoped, should then be able to finally crush the Rebellion and restore the Union under Republican leadership.[4]

Like the Federal army, the Confederate army in Virginia was also reorganized after the Seven Days' Battles. Because of its generally lackluster performance during the previous few weeks, Magruder's wing was disbanded and its constituent units were either distributed throughout Longstreet's and Jackson's commands or were retained in the Richmond defenses (Magruder himself was transferred to command the Department of the Trans-Mississippi's District of Texas). Whiting's and D.H. Hill's divisions were returned to Longstreet's wing, and there was talk that Jackson's and Longstreet's wings would become bona fide corps within the Army of Northern Virginia.[5]

The Louisiana troops serving in Virginia were also reorganized. General Taylor, on the recommendation of Jackson, was promoted to major general and transferred back to his home state to command the District of West Louisiana.[6] Before his departure, however, Taylor suggested that all Louisiana troops posted in Virginia be organized into two brigades—the 1st and 2nd Louisiana brigades—and that the remaining Louisiana battalions in Lee's army, Charles Dreux's 1st, Robert Harris' (formerly Wheat's) 2nd, William Bradford's 3rd, and Henri St. Paul's 7th should be disbanded and their men transferred to beef up the existing regiments.[7]

Both President Davis and General Lee agreed.[8] Taylor's old Louisiana Brigade thus became the 1st Louisiana Brigade and would now consist of the 5th, 6th, 7th, 8th, and the 14th Louisiana regiments. It would remain in Ewell's division of Jackson's wing.[9] Colonel Henry Forno's 5th and Colonel Valery Sulakowski's 14th regiments would be new to the brigade, and Taylor's old 9th Regiment would be transferred to the 2nd Brigade. The other Louisiana infantry units posted in Virginia—the 1st, 2nd, 10th, and 15th regiments and George Coppens's 1st Louisiana Zouave Battalion—were adjoined with the 9th Regiment to form the 2nd Louisiana Brigade, Brigadier General William Starke commanding.[10] The 15th Louisiana Regiment was a new outfit, formed around Bradford's and St. Paul's disbanded battalions (which included the Catahoula Guerrillas), and it was commanded by Lieutenant Colonel Francis Nicholls, who had been horribly wounded at Winchester while helping to lead the 8th Louisiana against the Central Heights.[11] Because Starke's brigade was placed in Winder's division, both Louisiana brigades were under Jackson's direct command.[12] On July 25, 1862, President Davis wrote to General Lee on disbanding the Tiger Battalion:

GENERAL: Yesterday evening I had a full conversation with General Taylor, and also with Major La Sere. General Taylor thinks the best arrangement which can be made of the Louisiana troops will be as proposed, to place the 5th, 6th, 7th, 8th, and the 14th Louisiana Regiments in a brigade, to promote Colonel Hays to be a brigadier, and assign him to the command of it.... General Taylor is decidedly in favor of breaking up Wheat's Battalion. He thinks the men would voluntarily transfer to other companies in service and that the officers should be disbanded. He reports favorably of Captain Atkins, who has commanded one of the companies, and thinks, if he desires to remain in the service, that he should be made an exception. Imperfect knowledge of the captain, limited to an examination of the evidence of his service in Italy and to observation of him on the field of Manassas, has led me to regard him as worthy of special consideration.[13]

On August 9, 1862, Special Order 185 formally disbanded Wheat's Special Battalion:

The battalion of Louisiana volunteers commanded by Major Wheat, deceased, having been reduced to not more than a hundred men, will be disbanded, and the men comprising the same will be transferred to the Louisiana regiments serving in Virginia.[14]

With disbandment, the sixty-four or so remaining officers and men of the Star Battalion were assigned not only to other Louisiana units serving in Virginia, but throughout the Confederacy.[15] For example, from the Walker Guards, Major Robert Harris "surrendered in May 1865 in Meridian, Mississippi, after serving in the Provost Department at Mobile, Alabama," Private James Byrnes was "transferred to Company D, 5th Louisiana," and Private George Smith was "captured at Hagerstown, Maryland, 1862." From the Tiger Rifles, Captain Alexander White was "captured at Vicksburg, 1863," Lieutenant Thomas Adrian was "promoted to lieutenant colonel in the 12th Tennessee Cavalry and was killed by a junior officer while serving around Knoxville in November, 1862," Private Peter Connor was "wounded in Dea's Brigade at Murfreesboro, Tennessee, December 31, 1862," and Dennis Quirk was "captured at Sharpsburg, September 17, 1862." From the Delta Rangers, Lieutenant Thaddeus Ripley was "captured near St. Louis, 1864," Private James Collins was "admitted to hospital in Shreveport, Louisiana, January 18, 1864," and Private Frederick Hamm became a "member of Capt. O.G. Jones's Battery, Texas Light Artillery." From the Old Dominion Guards, "musician (bugler) James Wallace [was] severely wounded and died at Murfreesboro," Private John Smith was "transferred to Company G, 6th Louisiana and died of wounds received near Battle House, Virginia, April 27, 1863," and Private James Taylor was "slightly wounded at Murfreesboro on January 3, 1863 while on picket duty." And finally, from Wheat's Life Guards, Captain Robert Going Atkins "served on General Jubal Early's staff" until 1864 when he returned to Ireland, Lieutenant Robert Grinnel "served as an assistant adjutant for Brig. Gen. James Archer, an assistant inspector general for Maj. Gen. Harry Heth, and escorted $9,000,000 of Confederate funds to Marshall, Texas, in 1865," Private John Long was "wounded and missing at

Murfreesboro," and James Dooley was "killed at Payne's Farm during Mine Run Campaign, November 27, 1863, assigned to the 1st Louisiana Regiment."[16]

Upon Taylor's transfer and the Tiger Battalion's disbandment, the 1st Louisiana Brigade was put under the command of Harry Thompson Hays of the 7th Regiment, who was promoted to the rank of brigadier general on July 25, 1862.[17] Soon after, Hays's brigade adopted, "erroneously," according to one veteran, the Special Battalion's *nomme de guerre*—Tigers—and it was thereafter known as "The Tiger Brigade."[18]

As to the fate of Wheat's doomed battalion, Major David French Boyd of the 9th Louisiana and Private William McClendon of the 15th Alabama summed it up best when they said:

> [The Tigers] were brave, desperate fighters, and on account of their bravery, and daring, their organization was destroyed [after Gaines' Mill].... They would fight in any other command to which they might be assigned, but as Wheat's Battalion, never again would they fire a gun.[19]

Had Wheat lived, there is little doubt that his intrepid little battalion, although reduced to a handful of officers and men after the Seven Days, would not only have survived reorganization, but would have been contorted into either the 15th "Louisiana Tiger" Regiment or the 1st Confederate Zouave Regiment (regulars), Wheat being commissioned its colonel, Atkins its lieutenant colonel, and Harris its major. And with the reputation the original Tigers had built since Manassas, Wheat probably would have eventually risen to the rank of brigadier general in the Army of Northern Virginia.

But this would not come to pass, as the 1st Louisiana Special Battalion, one of the most colorful, audacious, and combative units that took to the field in defense of Southern independence during the Civil War, was disbanded soon after Wheat's death. Originally raised from the waterfront of New Orleans, most of the Tigers, who were despairingly known before the war as being "adventurous wharf rats, cut throats, and bad characters generally," rose to become heroes of the Southern nation. Their spirited defense of Matthews' and Henry hills at the battle of First Manassas, for example, launching no less than three impetuous assaults in the face of a superior enemy, established their aggressive reputation for friend and foe alike. During the now-famous Valley Campaign, their uncanny fighting spirit was further proven as they seized the key positions at the battles of Front Royal, First Winchester, and Port Republic, enabling Jackson to vindicate his name and changing the course of the war in favor of the Southern Confederacy, at least for a while. During the Seven Days' Battles, the battalion's swan song, Wheat dared his Tigers to charge the strong Federal lines at Gaines' Mill, even though they numbered less than a hundred men. The Tigers, then, lived on life's edge. For them, whether on the docks of New Orleans, in the jungles of Nicaragua, or on battlefields of northern Virginia, there was no middle ground. It was either conquer or be conquered—Lincoln's life, or a Tiger's death.

Appendix I

Service Record of the 1st Louisiana Special Battalion

Wheat's battalion was organized at Camps Davis, Walker, and Moore, Louisiana, from April to June 1861. On June 6, 1861, it was officially mustered into Confederate service as the "1st Special Battalion, Louisiana Volunteers" with five companies: the Walker Guards, the Tiger Rifles, the Delta Rangers, the Old Dominion Guards, and the Rough and Ready Rangers. On June 9, a sixth company, the up-country Catahoula Guerrillas, was added. On June 13, 1861, with Maj. Wheat's insistence to get to Virginia as soon as possible, the state changed the battalion's nomenclature to the "2nd Battalion, Louisiana Volunteers." On August 12, 1862, due to combat losses and other factors, the battalion was officially disbanded and its sixty-four remaining men were transferred to other units throughout the Confederacy.

Battalion Staff

Major Chatham Roberdeau Wheat, Virginia born, and thirty-five years old upon the formation of the battalion. University of Nashville alum, Mexican War veteran, New Orleans attorney, Louisiana state representative, and renowned filibuster and soldier of fortune. Elected captain of the Old Dominion Guards on April 25, 1861, and major of the battalion at Camp Walker on May 10. On June 6, he was mustered into Confederate service with the rest of the battalion. At the battle of Manassas, he was "wounded in the left arm and breast ... the bullet passing immediately under and a little in front of the arm pits ... puncturing a lung before passing out the other side." At the battle of Gaines' Mill, he was killed outright and buried on the field where he fell. The next year, 1863, his family had his body disinterred and buried in Hollywood Cemetery, Richmond, where his grave site is still extant.

Major Robert Harris, the original captain of the Walker Guards, was promoted to command the battalion after Wheat's death at Gaines' Mill.

Battalion Adjutant (first): Lieutenant Richard Dickinson, originally from the Old Dominion Guards. Wounded in the leg at Manassas. Later promoted to captain and served in the Trans-Mississippi Department. Found guilty of assaulting a "Negro street vendor" in 1860.

Battalion Adjutant (second): Lieutenant Charles Pitman, originally from the Delta Rangers.

Battalion Quartermaster: Lieutenant Samuel Dushane, originally from the Tiger Rifles. Helped bury Wheat at Gaines' Mill. Later promoted to captain and served with Mosby's Partisan Rangers. Buried in the Dranesville, Virginia, United Methodist Cemetery, 11720 Sugarland Road.

Battalion Surgeon: Dr. William Love.

Sergeant Major (first): Bruce Putnam, originally from the Old Dominion Guards. Promoted to lieutenant after the battle of Manassas, he was assigned to Wheat's Life Guards.

Sergeant Major (second): James Wrigley, originally from the Walker Guards.

Ordnance Specialist: Sgt. H.H. Tabor, originally from the Delta Rangers.

Sutler (supplier): Solomon Solomon was a close friend and business associate of Obedia Miller's, a New Orleans attorney. His daughter, Clara, wrote in her diary about the formation of the battalion and her closeness to Miller.

Company A
Walker Guards

The Walker Guards were raised by Robert Harris from the New Orleans waterfront during the early months of the war, principally from among the Irish ship hands or dock workers. Many of these men, especially the officers, reportedly were former filibusters who had served with William Walker or Roberdeau Wheat in Nicaragua from 1856 through 1857. With Wheat's timely arrival to New Orleans in early April 1861, the Walker Guards consented to confederate with the Old Dominion Guards, the Tiger Rifles, the Delta Rangers, and the Rough and Ready Rangers, forming the base of the battalion. The battalion was mustered into service on April 24, 1861.

Capt. Robert A. Harris. Promoted to major upon Wheat's death at Gaines' Mill. Known to have been a former filibuster and to have run a bawdy gambling establishment before the war. After the battalion was disbanded, he served in the Provost Department at Mobile, Alabama, and surrendered in May 1865 in Meridian, Mississippi.

1st Lt. John Coyle. Wounded at Port Republic.

1st Lt. E.B. Sloan. Resigned Dec. 1861.

2nd Lt. Edward Cockroft. Wounded at Port Republic.

2nd Lt. W.V. Kinnan.

Sgt. William Campbell.

Sgt. George Johnson.

Sgt. T.W. Smythe.

Sgt. John Wrigley. Promoted to sergeant major in Oct. 1861.

Cpl. Morris Buckley. Captured at Front Royal and sent to Fort Delaware. Exchanged at Aikens Landing, VA, Aug. 5, 1862.

Cpl. T.T. Burne.

Cpl. Charles Byrnes.

Cpl. William Carson.

Cpl. Cornelius Hurley.

Cpl. Stephen Janey. Discharged Aug. 12, 1862, because of disease.

Cpl. William Jenkins. Died of disease July 5, 1862.

Cpl. Stephen Jenny. Deserted July 2, 1862.

Musician Charles Johnston (drummer).

Musician Henry Ward (drummer).

Pvt. Jacob Abel. Transferred to G/6th LA after battalion was disbanded Aug. 1862.

H.L. Addison.

Martin Baldwin.

Daniel Bane.

Charles Barnes. Deserted Aug. 1861.

James Barnes.

James Bawden. Deserted Aug. 1861.

Joseph Bawden.

T. Barnes.

Samuel Blake.

Henry Brooks.

James Brown.

Edward Buckley. Captured at Front Royal and sent to Fort Delaware. Exchanged at Aikens Landing, VA, Aug. 5, 1862.

James Byrnes. Severely wounded in left leg at Manassas. Transferred to D/5th LA

when battalion was disbanded in Aug. 1862.
Thomas Byrnes.
Charles Byrnes.
Benard Cantilla.
Thomas Comfort.
L.H. Cummings.
James Doane.
Sam Doyle.
Charles Edgecomb.
Louis Ellinghausen.
George Ellis.
George Fesenfelt.
James Flynn.
Charles Foster. Deserted Aug. 1861.
Christopher Gagens.
Theodore Girod.
William Gray.
John Haley. Killed at Manassas.
John Hanan.
Frank Hartman.
Haywood Henshaw.
John Hessing.
John Hinds.
J.A. Howard. Wounded severely in leg at Manassas.
William Howard.
John Hanan.
J. Huff. Captured at Front Royal and sent to Fort Delaware Exchanged at Aikens Landing, VA, Aug. 5, 1862.
L.H. Jennings.
Eldridge Johnson. Deserted April, 1862.
James Jordan.
Simon Kiefner. Discharged because of T.B. in 1862.
Thomas Kilraine. Deserted Nov. 1861.
Peter King.
William Lacey. Wounded in the leg at Manassas.
Simon Lebrick.
James Lynch. Consigned to hospital Aug. 1861 to Dec. 1861.
Martin Lynch.
William Lyons. Wounded at Manassas.
Robert Lytle.
Barney Martin.
John Mitchell. Consigned to hospital Aug. 1861 to Dec. 1861.
James Murphy. Later captured Oct. 16, 1862 at Paris, Kentucky.
Timothy O'Brien.
Henry Ott.
Henry Raine. Wounded in leg at Manassas.
Peter Reynolds.
David Richards.
John Rodens.
Thomas Ryan. Consigned to hospital Aug. 1861 to Sept. 1861. Subsequently discharged on a surgeon's certificate.
Charles Shields.
James Shields. Captured at Port Republic June 1862 and sent to Fort Delaware. Exchanged at Aikens Landing, VA, Aug. 1862.
Frank Smith.
George Smith. Later captured Hagerstown, MD, 1862.
Lewis Stanley.
George Steele. Captured at Front Royal and sent to Fort Delaware. Exchanged at Aikens Landing, VA, Aug. 5, 1862.
Charles Stratton. Later captured at Winchester.
John Switzer. Captured at Port Republic June 1862 and sent to Fort Delaware. Exchanged at Aikens Landing, VA, Aug. 5, 1862.
John Tally. Deserted Oct. 1861.
Charles Tidmarsh. Deserted March 1862.
Melvin Whitcomb.
Richard Whitcomb.
Joseph Woop.
George Wrigley. Deserted Oct. 1861.
William Wrigley.
John Young. In hospital Oct. 1861. Later captured at Fredericksburg.

Company B Tiger Rifles

Known felon and riverboat pilot Alexander White raised the Tiger Rifles from the New Orleans waterfront. The company consisted almost exclusively of Irish (and to a lesser extent German) ship hands, stokers, stevedores, or dock workers. With Wheat's arrival to New Orleans in early April 1861, the Tigers consented to join with the Old Dominion Guards, the Walker Guards, the Delta Rangers, and the Rough and Ready Rangers, forming the base of the battalion. The battalion was mustered into Confederate service on April 27, 1861. The Tiger Rifles, according to Richard Taylor, "was the largest [company of the battalion] ... giving character to all" and its men were uniformed as Zouaves throughout most of the battalion's existence.

Capt. Alexander White. Mexican War veteran, convict, riverboat pilot, and proud husband. Confined July 1861 to Aug. 1861 for wounding Capt. William McCausland in a duel. Wounded in the thigh at Port Republic. Later captured at Vicksburg.
1st Lt. Thomas Adrian. Mexican War veteran who reportedly "loved war." Wounded in leg at Manassas while leading a platoon of Zoauves on Matthews' Hill. After disbandment, was promoted to lieutenant colonel in the 12th Tennessee Cavalry and was killed by a junior officer while serving around Knoxville in November 1862.
2nd Lt. Edward Hewitt. Detached on recruiting duty Nov. 1861 to Dec. 1861. Suffered a "gunshot and concussion" at Port Republic. Sent home June 13, 1862 on a surgeon's certificate.
1st Sergeant Robert Richie. Led the Tigers steadily on Henry Hill. After disbandment, he was promoted lieutenant and served in the Trans-Mississippi Department.
Sgt. Joseph Cooper. Killed by accident Aug. 23, 1861.
Sgt. William Keller.
Sgt. William Kelley. Deserted 1862.
Sgt. Charles Lewis.
Sgt. Samuel Waits.
Cpl. John Boyle.
Cpl. John W. Carroll.
Cpl. William Granger.
Cpl. William Lithgow.
Cpl. Cornelius Malloy.
Cpl. Joseph Nichols.
Pvt. Herman Albertstein.
John Beggs.
Lewis Berger. Deserted June 10, 1861 with Jourdan Stewart at Tangipahoa, LA, while en route to Manassas, VA.
Robert Bristol.
James Brown. Hospitalized for chronic diarrhea March 1862 to April 1862.
Stephen Burke.
James Burnes. Wounded at Seneca Falls (Potomac), July 14, 1861, in the leg, which was amputated at thigh in a Charlottesville hospital by Dr. Samuel Fisher.
Edward Carr.
William Cline.
Daniel Corcoran.
Dennis Corcoran. Executed for mutiny Dec. 9, 1861 at Camp Florida with Michael O'Brien.
Charles Connelly.
Peter Conner. Later wounded while in Dea's Brigade, Murfreesboro, TN, Dec. 31, 1862.
William Cook.
John Cotter.
Robert Cummings. Detached on recruiting duty with 1st Lt. Hewitt Nov. 1861 to Dec. 1861.
James Curren.
Edward Daily (1).
Edward Daily (2).
Patrick Deary. Died of pneumonia Jan. 30, 1862.
John Devlin.
William Douglas.
John Flanagan.
John Evans. Deserted Sept. 1861.
Stephen Foley.
John Fossie.
Henry Fraeling.
Morris Gallion.
John Gerroghty.
Thomas Green. Wounded in leg at Manassas.
James Hamilton.
Thomas Harris.
Richard Hawkins. Wounded in chest at Manassas and died two days later.
James Hays.
Edward Jackson. Killed at Manassas.
John Johnson.
Michael Kane.
James Keefer. Killed at Manassas.
Michael Keefe. Killed at Manassas.

Henry Kelley. Deserted 1862.
James Langtry.
Patrick Larkin.
William Ler. Killed at Manassas.
Michael Lyman. Hospitalized in Richmond for chronic rheumatism Oct. 1861. Discharged on a surgeon's certificate.
John McCarthy (1).
John McCarthy (2).
John McCarthy (3).
Lemuel Miller.
Leonard Miller.
Hugh McDonald. Died of wounds received by 4th S.C. at Manassas.
Robert Morgan.
Charles Mortimer. Captured at Front Royal and sent to Fort Delaware. Exchanged at Aikens Landing, VA, Aug. 5, 1862.
Stephen Mulchahie.
Charles Murray.
Wesley Nichols.
John Nugent.
Michael O'Brien. Executed for mutiny on Dec. 9, 1861 at Camp Florida with Dennis Corcoran.
James O'Conner.
John O'Donnel.
Joseph Perkins. Wounded at Malvern Hill.
James Purcell. Killed accidentally by Thomas Riggs of the Old Dominion Guards, Oct. 4, 1861.
Dennis Quirk. Later captured at Sharpsburg.
John Reynolds. Deserted July 1861.
James Riley.
William Rush.
Daniel Ryan. Deserted Oct. 1861.
Archibald Scott.
James Shaughnessey.
George Shiveley.
Hugh Smith.
John Smith. Deserted Aug. 1861.
William St. Clair. Accidentally shot, Oct. 15, 1861, at Camp Beauregard.
Jourdan Stewart. Deserted July 24, 1861 with Lewis Burger at Tangipahoa, LA, June 10, 1861, while en route to Manassas, VA.
Michael Sullivan. Deserted Sept. 1861.
John Thompson.
John Travers. Held in the brigade guardhouse for murdering Pvt. James Purcell of D/6th LA on Oct. 20, 1861.

Jacob Wallace. Wounded at Manassas.
Samuel Wayts.
Michael Welsh. Missing, possibly deserted, at Manassas.
Benjamin White.
Daniel Whitney.
Henry Wilcox.
John Williams.
Thomas Williams.
William Williams.
James Wilson. Died of wounds received by 4th S.C. at Manassas.

Company C
Delta Rangers

Henry Gardner from New Orleans raised the Delta Rangers during the early months of the war. Much like the volunteers from the Tiger Rifles and the Rough and Ready Rangers, the Delta Rangers primarily consisted of immigrant ship hands or dock workers. The Rangers were mustered into Confederate service on April 28, 1861.

Capt. Henry Gardner resigned his commission on June 1, 1862, in the wake of Gaines' Mill. Along with Austin Eastman, he was signatory of a document that requested Governor Moore to convene a secession convention in early 1861.
1st Lt. Austin Eastman. Resigned Jan. 11, 1862. Probably later drafted as a private and served with another unit. Carried the battalion's colors at Manassas.
1st Lt. Frank McCarthy. Killed at Port Republic.
1st Lt. Thaddeus Ripley. Wounded at Port Republic. Later captured St. Louis, MO, April 9, 1864.
2nd Lt. Charles Pitman. Battalion adjutant from July 1861 through February 1862. Killed at Gaines' Mill.
Sgt. Michael Horan.
Sgt. A.A. Overby.
Sgt. R.P. Price.
Cpl. J.B. Beeler. Later captured at Sharpsburg.

Cpl. John Collins. Later deserted Aug. 7, 1862.
Cpl. Peter Cristy.
Cpl. William Krans.
Cpl. Thomas Lennard. Deserted Oct. 1861.
Musician James Byrd (drummer). Deserted March 1862.
Pvt. James Arnold. Captured at Front Royal and sent to Fort Delaware. Exchanged at Aikens Landing, VA, Aug. 5, 1862.
William Black.
James Brady.
James Brooks.
Charles Buck.
James Burke.
James Burnes. Deserted Sept. 1861.
Peter Burnes.
James Byrd. Deserted April, 1862.
Jeremiah Callahan.
James Carey. Died of disease 1862.
John Carroll.
Charles Christy.
Peter Christy.
James Clark.
James Collins.
Michael Connally.
Frederick Dietrick.
Lawrence Delaney.
John Dougherty. Deserted April 1862.
William Duffy.
John Eckler. Captured at Port Republic.
John Evans.
Edward Ferry.
John Fitz. Died of diarrhea, Aug. 17, 1862.
August Good.
Luke Gordon.
James Grant.
Frederick Hamm. Later served in the Texas Light Artillery.
Edward Harris. Died of disease July 6, 1862.
Thomas Hayes. Captured at Manassas.
William Hickey.
Thomas Higgins.
William Hodgson.
John Holmes.
Frank Johnson.
John Johnson.
Mark Jordan. Wounded around Richmond, June 20, 1862.
Richard Kane. Captured at Front Royal and sent to Fort Delaware. Exchanged at Aikens Landing, VA, Aug. 5, 1861.
James Kelley.
Thomas Lee. Captured at front Royal and sent to Fort Delaware. Exchanged at Aikens Landing, VA, Aug. 5, 1861.
William Lemmon.
Thomas Leonard. Deserted March 1862.
Patrick Lynch. Wounded in hand at Manassas.
Patrick Mahar.
Frank Mallen. Wounded at Winchester, VA.
Thomas Maloney. Wounded around Richmond, 1862.
John Martin.
Patrick Matthews.
Thomas McGrath. Deserted March 1862.
Frank McGuire.
George Miller.
John Moran. Wounded in hand and groin at Manassas.
Frank Mullen.
Thomas Mullen.
Thomas Mulligan.
Thomas Newell. Deserted March 1862.
William Nixon. Wounded in shoulder at Manassas.
Charles O'Neal.
William Owens.
Charles Pendergast.
John Powers. Lists occupation as shoemaker.
Timothy Raine. Killed around Richmond, 1862.
Herman Rose. Wounded in the head at Manassas.
Dennis Ryan. Wounded in action around Richmond.
Patrick Ryan. Captured at Strasburg.
Robert Smith.
John Sydney. Deserted March 1862.
H.H. Tabor. Arrested at Manassas Aug. 1861. Battalion ordnance sergeant after January 1862.
William Thomson.
Thomas Tracy.
Francis Vestphol. Deserted Oct. 1861.
Peter Walsh.
James Watson. Wounded at Manassas.
Peter Welsh.
John Wilson.
John Winn.
Connally Wright.

Company D (First) Catahoula Guerrillas

Pennsylvania-born Jonathan W. Buhoup raised the Catahoula Guerrillas from the town of Trinity in Catahoula Parish. Unlike the rest of the battalion, the Guerrillas were generally more up-scale farmers, merchants, clerks, lawyers, pharmacists, physicians, artisans, overseers, or laborers from northern Louisiana. The Guerrillas, originally outfitted as cavalrymen, were slated to join the 8th Louisiana Regiment at Camp Moore in late May 1861. But when Capt. Buhoup failed to win a field commission in that regiment, he lobbied the Guerrillas to throw in with Wheat's nascent battalion in hopes of getting a better deal. Buhoup's company joined the 1st Louisiana Special Battalion on or about June 8, 1861. After the battle of Manassas, on November 1, 1861, Buhoup had his company transferred again, first to Major Henri St. Paul's 7th Louisiana Battalion and then to the 15th Louisiana Regiment. The Old Dominion Guards, the original Company E, became the new Company D. Buhoup never attained his coveted field commission. The records of the Guerrillas are far more complete because the Guerrillas were the only company of Wheat's battalion to last throughout the war. The men included here are those who most probably served under Wheat. "M" means "married," "U.M." means "unmarried," and "N.O." means "New Orleans."

Capt. Jonathan W. Buhoup. Pennsylvania-born. Age 35. Married merchant from Trinity. Died in N.O. while on recruiting duty Jan. 1862.
1st Lt. Moses Liddell. Later served on the staff of his father, Brig. Gen. St. John Liddell, in the Trans-Mississippi.
2nd Lt. Samuel Spencer. Age 24. M. lawyer from Harrisonburg.
2nd Lt. William Guss. Pennsylvania-born. Age 23. U.M. clerk from Trinity.
1st Sgt. Robert Walters. Indiana-born. Age 21. U.M. merchant from Tooly. Later promoted to 1st Lt.
Sgt. Joseph H. Dale. Mississippi-born. Age 22. U.M .clerk from Trinity.
Sgt. Benjamin Hughes.
Sgt. Hiram Sample. Pennsylvania-born. Age 20. U.M. farmer from Trinity.
Sgt. Riley Sands.
Cpl. James Brown.
Cpl. Benjamin Hardesty.
Cpl. John F. Napier. South Carolina–born. Age 23. U.M. tin smith from Trinity.
Cpl. Alfred Stone. Louisiana-born. Age 20. U.M. overseer from Trinity.
Cpl. Samuel Walker. Louisiana-born. Age 19.
Musician (drummer) Edward Gill.
Pvt. Robert Allison.
Hugh Anderson. Killed at Manassas.
Robert Arlinson.
Elijah Ballard.
Samuel Barfield. Wounded in back and face at Manassas.
L.W. Barfield.
Noah Barlow.
William Barnum. New York–born. Age 26. U.M. carpenter from Trinity.
Lambert Bawden. Consigned to hospital Sept. 1861 through Oct. 1861.
Zachariah Blackman. Mississippi-born. Age 19. U.M. blacksmith from Trinity. Discharged because of consumption (i.e., tuberculosis).
Samuel Bloch. German-born. Age 21. U.M. merchant from Trinity.
James Bolan.
William Bristol. Louisiana-born. Age 20. U.M. farmer from Trinity.
Isaac Newton Brown. Age 24. M. butcher from Trinity. Later promoted 2nd Lt.
Charles Brunson. Louisiana-born. Age 29. M. farmer from Trinity.
Edward Buckley.
Nathan Calhoun. South Carolina–born. Age 20. U.M. farmer from Trinity.
J. Carey.
Edward Clark. Irish born. Age 20. U.M. laborer from Trinity.
Hogan Clark.
Martin Conway.
John Croak.
O.B. Crooks.
Hiram Codaback. New York–born. Age 26. U.M. machinist from Trinity.

Francis Cunningham.
Joseph Dale.
George Davis.
Andy Day.
John Dobley.
John Elam. Mississippi-born. Age 20. U.M. farmer from Trinity.
Henry Fisher.
James Flynn. Irish-born. Age 27. U.M. laborer from Trinity.
Thomas Flynn. Wounded in leg at Manassas. Died of wound.
Thomas Gibbs.
Drury Gibson. Louisiana-born. Age 22. U.M. Physician from Trinity. Later promoted to captain and served as surgeon of the 15th Louisiana.
Vernon Gibson.
Thomas Gillick.
John Gines.
Daniel Goss. Georgia-born. Age 22. U.M. farmer from Trinity.
Charles Greer. N.O.–born. Age 19. U.M. farmer from Trinity.
Edward Greer. Georgia-born. U.M. overseer from N.O.
George Grover.
Francis Guice. Mississippi-born. Age 26. M. farmer from Trinity.
James Halping.
George Hammaker.
James Hancock. Alabama-born. Age 30. U.M. farmer from Trinity.
Alfred Harvey.
Thomas Hazzard. Massachusetts-born. Age 29. U.M. clerk from Trinity.
Edward Hicks. Missouri-born. Age 20. U.M. clerk.
Dennis Hogan.
James Holloway.
Remy Jardnell. Baker from Ascension Parish.
Franklin Kessler. New York–born. Age 27. U.M. molder from Trinity.
Josiah Lincoln. New York–born. Age 27. U.M. carpenter from Trinity.
Michael Manning. Alabama-born. Age 21. U.M. overseer from Trinity.
James McClure. Age 21.
William McCoy. Kentucky-born. Age 23. U.M. farmer from White Springs.
Patrick McQuaid. Irish-born. Age 26. U.M. laborer from Trinity.

Patrick Melville. Irish-born. Age 29. U.M. laborer from Trinity.
Stephen Morgan.
William Morris. Wounded in shoulder at Manassas.
Claudius Nelder. Louisiana-born. Age 17. U.M. farmer from Trinity.
William Noyes. Louisiana-born. Age 27. U.M. farmer from Concordia.
Patrick O'Conner.
John O'Hara. Irish-born. Age 27. U.M. laborer from Trinity. Died in hospital 8/61. Buried in Hollywood Cemetery as "JO Haira."
Jesse Peebles. Died in hospital, 1861.
Robert Penticost.
John Phillips. Louisiana-born. Age 20. U.M. farmer from Baton Rouge.
Thomas Rawlings. Louisiana-born. Age 25. M. farmer from Trinity.
John Rhinehart. Louisiana-born. Age 21. U.M. farmer from Trinity.
Daniel Shay. Irish-born. Age 43. U.M. tailor from Jackson.
James Shay. Irish-born. Age 36. U.M. laborer from Trinity.
John Shultzer. German-born. Age 25. M. clerk from Trinity.
Charles Smith (Schmidt). German-born. Age 19. U.M. butcher from Trinity.
John Spann. Age 20.
Charles Spencer. New York–born. U.M. clerk farmer Trinity.
James Spencer.
Elias Stone. Louisiana-born. Age 20. U.M. physician from Trinity. Killed at Manassas.
William "Hall" Stone. Louisiana-born. Age 19. U.M. overseer from Trinity. Shot through neck and killed at Manassas.
Madison Summerlin.
Patrick Sweeney. Died of pneumonia at Camp Moore, June 5, 1861.
James Taylor. Later wounded at Stones River while on picket.
Oliver Tresler.
Samuel Walker.
Sylvanus Walker. Georgia-born. Age 24. U.M. farmer from Trinity.
John Ward.
Samuel Warwick. Died of pneumonia, Aug. 21, 1861.

W. Warwick.
William Welsh.
Patrick Wheelan.
Henry White.
Napoleon Williamson. Later killed at 2nd Manassas.
Chester Woods. Captured at Manassas and sent to Fort Delaware. Exchanged at Aikens Landing, VA, Aug. 5, 1862.
James Woods.

Company E (First) and D (Second) The Old Dominion Guards

The Old Dominion Guards were raised in New Orleans by the renowned soldier of fortune and Southern partisan Roberdeau Wheat and a New Orleans attorney named Obedia Plummer Miller. The Guards were one of the original five companies of the battalion, being mustered into Confederate service on April 27, 1861. On or about November 1, 1861, when the Catahoula Guerrillas transferred out of the battalion to seek greener pastures, the Old Dominion Guards were moved over to become Wheat's Company D (second). The Guards consisted mostly of Irish dock workers or expatriate Virginians.

Capt. Obedia Plummer Miller was a New Orleans attorney and friend of Solomon Solomon's, the battalion's sutler. He was horribly wounded in the ankle at Manassas and never returned to the Special Battalion. According to Clara Solomon, "Obed" grew jealous of Wheat and gained a commission from the Confederate government to raise a company of cavalry. Calling his command "Capt. Miller's Independent Mounted Rifles" or the "Wild Cats," Miller was assigned to the 9th Virginia Cavalry. But like Wheat's battalion, the Mounted Rifles were disbanded after Miller was killed in late 1862.

1st Lt. William Foley was an associate of Obedia Miller's. He took command of the company after Miller was wounded at Manassas. Killed at Gaines' Mill while leading his company. Along with Henry Gardner, Foley was signatory to a document that asked Governor Moore to convene a secession convention in early 1861.

2nd Lt. Henry S. Carey. Born in Virginia and a professed relative of Thomas Jefferson. Wounded in the thigh at Manassas. Later assigned to Wheat's Life Guards.

2nd Lt. John Keenan. The former drummer of the company.

2nd Lt. Alvan Read. On sick leave Nov. 1861 through Dec. 1861.

Sgt. John McSweegan.
Sgt. David O'Keefe.
Sgt. Daniel Ross. Wounded in leg at Manassas.
Cpl. Thomas Mulready.
Cpl. James Gordon.
Musician (bugler) William E. Wallace.
Pvt. Martin Barnes.
James Barrett. Consigned to hospital Nov. 1861 through Dec. 1861.
William Bennett.
Martin Bolwin.
Frederick Bossey.
Benjamin Burton.
James Carroll.
John Carroll.
William Casey.
James Conner. Captured at Front Royal and sent to Fort Delaware. Exchanged at Aikens Landing, VA, Aug. 5, 1862.
Patrick Connerty. Wounded in leg at Manassas.
Andy Day.
Robert Deshelter.
Thomas Daugherty.
Dennis Dowdy.
Joseph Fanning.
John Flanagan.
Thomas Ford. Discharged on surgeon's certificate, Oct. 25, 1861.
Joseph Gallander.
William Gardner.
William Gillespie.
C. Gribble. Deserted.
George Hamilton. Irish-born. Age 34. U.M. clerk from N.O. Later served with 8th LA.

John Haman.
J.H. Hutchinson. Wounded in face at Manassas.
August Johnson. Shot and supposed to be killed but missing in action at Manassas.
John Kuntz. Wounded in back and captured at Manassas.
John McCluskey.
James McDermott.
Henry McQuaid.
John Meyer.
Fritz Mirb.
Edward Morris.
James McDermott. Wounded in back at Manassas.
Peter McKune.
John Murphy. Captured at Port Republic and sent to Fort Delaware. Later exchanged at Aikens Landing, VA, Aug. 5, 1862.
Linus Musgrave.
James Nash.
Charles Newman.
Cornelius O'Brian.
Thomas O'Donnel.
Daniel O'Neill. Discharged on surgeon's certificate, Oct. 25, 1861.
Henry S. Orr.
Jacob Penticost. Wounded severely in neck at Manassas.
John Randel.
John Reynor. Wounded in thigh at Manassas.
Cornelius Reilly.
John Richards.
Edward Riggs.
Thomas Riggs. Accidentally shot and killed James Purcell of the Tiger Rifles on Oct. 4, 1861.
Thomas Rocks. Captured at Port Republic and sent to Fort Delaware. Later exchanged at Aikens Landing, VA, Aug. 5, 1862.
Henry Rose.
Frederick Schultz. Wounded in shoulder at Manassas.
James Shehan. Wounded at Front Royal and then captured May 30, 1862.
John Shine.
George Smith.
John Smith.
Patrick Sullivan.
William Tiller.
Joseph Trunzler.
David Vance. Wounded in knee at Manassas.
Jerry Van Riper.
John Walden.
John Walker. Wounded in thigh at Manassas.
Johannes Wallen.
James Welch. Died of disease, Feb. 9, 1862.
John Wright.

Company E (Second) Wheat's Life Guards

Wheat's Life Guards were originally raised by Henry Chaffin of New Orleans, who called the company the Rough and Ready Rangers. Chaffin was apparently a friend of Obedia Miller's and agreed to adjoin with Wheat at Camp Davis. Unable to fill its muster at Camp Moore, the Rough and Readies were disbanded, and the dishonored Chaffin handed control of the company over to George Hanna, who renamed the organization the Orleans Claiborne Guards. Still, the company was plagued, and because Hanna was unable to sufficiently fill his quota, the Guards were not mustered into Confederate service until after the battle of Manassas. In October 1861, the Guards were finally attached to Wheat's Battalion, effectively replacing the outgoing Catahoula Guerrillas (although it was officially designated Company F for a few weeks). Wheat immediately brushed the inept Hanna aside and presented the Guards with Robert Going Atkins, his Irish aide-de-camp, fellow Garibaldini, and noted hero of the battle of Manassas. Atkins quickly renamed the company Wheat's Life Guards and it officially became Company E (second), 1st Louisiana Special Battalion. Bruce Putnam, the battalion's sergeant major at the time, was commissioned a 2nd Lt. in the Life Guards and was sent back to New Orleans to try to fill the company's muster roll.

Captain Robert Going Atkins was an Irish soldier of fortune who had served with Wheat in Italy under Giuseppe Garibaldi. Enlisted in the battalion just before the battle of Manassas and served as Wheat's aide-de-camp. He was commissioned a 2nd lieutenant in Sept. 1861 by the Confederate government for his actions at Manassas and was "elected" by the men of the Rough and Ready Rangers to be their captain. After the battalion was disbanded in Aug. 1862, Atkins served on Brig. Gen. Jubal Early's staff. In 1864, he returned to Ireland and after the war, moved to Arkansas, where he died and is buried.

1st Lt. Robert Grinnel. Wounded in hand and captured at Front Royal, VA. Sent to Fort Monroe. Exchanged Aug. 5, 1862 at Aikens Landing, VA. Later served as an assistant adjutant for Brig. Gen. James Archer and an assistant inspector general for Maj. Gen. Harry Heth. He also escorted $9,000,000 of Confederate funds to Marshall, Texas, in 1865.

2nd Lt. Henry S. Carey originally served with the Old Dominion Guards during the battle of Manassas and was shot in the foot and bayoneted in the thigh.

2nd Lt. Bruce Putnam originally served as Wheat's sergeant major at Manassas. Wounded at Port Republic.

1st Sgt. John Tomlin.
Sgt. E. Cox
Sgt. John McLaughlin.
Sgt. Andrew Murphy. Captured at Front Royal and sent to Fort Delaware. Exchanged Aug. 5, 1862 at Aikens Landing, VA.
Sgt. Charles Seeley.
Sgt. John Sheridan.
Cpl. Francis Foley. Enl. N.O. June 26, 1861. Captured at Front Royal and sent to Fort Delaware. Exchanged Aug. 5, 1862 at Aikens Landing, VA.
Cpl. Byron McMannis.
Musician James Russell.
Pvt. James Bear.
George Bell. Enl. N.O. Sept. 23, 1861.
John Bell. Enl. N.O. Sept. 23, 1861.
Patrick Brannon.
D. Butler

Charles Caldwell. Enl. N.O. Sept. 23, 1861.
John Carr
Thomas Caughlin. Enl. N.O. Sept. 23, 1861. Captured at Front Royal and sent to Fort Delaware. Exchanged Aug. 5, 1862 at Aikens Landing, VA.
L.L. Cohen.
L.W. Conklin.
M. Conner.
Joseph Cox. Enl. N.O. Sept. 23, 1861.
Edward Cummings. Captured at Front Royal and sent to Fort Delaware. Exchanged Aug. 5, 1862 at Aikens Landing, VA.
James Darley.
Peter Davis. Enl. N.O. June 26, 1861.
Charles Dennings.
James Dooley. Enl. N.O. June 26, 1861. Later assigned to the 1st LA; killed at Payne's Farm at Mine Run, Nov. 27, 1863.
John Dorley. Enl. N.O. June 26, 1861.
James Duggan.
James Dunn.
Larry Dunn.
J.M. Earhart. Enl. N.O. June 26, 1861.
Asa Ferguson.
Patrick Finnerty. Born Irish. UM laborer from N.O. Enl. N.O. June 26, 1861. Later assigned C/7th LA.
Bradley Fisk. Enl. N.O. June 26, 1861.
Patrick Flanny.
Michael Foley.
George Gillmore.
C Gribble.
James Hallen. Enl. N.O. June 16, 1861.
W. Halley. Enl. N.O. Sept. 23, 1861. Died of pneumonia Dec. 2, 1861.
J.B. Hardy.
Timothy Harrigan. Enl. N.O. June 26, 1861.
Thomas Hastings. Enl. N.O. June 26, 1861. Deserted.
John Hennessy. Enl. N.O. June 26, 1861. Deserted.
D. Higgins. Enl. N.O. June 26, 1861. Deserted.
Henry Jones.
William Jones.
Thomas Kehoe. Enl. N.O. June 26, 1861. Deserted.
William Lake.
John Long.

Sylvester Langdon.
Jacob Lapare.
Giacasonme Lapiere.
J. Lasperrie.
Andrew Lindsey. Enl. N.O. June 23, 1861.
John Long. Later wounded and missing. Murfreesboro, Tennessee.
Martin Lynch. Enl. N.O. June 23, 1861.
Thomas Mercer.
James McCue. Enl. N.O. June 23, 1861. Consigned to hospital Oct. 1861.
Andrew Murphy. Enl. N.O. June 23, 1861. Captured at Port Republic and sent to Fort Delaware. Later exchanged at Aikens Landing, VA, Aug. 5, 1862.
Jefferson Musser.
Zachariah Nash. Enl. N.O. June 23, 1861.
Tobias Quillian. Enl. N.O. Sept. 23, 1861.
John Rhoder. Enl. N.O. Sept. 23, 1861.
John Rice. Enl. N.O. June 23, 1861.
John Ryan. Enl. N.O. June 23, 1861.
Herman Spohr.
T. Woodroe. Enl. N.O. Sept. 23, 1861.
G. Woods. Captured at Port Republic and sent to Fort Delaware. Later exchanged at Aikens Landing, VA, Aug. 5, 1862.

Appendix II
Uniforms and Accoutrements of the Battalion

1861

The Walker and Old Dominion Guards

- Broad brimmed felt hats of various earthen tones
- Red flannel "battle" or "Garibaldi" shirts with five brass buttons, angled collars, and an exterior pocket on each breast
- Cotton shirts of various patterns (e.g., checked), worn beneath the battle shirts
- Jean-wool trousers "of the mixed color of pepper and salt"
- .69 caliber M1842 muskets or M1816 conversion (i.e., flint to percussion lock) muskets
- Some bowie knives and pistols, reportedly the men's own
- Louisiana "Pelican plate" belts, cartridge boxes with slings, cap boxes and knapsacks manufactured by the New Orleans–based Magee and Kneass Leather Company, and C.S. "tin drum" canteens

The Tiger Rifles

- Dark blue or light brown wool Zouave jackets with red cotton trim (the city more than likely ran low on blue wool, thus the brown wool, too)
- Red flannel fezzes with red tassels
- Red flannel band collar shirts with five white porcelain buttons
- "Wedgwood blue and cream" 1½" vertically striped cottonade (Hamilton mattress ticking) pantaloons, cut in the Zouave fashion
- Blue and white horizontally striped stockings
- White canvas leggings (buttoned)
- .54 caliber Robbins and Lawrence (contract) M1841 "Mississippi" Rifles
- 21" long bowie knives with "sturdy handles" and other personal sidearms
- Louisiana "Pelican plate" belts, cartridge boxes with slings, cap boxes and knapsacks manufactured by the New Orleans–based Magee and Kneass or James Cosgrove Leather Companies, and C.S. "tin drum" canteens
- Before they received A. Keene Richards's stunning Zouave uniform, the men of the Tiger Rifles reportedly "painted a motto or picture of some sort on [their] ... broad brimmed hat[s] such as: A picture of Mose, preparing to let fly with his left hand and fend with his right, and the words, 'Before I Was a Tiger.'" Other slogans included: "Lincoln's Life or a Tiger's Death," "Tiger Bound for Happy Land," "Tiger Will Never Surrender," "A Tiger Forever," "Tiger in Search of a Black Republican," "Tiger By Nature,"

"Tiger," "Tiger — Try Me," "Arlington Heights," "Old Man Tiger," "Royal Bengal Tiger," "Tiger Drummer Boy," "Tiger Ready for a Spring," "Tiger — Win or Die," "Tiger During the War," "Tiger on the Muscle," "Tiger Never Say Die," "Living Tiger," "Abe's Tiger," "Tiger For Action," "Tiger — As You Are," "Tiger in Disguise," "Old Tiger," "Young Tiger," "Tiger on the Leap," "Tiger in Search of Abe," or "Sure Death to Lincoln."

The Delta Rangers

- Gray or dark blue wool kepis with stiff black bills and white cotton havelocks
- Red flannel battle or "Garibaldi" shirts with five brass buttons, angled collars, and exterior pockets on each breast
- Cotton shirts of various patterns, worn beneath the battle shirts
- Jean-wool trousers "of the mixed color of pepper and salt"
- .69 caliber M1842 muskets or M1816 conversion muskets
- Some bowie knives and pistols of the men's own
- Louisiana "Pelican plate" belts, cartridge boxes with slings, cap boxes and knapsacks manufactured by the New Orleans–based Magee and Kneass or James Cosgrove Leather Companies, and C.S. "tin drum" canteens

The Rough and Ready Rangers

- Probably gray wool short jackets with matching trousers
- Gray wool kepis or broad-brimmed civilian hats
- .69 caliber M1842 muskets or M1816 conversion muskets
- Some bowie knives and pistols, reportedly the men's own
- Louisiana "Pelican plate" belts, cartridge boxes with slings, cap boxes and knapsacks manufactured by the New Orleans–based Magee and Kneass Leather Company, and C.S. "tin drum" canteens

The Catahoula Guerrillas

- Gray wool short jackets with matching mounted trousers
- Possibly riding boots
- Gray wool kepis
- M1841 "Mississippi" Rifles
- Louisiana "Pelican plate" belts, cartridge boxes with slings, cap boxes and knapsacks manufactured by the New Orleans–based Magee and Kneass Leather Company, and C.S. "tin drum" canteens

The Officers

Most of the company-grade officers of the battalion probably uniformed themselves in gray wool single-breasted short jackets with matching trousers, red or blue wool kepis with stiff black leather bills, scarlet officer's sashes, and white canvas leggings worn over or under the trousers. Those of the Tiger Rifles more than likely wore blue wool single breasted frock coats or short jackets with red wool trousers, red wool kepis with stiff black leather bills, scarlet officer's sashes, and white canvas leggings worn over or under the trousers. Because they were responsible for arming themselves, the officers acquired presentation or issue swords and privately purchased pistols. Lieutenant William Foley of the Old Dominion Guards reportedly armed himself with a carbine. As for Wheat, he chose the uniform of a field grade officer (major to colonel) in the Army of Louisiana, viz.: a red wool kepi bedecked with appropriate Austrian gold lace, a double-breasted dark blue wool frock coat with brass shoulder scales, and dark blue wool trousers. He also sported a buff general's sash, no doubt to commemorate his past commissions in the Mexican and Italian armies.

Flags and Banners

- The Walker Guards' banner consisted of "a dark blue silk flag with a white crescent in the center."

- The Tiger Rifles' flag was most probably made of green silk and consisted of a "gamboling lamb" device with "Gentle As" written above it.
- The Delta Rangers' flag, which served as the battalion's color at First Manassas through the luck of the draw, was a rectangular silk "Stars and Bars" with eight celestial bodies.

1862

The Walker, Old Dominion, and Wheat's Life Guards, and the Delta Rangers

The men from these companies reportedly wore the uniform that was issued to them by their state government in the autumn of 1861: two shirts, one checked and one flannel; one bluish-gray jean-wool short jacket with nine Louisiana State buttons and epaulettes, trimmed with black cotton tape; matching trousers; white canvas leggings (buttoned); blue-gray jean-wool kepis with stiff black bills and trimmed with black wool; and one variously colored jean-wool overcoat. Many of the men apparently chose to continue to wear their distinctive red flannel Garibaldi shirts, however, and they probably kept their issue jackets in a bedroll or pack until discarded. As in 1861, they were armed with either M1842s or M1816 conversion muskets with socket bayonets.

Captain Gardner of the Delta Rangers reportedly sported a "badge of the battalion one of the prettiest imaginable designs — a little silver crescent in a concavity of which revolved a silver star upon a pivot on which was inscribed on one side 'The Star Battalion from the Crescent City' in a revolution — on the reverse side 'Wheat's New Orleans Battalion.' It was a cunning little ornament."

The Tiger Rifles

The Tigers tried to retain their distinctive Zouave visage as best they could and most probably looked like an eclectic band of brigands who were preparing to celebrate *Mardi Gras*. The men either wore their original but now faded blue or brown wool Zouave jackets with red cotton trim or new jean-wool issue jackets which were modified to more closely match their original uniforms. For trousers, they either continued to wear their sturdy white and blue-striped cottonade pantaloons with white canvas leggings or replaced them with their government-issue jeans. For headgear they would have donned either their distinctive red fezzes of Manassas fame, if available, broad brimmed hats of various earthy tones, or issue kepis. They also seemed to have supplemented their accoutrements with captured Federal packs, blankets, and gum blankets. They were still armed with M1841s and bowie knives. The officers at this time most probably uniformed themselves in gray wool frock coats or jackets with Louisiana State buttons and matching trousers, red wool kepis, white canvas leggings (worn under or over the trousers), and red officer's sashes. And as before, they were most likely armed with presentation or issue swords and pistols. Capt. Alexander White also had a relatively large "Bengal Tiger" device attached to the front of his kepi with brass letters "RIFLES" below it.

Flags and Banners

The battalion was issued a square "Army of Northern Virginia Battle Flag" with twelve stars and yellow edging in the autumn of 1861. After the battle of Gaines' Mill, the swan song of the battalion, one Georgia private described this banner as looking "like it had been used to clean out chimneys and afterwards drawn through a briar patch. It was simply torn into shreds by the enemy's bullets."

Appendix III

Wheat's Official Report of the Battle of Manassas

Report of Maj Chatham Roberdeau Wheat, First Special Battalion Louisiana Volunteers, of the Battle of Manassas, Virginia, July 21, 1861

Manassas, August 1, 1861

Sir:

    I beg leave herewith, respectfully, to report the part taken by the First Special Battalion of Louisiana Volunteers, which I had the honor to command in the battle of July 21.

    According to your [Colonel Nathan Evans's] instructions, I formed my command to the left of the Stone Bridge, being thus at the extreme left of our lines. Your order to deploy skirmishers was immediately obeyed by sending forward Company B under Captain White. The enemy threatening to flank us, I caused Captain Buhoup to deploy his Company D as skirmishers in that direction.

    At this conjuncture, I sent back, as you ordered, the two pieces of artillery which you had attached to my command, still having Captain Alexander's troop of cavalry with me. Shortly after, under your orders, I deployed my whole command to the left, which movement, of course, placed me on the right of the line of battle.

    Having reached this position, I moved by the left flank to an open field, a wood being on my left. From this covert, to my utter surprise, I received a volley of musketry which unfortunately came from our own troops, mistaking us for the enemy, killing three and wounding several of my men [sic]. Apprehending instantly the real cause of the accident, I called out to my own men not to return the fire. Those near enough to hear, obeyed; the more distant, did not.

    Almost at the same moment, the enemy in front opened upon us with musketry, grape, canister, round shot and shells. I immediately charged upon the enemy and drove him from his position. As he rallied again in a few minutes, I charged him a second and a third time successfully.

    Finding myself now in the face of a very large force — some 10,000 or 12,000 in number — I dispatched Major Atkins to you for more reinforcements and gave the order to move by the left flank to the cover of the hill; a part of my command, [by] mistake, crossed the open field and suffered severely from the fire of the enemy.

Advancing from the wood with a portion of my command, I reached some haystacks under cover of which I was enabled to damage the enemy very much. While in the act of bringing up the rest of my command to this position, I was put *hors de combat* by a Minie ball passing through my body and inflicting what was at first thought to be a mortal wound and from which I am only now sufficiently recovered to dictate this report. By the judicious management of Captain Buhoup I was borne from the field under the persistent fire of the foe, who seemed very unwilling to spare the wounded. Being left without a field officer, the companies rallied under their respective captains and, as you are aware, bore themselves gallantly throughout the day in the face of an enemy far outnumbering us.

Where all behaved so well, I forbear to make invidious distinctions, and contenting myself with commanding my entire command to your favorable consideration, I beg leave to name particularly Major Atkins, a distinguished Irish soldier, who as a volunteer Adjutant, not only rendered me valuable assistance but with a small detachment captured three pieces of artillery and took three officers prisoners. Mr. Early, now Captain Early, as a volunteer adjutant, bore himself bravely and did good service. My adjutant, Lieutenant Dickinson was wounded while gallantly carrying my orders through a heavy fire of musketry. Captain Miller of Company E, and Lieutenants Adrian and Carey were wounded while leading their men into the thickest of the fight.

> All of which is respectfully submitted C.R. WHEAT,
> Major, First Special Battalion, Louisiana Volunteers.
> N.G. EVANS, Brigadier-General of Confederate States of America.

Chapter Notes

Chapter 1

1. Charles Dufour, *Gentle Tiger: The Gallant Life of Roberdeau Wheat* (Baton Rouge, Louisiana: Louisiana State University Press, 1957), 7–12; Clara Solomon, *The Civil War Diary of Clara Solomon: Growing Up in New Orleans, 1861–62,* ed. Elliot Ashkenaski (Baton Rouge, Louisiana: Louisiana State University Press, 1995), 435; Leo Wheat, "Memoir of General C. R. Wheat, Commander of the 'Louisiana Tiger Battalion,'" *Southern Historical Society Papers* (hereafter SHSP") 17 (January–December 1889): 47–49.

2. Dufour, 19–20; SHSP, 49; Michael D. Jones, "Chatham Roberdeau Wheat and His Louisiana Tigers," *Blue and Gray Magazine,* November 1985, 24; Richard Taylor, *Destruction and Reconstruction: Personal Experiences of the Civil War,* ed. Michael Parrish (New York: Da Capo Press, 1995), 25.

3. Stephen W. Sears, *George B. McClellan: The Young Napoleon* (New York: Da Capo Press, 1999), 16.

4. Dufour, 25–27; SHSP, 47. The night before the new company left Vera Cruz, Wheat was "seized with vomito, or yellow fever. In a hammock swung between two mules he was carried up to Jalappa [sic], where he arrived in an insensible condition." See SHSP, 47.

5. SHSP, 48; Michael Jones, 24–25.

6. Dufour, 32–39; SHSP, 48.

7. Dufour, 26; SHSP, 48; Earl Niehaus, *The Irish in New Orleans, 1800–1860* (Baton Rouge, Louisiana: Louisiana State University Press, 1965), v. One component of the "Compromise of 1850," as framed by Senate majority leader Henry Clay (Whig) and Speaker of the House Stephen Douglas (Democrat), was that all federally-controlled western land would henceforth be open to "popular sovereignty."

8. SHSP, 48–49.

9. Charles Bridges, "The Knights of the Golden Circle, A Filibustering Fantasy," *Southwestern Historical Quarterly,* January 1941, 288; George Fitzhugh, "Acquisition of Mexico—Filibustering," *De Bow's Review,* December 1858, 10–13; John Franklin, *The Militant South: 1800–1860* (Cambridge, Massachusetts: Harvard University Press, 1956), 99–102, 115; Robert May, *The Southern Dream of a Caribbean Empire, 1854–1861* (Baton Rouge, Louisiana: Louisiana State University Press, 1973), 3–45; Crenshaw Ollinger, "The Knights of the Golden Circle," *American Historical Review,* October 1941, 34; Frederic Rosengarten, *Freebooters Must Die! The Life and Death of William Walker, the Most Notorious Filibuster of the Nineteenth Century* (Wayne, Pennsylvania: Haverford House Publishers, 1976), 14; May, 9.

10. Franklin, 99; May, 3–9; William Scroggs, *Filibusters and Financiers: The Story of William Walker and His Associates* (New York: Russell and Russell, 1916), 4.

11. William Walker, *The War in Nicaragua* (Mobile, Alabama: S.H. Goetzel, 1860), 271–80.

12. Fitzhugh, 613–24; Franklin, 5–155; May, 22–45, 90–91; Rosengarten, 10–26; SHSP, 48, 50; Taylor, 26, Walker, 23–24, 261–85; William Barney, *The Passage of the Republic: An Interdisciplinary History of Nineteenth-Century America* (Lexington, Massachusetts: Heath, 1987), 121–190; Albert Carr, *The World and William Walker* (New York: Harper and Row, 1963), 4–5; William Freehling, *The Road to Disunion: Secessionists at Bay, 1776–1854* (New York: Oxford University Press, 1990), 3–565; Gary Gallagher, *The Confederate War: How Popular Will, Nationalism, and Military Strategy Could Not Stave Off Defeat* (Cambridge, Massachusetts: Harvard University Press, 1997), 1–113; David Heidler, *Pulling Down the Temple: The Fire-Eaters and the Destruction of the Union* (Mechanicsburg, Pennsylvania: Stackpole Books, 1994), 1–183; James McPherson, *Battle Cry of Freedom: The Civil War Era* (New York: Oxford University Press, 1988), 78–114, and *Drawn with the Sword*

(New York: Oxford University Press, 1996), 33–37; Laurence Oliphant, *Patriots and Filibusters* (London: William Blackwood and Sons, 1860), 5–22; Alexander Powell, *Gentlemen Rovers* (New York: Scribner's, 1913), 10–54; Kenneth Stampp, *The Causes of the Civil War* (New York: Simon and Schuster, 1991), 13–244.

13. George Fitzhugh, "Acquisition of Mexico: Filibustering," *De Bow's Review,* December 1858, 36–40.

14. William Walker, "General Walker's Policy in Central America," *De Bow's Review,* August 1860, 162.

15. Franklin, 105; May, 25–27; McPherson, 105; Rosengarten, 13–14.

16. May, 25–27.

17. Franklin, 106–07; Robert May, *John A. Quitman: Old South Crusader* (Baton Rouge, Louisiana: Louisiana State University Press, 1985), 236–39.

18. Dufour, 40–50; May, 29; Rosengarten, 15–16.

19. Rosengarten, 16.

20. Dufour, 52; May, 27–28; Rosengarten, 16–17.

21. Dufour, 53–54; May, 27; McPherson, 106; Rosengarten, 16–17; www.rose-hulman.edu/~delacoy/clayton5.htm.

22. Dufour, 54; May, 27; McPherson, 106; New Orleans *Orleanian,* June 8, 1850; Rosengarten, 16–17.

23. Dufour, 61–69; SHSP, 48; Charles Brown, *Agents of Manifest Destiny: The Lives and Times of the Filibusters* (Chapel Hill, North Carolina: University of North Carolina Press, 1980), 151–55.

24. Dufour, 77–89; SHSP, 52.

25. Carr, 36–61, 74–75; New York *Daily News,* February 28, 1856; Rosengarten, 23, 40, 59; Scroggs, 14–17; SHSP, 51–52.

26. Rosengarten, 71–75; Scroggs, 82; Walker, 13–41.

27. John De Bow, "The Walker Expedition, 1856: The Regenerator of Central America," *De Bow's Review,* February 1858, 1–2.

28. Rosengarten, 57–72; Scroggs, 71–72.

29. Rosengarten, 57–72.

30. Carr, 42–55, 94–95; Rosengarten, 37–45; Scroggs, 79–84; Walker, 24–30, 75.

31. Carr, 125; Rosengarten, 77–78, 153; Scroggs, 7, 86–88, 139; Walker, 23, 32; Charles Doubleday, *The "Filibuster" War in Nicaragua* (New York: Putnam, 1886), 1–3.

32. Rosengarten, 81–82; Scroggs, 139; Walker, 32–41, 63–68.

33. Rosengarten, 81–83; Walker, 40–44.

34. Walker, 44–46.

35. Ibid., 47–48.

36. Ibid., 50–51.

37. Ibid.

38. Rosengarten, 88–91; Walker, 52–53; Walker, "General Walker's Policy," 154–56.

39. Walker, 55–57.

40. Rosengarten, 88–91; Walker, 76–86, 107; Walker, "General Walker's Policy," 154–56.

41. Walker, "General Walker's Policy," 154–56.

42. Rosengarten, 88–91; Walker, 251–81; Walker, "General Walker's Policy," 154–56.

43. Carr, 37; Rosengarten, 88–91; Scroggs, 224; Walker, 259–265; Walker, "General Walker's Policy," 154–56.

44. Walker, 260–61.

45. Carr, 141; May, 29, 90–93, 100–101; Scroggs, 7; Walker, 106–07.

46. Rosengarten, 91–121; Walker, "General Walker's Policy," 157.

47. Walker, 109–111.

48. Carr, 133–189; May, 94–95; Rosengarten, 96–145; Walker, 63, 111–251; Walker, "General Walker's Policy," 157.

49. Rosengarten, 143–50.

50. William Walker, "Walker's Expedition of 1856," *De Bow's Review,* February 1858, 36–38.

51. Rosengarten, 143–50; Walker, 281–313.

52. Dufour, 92–99; Doubleday, 176–91; May, 92; Oliphant, 173; Rosengarten, 168–70, 184; Walker, 355–366.

53. Doubleday, 192–95; Dufour, 94–99.

54. Doubleday, 195–98; Dufour, 99; May, 109–110; Rosengarten, 171–76; Walker, 423–429.

55. New Orleans *Daily Picayune,* October 23, 1852; Franklin, 121–22.

56. Rosengarten, 178–79.

57. Dufour, 100–08; Rosengarten, 180.

58. Franklin, 123–125; May, 113–114; Rosengarten, 182–87; John De Bow, "Advancement of Agricultural Interest of the South," *De Bow's Review,* February 1859, 14–15.

59. Carr, 230; May, 113–128; Rosengarten, 182–97.

60. May, 128–35; Rosengarten, 205–208.

61. Dufour, 109–114; Taylor, 26; Michael Bacarella, *Lincoln's Foreign Legion: The 39th New York Infantry, The Garibaldi Guard* (Shippensburg, Pennsylvania: White Mane, 1996), 1–14.

62. Bacarella, 1–17; SHSP, 53.

63. Bacarella, 20–25; Dufour, 113–115.

64. Bacarella, 14, 21–28; Dufour, 115–16; SHSP, 53–54; Taylor, 26; Henry Kyd Douglas, *I Rode with Stonewall,* ed. Philip van Doren Stern (Chapel Hill, North Carolina: University of North Carolina Press, 1940), 86.

Chapter 2

1. Ron Field, *The American Civil War: Confederate Army* (London, England: Brassey's

Publications, 1998), 50–55; U.S. War Department, *The War of the Rebellion: A Compilation of the Official Records of the Union and Confederate Armies, 1861–65* (Washington, D.C.: Government Publishing Office, 1880–1901), Series 4, Vol. 1, 272. Wheat reportedly stopped in Montgomery, Alabama, capital of the newly-proclaimed Southern Confederacy, seeking a commission. Since the Confederate government lacked the power to commission officers, Wheat continued his journey to New Orleans. His native state, Virginia, had not yet seceded from the United States. See SHSP, 48.

2. Field, 50; Napier Bartlett, *Military Record of Louisiana* (Baton Rouge, Louisiana: Louisiana State University Press, 1964), 20; Ella Lonn, *Foreigners in the Confederacy* (Chapel Hill, North Carolina: University of North Carolina Press, 1940), 100, 113.

3. Jefferson Davis Bragg, *Louisiana in the Confederacy* (Baton Rouge, Louisiana: Louisiana State University Press, 1952), 58.

4. Michael McAfee, *Zouaves: The First and the Bravest* (Gettysburg, Pennsylvania: Thomas Publications, 1991), 9, 20; www.zouave.org.

5. As cited in www.zouave.org/origins.html.

6. McAfee, 9, 20; www.zouave.org/origins.html.

7. Paddy Griffith, *Battle Tactics of the American Civil War* (Yale University Press, 1987), 50–75; "Phasalia and Manassas," *Southern Literary Messenger* 33.4 (Richmond, Virginia: T. W. White, 1863): 297.

8. As cited in www.zouave.org/craze.html.

9. Field, 50–55; McAfee, 25–26; J. W. Minnich, "Picturesque Soldiery," *Confederate Veteran* (henceforth "*CV*") 31 (August 1923): 295; Robin Smith, *American Civil War Zouaves* (London, England: Osprey Publishing, 1996), 48–49.

10. Bartlett, 253; Arthur Bergeron, Guide to Louisiana Confederate Units, 1861–65 (Baton Rouge, Louisiana: Louisiana State University Press, 1989), 151; Field, 55; McAfee, 25–26; *CV*, 295; Smith, 48–49.

11. SHSP, 57.

12. New Orleans *Daily Crescent*, April 18, 1861.

13. Bartlett, 253; Bergeron, 149–50; Dufour, 120–22; Solomon, 17–18, 25, 197; SHSP, 54, 57; Taylor, 24–25; Andrew Booth, *Record of Louisiana Confederate Soldiers and Louisiana Confederate Commands* (Baton Rouge, Louisiana: Louisiana State University Press, 1985), 251–52; Ross Brooks, "'Part Irish and the Rest the Flower of Southern Chivalry': Clothing, Arms, and Equipment of the 1st Special Battalion, Louisiana Infantry 1861–62," *Military Collector and Historian*, Fall 1999, 98, 113; Company of Military Historians, *Military Uniforms in America*, volume 3, *Long Endure: The Civil War Period,*

1852–1867 (Novato, California: Presidio Press, 1984), 94–95; "First (Wheat's) Special Battalion, Infantry," *Compiled Service Records of Confederate Soldiers Who Served in Organizations from the State of Louisiana*, Record Group 108, M320, Rolls 100 and 101 (National Archives, Washington, D.C.); Janet Hewitt, ed., "Louisiana Troops (Confederate)," *Supplement to the Official Records of the Union and Confederate Armies*, (Wilmington, North Carolina: Broadfoot, 1994) part 2, vol. 23, 701; Jack Holmes, "The Not So Gentle Louisiana Tigers," *Civil War Times Illustrated*, May 1963, 22–25; Michael Jones, "Chatham Roberdeau Wheat and His Louisiana Tigers," *Blue & Gray Magazine*, November 1985, 24–30; William Oates, *The War Between the Union and the Confederacy and Its Lost Opportunities with a History of the 15th Alabama Regiment and the Forty-Eight Battles in Which It Was Engaged* (Dayton, Ohio: Morningside Publishing, 1974), 81; *Daily Picayune*, August 13, 1861; J.B. Roden, "Trip from Louisville to New Orleans," *Confederate Veteran* 18 (May 1910): 237; Randy Steffen and Ronald Youngquist, "1st Special Battalion, Louisiana Infantry (Wheat's Tigers), 1861–1862," *Military Collector & Historian Magazine*, Spring 1959, 12–13; Richard Steuart, "Wheat's Tigers and Others," *Confederate Veteran* 31 (September 1923): 326.

14. Niehaus, 43–49; Frederick Law Olmstead, *The Cotton Kingdom: A Traveller's Observations on Cotton and Slavery in the American Slave States, 1853–1861,* ed. Arthur Schlesinger (New York: Da Capo Press, 1996), 223; Robert Shugg, *Origins of Class Struggle in Louisiana: A Social History of White Farmers and Laborers During Slavery and After, 1840–1875* (Baton Rouge, Louisiana: Louisiana State University Press, 1965), 76, 119, 174–175; Edward Sullivan, *Rambles and Scrambles in North and South America* (London, England: n.p., 1852), 216.

15. Niehaus, 48–49; Shugg, 41.

16. *CV* 17:237, 31:326; New Orleans *Daily Crescent*, April 15–18, 1861; New Orleans *Daily Item*, August 25, 1896; New Orleans *Daily Picayune*, August 6, 1861; Dufour, 121; Solomon, 19–21; Taylor, 24; Walker, 203, 224–225.

17. New Orleans *Daily Crescent*, April 23, 1861.

18. New Orleans *Bee*, August 1, 1861; Brooks, 101–104; *CV* 17:237, 31:295, 326; New Orleans *Daily Crescent*, May 9 and 29, 1861; New Orleans *Daily Delta*, May 12 and June 22, 1861; New Orleans *Daily Item*, August 25, 1896; Field, 52; McAfee, 21; Oates, 81; Rosengarten, 215; SHSP, 54; Taylor, 24. Other slogans were: "Tiger by Nature," "Tiger," "Tiger — Try Me," "Arlington Heights," "Old Man Tiger," "Royal Bengal Tiger," "Tiger Drummer Boy," "Tiger Ready for a Spring," "Tiger — Win or Die," "Tiger During

the War," "Tiger on the Muscle," "Tiger Never Say Die," "Living Tiger," "Abe's Tiger," "Tiger for Action," "Tiger — As You Are," "Tiger in Disguise," "Old Tiger," "Young Tiger," "Tiger on the Leap," "Tiger in Search of Abe," or "Sure Death to Lincoln."

19. Brooks, 98–103; New Orleans *Daily Picayune*, April 18, 1861; New Orleans *Sunday Delta*, May 12 and June 9, 1861; *Washington Evening Star*, August 23, 1861. The impressed Yankees apparently deserted the first chance they could.

20. Brooks 104–06; *Cincinnati Enquirer*, December 1, 1895; *CV* 17:237, 31:295, 326; New Orleans *Daily Crescent*, May 9, 1861; New Orleans *Daily True Delta*, June 30, 1861; New Orleans *Sunday Daily Delta*, December 29, 1861; Dufour, 124; Field, 50–55; McAfee, 21; *Montgomery [Alabama] Weekly Advertiser*, August 1, 1861; SHSP, 54; "Crossing the Manassas Gap Railroad and the Alexandria & Washington Turnpike at White Plains—Arrival of Reinforcements for Beauregard at the Camp of the Tiger Zouaves of Louisiana," *Harper's Weekly Magazine of Civilization*, September 28, 1861, 617; León Fremaux, "The Tiger Rifles: Wheat's Battalion [drawing]," Natalie Nelson Collection, Manassas National Battlefield Park; James Harrold, "Surgeons of the Confederacy," *Confederate Veteran* 40 (May 1932): 174; Bradley Johnson, "Memoir of the 1st Maryland Regiment," *Southern Historical Society Papers* 10 (January and February 1882): 54; "A Louisiana 'Tiger,' *Battles and Leaders of the Civil War* (New York: The Century Company, 1887), 1:196; William Todd, *The Seventy-Ninth Highlanders, New York Volunteers, in the War of the Rebellion, 1861–65* (Albany, New York: Press of Brandon, Baton, 1886), 44. It is most probable that A. Keene Richards was a friend of White's or Wheat's, thus the generous support. The *Delta* article on December 29, 1861, implied that White was simply a passerby who was "impressed by their appearance." I find such objectivity doubtful. My statement that "the first platoon was apparently outfitted and blue jackets and the second in brown" is not derived from a single source per se, but is a conclusion that I have reached after piecing together all of the known sources. It is quite possible that blue wool had simply run out in the city by the time the Tiger Rifles were having their uniforms made, thus the brown. Although some have suggested that the blue jackets simply faded after the battle of Manassas, I know of no period blue wool dye that degenerated that quickly or that radically to the tan-brown that is in Fremaux's drawing.

21. Brooks, 104; New Orleans *Daily Delta*, September 29, 1861; Dufour, 124.

22. Brooks, 99; New Orleans *Daily Crescent*, May 9, 1861; Dufour, 145; SHSP 17:54.

23. Brooks, 98, 100; *CV* 31:295; Dufour, 124–26; New Orleans *Bee*, May 31, 1861; New Orleans *Daily Picayune*, May 1, 1861; New Orleans *Daily True Delta* August 8, 1861; *War of the Rebellion: A Compilation of the Official Records of the Union and Confederate Armies, 1861–65*. 130 vols. Washington, D.C.: Government Printing Office, 1880–1901. Hereafter cited as "*OR*." Series 4, 1:272; London *Times*, June 19, 1861; *Echoes of Glory: Arms and Equipment of the Confederacy* (Alexandria, Virginia: Time Life Books, 1991), 35.

24. B.B. Brezeale, "Co. J, 4th South Carolina Infantry at the Battle of First Manassas," Manassas Battlefield National Park; Brooks 100; *CV* 31:295, 326, 421; New Orleans *Daily Crescent*, August 1, 1861; New Orleans *Daily Delta*, August 27, 1861; "Phasalia and Manassas," *Southern Literary Messenger* 33 (1863): 297–98; Stuart Brown, *The Guns of Harpers Ferry* (Virginia Book, 1968), 93; Robert Howison, "History of the War, Chapter VI," *Southern Literary Messenger* 37.5 (Richmond, Virginia, T. W. White, 1863), 261; Berrien Zettler, *War Stories and School Days Incidents for Children* (New York: Neale Publishing, 1912), 78.

25. Robert Krick, *Conquering the Valley: Stonewall Jackson at Port Republic* (New York: William Morrow, 1996), 413; William McClendon, *Recollections of War-Times by an Old Veteran While Under Stonewall Jackson and Lieutenant General James Longstreet: How I Got In and How I Got Out* (Montgomery, Alabama: The Paragon Press, 1909), 37.

26. Bergeron, 150–51; Brooks, 98; New Orleans *Daily Picayune*, May 25, 1861; Dufour, 125; Jones, 5, 8–9; "Drury Gibson to May Cotton, June 6, 1861," as cited in Debra Laurence, "Letters from a North Louisiana Tiger," *North Louisiana Historical Association Journal*, Fall 1979, 130–131; Stewart Sifakis, *Compendium of the Confederate Armies: Louisiana* (New York: Facts on File, 1995), 61.

27. Brooks, 100–02; *Compiled Service Records of Confederate Soldiers Who Served in Organizations From the State of Louisiana*, Record Group 108, M320, rolls 100 and 101, National Archives, Washington, D.C. Hereafter cited as "*CSR*."; Dufour, 125; Jones, 5, 8–9; Sifakis, 46–47. The 1st Louisiana Cavalry Regiment wasn't formed until September 1861. It fought along the Mississippi River and was surrendered by Lt. Gen. Richard Taylor on May 4, 1865.

28. Jones, 8–9.

29. New Orleans *Daily Delta*, August 25, 1896; Dufour, 124; Jones, 249; Sifakis, 61–62; Lucy Buck, *Sad Earth, Sweet Heaven: The Diary of Lucy Rebecca Buck During the War Between the States*, William Buck, ed. (Birmingham, Alabama: Buck Publishing, 1992), 82.

30. Brooks, 98; New Orleans *Daily Delta*, June 21, 22, and July 4, 1861; Sifakis, 61.

31. New Orleans *Daily Crescent*, June 22, 1861; New Orleans *Daily Delta*, August 25, 1896; Dufour, 125–26; Henry E. Handerson, *Yankee in Gray: the Civil War Memoirs of Henry E. Handerson, with a Selection of His Wartime Letters* (Cleveland: Press of Western Reserve University, 1962), 89; Solomon, 33.

Chapter 3

1. New Orleans *Daily Delta*, June 22, 1861; Dufour, 126; Gibson, 132; OR 51, 2:32; Robert Withers, *Autobiography of an Octogenarian* (Roanoke, Virginia: The Stone Printing and Manufacturing Company Press, 1907), 139.

2. Gibson, 132; OR 2:107, 51, 2:32.

3. CSR; Dufour, 126; OR 2:107–122.

4. OR 2:439–41, 559, 51, 2:26–27; Earl McElfresh, *The Manassas Battlefields* (Olean, New York: McElfresh Map, 1996).

5. McElfresh; OR 2:558–64; 51, 2:27; John Hennessy, *The First Battle of Manassas: An End to Innocence* (Lynchburg, Virginia: Howard, 1989), 39–40, 134. During the war, one cannon and its crew, commanded by a sergeant or "gunner," was called an artillery platoon; two platoons equaled a section, commanded by a lieutenant; and three sections equaled an artillery company. When the company deployed into line of battle, it was called a battery.

6. OR 2:186–87; *Battles and Leaders of the Civil War* (henceforth "B&L") 1:179–183, 205; JoAnna McDonald, *"We Shall Meet Again": The Battle of First Manassas (Bull Run), July 18–21, 1861* (Shippensburg, Pennsylvania: White Mane Publishing, 1998), 10. During the summer of 1861, the Confederates had two armies deployed across northern Virginia: Brig. Gen. Joseph E. Johnston's 10,000-man Army of the Shenandoah at Winchester and Brig. Gen. P.G.T. Beauregard's 23,000-man Army of the Potomac, at Manassas. The U.S. Army in the east was similarly organized: Brig. Gen. Irwin McDowell's 35,000-man Army of Northeastern Virginia was posted at Alexandria, facing Beauregard, and Maj. Gen. Robert Patterson's 14,000-man Army of Pennsylvania was positioned at the head of the Shenandoah Valley at Martinsburg, facing Johnston. For the battle of Manassas, Maj. Gen. Robert E. Lee, commander of all Confederate forces in Virginia, boldly ordered Johnston to abandon Winchester "if practicable" and to reinforce Beauregard with most of his army. This is where I get the figure of 30,000 for the Confederate Army of the Potomac. And although Johnston was senior in rank during the battle, he allowed Beauregard to command the "left wing" that did most of the fighting on July 21.

7. B&L 1:183; Samuel Bates, *Martial Deeds of Pennsylvania* (Philadelphia: T.H. Davis & Co., 1976), 128. Richardson's division consisted of his own brigade and Col. Thomas Davies's brigade. McDowell kept Col. Louis Blenker's brigade in reserve at Manassas and two others, under Brig. Gen. Theodore Runyon, at Alexandria.

8. B&L 1:205; Gibson, 134; OR 2:346, 361, 560; James M. Catlett and T. B. Warder, *Battle of Young's Branch or, Manassas Plain, Fought July 21, 1861* (Richmond, Virginia: Enquirer Book and Job Press, 1862), 18.

9. OR 2:560–6; Roberdeau Wheat, "Report of Maj. C.R. Wheat, First Special Battalion Louisiana Volunteers, of the First Battle of Bull Run Virginia, July 21, 1861," *Supplement of the Official Records of the Union and Confederate Armies*, part I, volume 2 (Wilmington, North Carolina: Broadfoot Publishing, 1992), 194.

10. B&L 1:205–08; Hennessy, 6, 40; OR 2:369, 559–60.

11. B&L 1:205–08; Hennessy, 6, 40; OR 2:559–605; E. P. Alexander, *Military Memoirs of a Confederate* (New York: Da Capo Press, 1983), 30–31.

12. B&L 1:205–6; OR 2:559–60, 51, 2:27.

13. OR 2:488, 559–64; Catlett and Warder, 18–19; Wheat, "Report" 2:194.

14. Dufour, 137; OR 2:488, 559–61, 563–64; Wheat, "Report" 2:194.

15. Dufour, 137; OR 2:559–61, 563; McElfresh; Wheat, "Report" 2:194.

16. Dufour, 137; OR 2:560–61; Wheat, "Report" 2:194.

17. CSR; Dufour, 137; OR 2:560–61; Wheat, "Report" 2:194.

18. Dufour, 137; Wheat, "Report" 2:194.

19. OR 2:383, 395.

20. McElfresh; OR 2:395, 559–61; Wheat, "Report" 2:194; Elijah Hunt Rhodes, *All for the Union: A History of the Second Rhode Island Infantry in the War of the Great Rebellion* (Lincoln, Nebraska: University of Nebraska Press, 1986), 26.

21. B&L 1:185; Hennessy, 51; OR 2:346, 395, 489; 559–63; Dufour, 137.

22. B&L 1:185; OR 2:346, 395, 559; Dufour, 137; Wheat, "Report" 2:194.

23. Gibson, 134; Wheat, "Report" 2:194.

24. Dufour, 137; Hennessy, 54; OR 2:559; Wheat, "Report" 2:194. Wheat may also have chosen to attack because he thought the Federals were retreating. Just before he ordered the charge, the Second Rhode Island shifted left to allow the 1st Rhode Island to come into line.

25. Dufour, 137; Hennessy, 54; OR 2:559; Wheat, "Report" 2:194.

26. *OR* 2:394–400. Hunter totally botched the Federal deployment atop Matthews' Hill. For example, when the 2nd Rhode Island first came into contact with the Tigers, instead of allowing Burnside to deploy his brigade atop Matthews' Hill, Hunter, a cavalryman from the old army, simply took over the Rhode Islander's job and then, to add insult to injury, gave confusing orders to his regiments. This is one reason why the 2nd Rhode Island fought so long unsupported. Hunter also misdirected the 2nd New Hampshire and was slow to bring up Porter's brigade. If he had acted even as a mediocre division commander and not as a poor brigade commander, there is little doubt that his men would have swept the Tigers and others aside after only one hour of fighting and not two. He was later called "Black Dave" for his destructive exploits in the Shenandoah Valley in 1864.

27. *CSR*; Dufour, 137–38; *OR* 2:559–61; *Providence Evening Press*, July 31, 1861; Rhodes, 26, 37; Wheat, "Report" 2:194. The Tiger Rifles who brandished their bowie knives no doubt slung their Mississippi rifles.

28. *CSR*; Dufour, 137–38; *OR* 2:559–61; *Providence Evening Press*, July 31, 1861; Rhodes, 26, 37.

29. *OR* 2:394–96, 559–61.

30. *B&L* 1:207, 232–33; *OR* 2:469, 569. Brig. Gen. Barnard Bee's brigade, Army of the Shenandoah, consisted of the 2nd and 11th Mississippi, the 4th Alabama, and the 6th North Carolina.

31. *B&L* 1:185, 232–33; *OR* 2:499, 559; Wheat, "Report" 2:194.

32. *OR* 2:559–61; Wheat, "Report" 2:194.

33. New Orleans *Daily Delta*, July 28 and August 15, 1861; Dufour, 138; *New York Times*, August 4, 1861; McDonald, 3; Catlett and Warder, 46–47; Wheat, "Report" 2:194; *OR* 2:401; Martin Haynes, *A History of the Second Regiment, New Hampshire Volunteer Infantry in the War of the Rebellion* (Lakeport, New Hampshire: 1896), 26–27.

34. Wheat, "Report" 2:194. The tough 2nd New Hampshire Regiment, along with Major George Sykes's battalion of army regulars, acted as McDowell's rear guard during the retreat. Like the 2nd Rhode Island, it was one of the precious few Federal units to send Tigers packing.

35. Brooks, 99; *CSR*; New Orleans *Daily Delta*, December 12, 1861; *OR* 2:559; Wheat, "Report," 193; and "Francis Shober to wife, July 26, 1861," as cited in Dufour, 142. Shober writes: "[Wheat's] wound is through and through the chest, immediately under and a little in front of the arm pits; one of his lungs is perforated and he suffers great pain in throwing off the matter of it." The *CSR* of the Special Battalion reports that Wheat was "wounded at First Manassas, July 21, 1861 in the breast and arm." Col. Evans erroneously reported that Wheat was "shot through both lungs" and questioned his recovery.

36. New Orleans *Sunday Delta*, December 29, 1861.

37. *B&L* 1:206, 233; *OR* 2:559–61, 394; Wheat, "Report" 2:194; Catlett and Warder, 46. After it threw back the Tigers at Rosefield, the 2nd New Hampshire pulled back up Dogan's Ridge and deployed to the right of Reynolds's guns as it was originally intended. While in this position, its commander, Col. Gilman Marston, was wounded.

38. Catlett and Warder, 46.

39. New Orleans *Daily Delta*, July 28 and August 15, 1861; *OR* 2:469, 559–61, 569; Wheat, "Report" 2:194; and Catlett and Warder, 46.

40. *B&L* 1:207; *OR* 2:346, 384, 561, 563; Wheat, "Report" 2:194.

Chapter 4

1. *B&L* 1:210; McDonald, 76–78; *OR* 2:559–61. A West Point graduate and Mexican War veteran, Thomas Jackson was the artillery instructor at the Virginia Military Institute (V.M.I.) when his state seceded from the Union. After the battle, "Stonewall" Jackson was promoted to major general and given command of the Valley District, Department of Northern Virginia.

2. *B&L* 1:210; McDonald, 76–78; *OR* 2:481, 515–16, 559–61, 552, 566–67.

3. *B&L* 1:185, 210; *OR* 2:481, 515–16, 552, 559, 566–67.

4. Ibid.

5. *B&L* 1:186; Hennessy, 77–79; McDonald, 97; *OR* 2:346; L. Van Loan Naisawald, *Grape and Canister: The Story of the Field Artillery of the Army of the Potomac, 1861–65* (Mechanicsburg, Pennsylvania: Stackpole Books, 1999), 10.

6. Ibid.

7. *B&L* 1:233–34; Alexander, 35.

8. *B&L* 1:134–35, 186; Hennessy, 77–80; Naisawald, 10; *OR* 2:346, 516. "Spring Hill" was owned and occupied by the "Widow Judith Henry" during the battle.

9. Ibid.

10. *B&L* 1:212–13; *OR* 2:384, 483.

11. Hennessy, 83; McDonald, 107; Naisawald, 10.

12. Alexander, 39; *B&L* 1:212; Hennessy, 83–84; McDonald, 107.

13. *B&L* 1:213; Hennessy, 97–100; *OR* 2:346.

14. Hennessy, 100–101 and McDonald, 119–29. During this melee, Capt. Ricketts was

wounded and captured. Released five months later, he was promoted to brigadier general and commanded a division of infantry in McDowell's Army of the Rappahannock.

15. Hennessy, 101.
16. Withers, 148.
17. New Orleans *Daily Delta*, July 28 and August 15, 1861; Hennessy, 107; *OR* 2:559–61.
18. Baltimore *Sun*, July 25, 1861; *CV* 31:326, 295; Dufour, 137; Howison, 261; *New Orleans Commercial Bulletin*, July 25, 1861; New Orleans *Daily Delta*, July 28, 31, and August 15, 1861; "Phasalia," 297–98; Richmond *Dispatch*, July 31, 1861; Richmond *Examiner*, August 1, 1861.
19. New Orleans *Daily Delta*, August 15, 1861.
20. "Phasalia," 297–98.
21. Hennessy, 102–105; McDonald, 152–54; *OR* 2:546–47.
22. New Orleans *Daily Delta*, August 15, 1861; Hennessy, 102–105; McDonald, 150–54.
23. *CV* 17:237.
24. Todd, 44.
25. *OR* 2:493.
26. New Orleans *Daily Crescent*, August 1, 1861.
27. Bartlett, 51–52; *CSR*; Dufour, 147; *OR* 2:570; Wheat, "Report" 2:194.
28. *CSR*.
29. SHSP 55.
30. New Orleans *Daily Picayune*, July 23, 1861.

Chapter 5

1. New Orleans *Bee*, August 9, 1861; New Orleans *Daily Delta*, August 3, 1861; New Orleans *Daily Picayune*, July 25, 26, and 29, 1861; "Francis Shober to wife, July 26, 1861," as cited in Dufour, 143.
2. New Orleans *Daily Crescent*, August 1, 1861; "Francis Shober to wife, July 26, 1861," as cited in Dufour, 143.
3. Bartlett, 50–51; New Orleans *Daily Item*, August 25, 1896; New Orleans *Daily Picayune*, August 6, 1861; Roden, "Trip from Louisville," 237; Solomon, 195, 214–21, 432, 250; Steuart, 326; Taylor, 24. Obedia Miller never returned to the Special Battalion. According to Clara Solomon, "Obed" was jealous of Wheat and gained a commission from the Confederate government to raise a company of cavalry from New Orleans. Calling his command "Capt. Miller's Independent Mounted Rifles" or the "Wild Cats," it was assigned to the 9th Virginia Cavalry. But like Wheat's Battalion, the Independent Mounted Rifles were disbanded after its founder, in this case Miller, was killed in late 1862.
4. "James Barbour to Governor Letcher, August 12, 1861," as cited in Dufour, 149–50.
5. Handerson, 33, 91; *OR* 2:999–1000. "Old Bald Head," "Bald Dick," or "Old Baldy" was 42 years old when he was given command of the division. Born to a once-proud planter family from northern Virginia (original name Llewellen), Ewell attended West Point and served with distinction in the 2nd U.S. Dragoons during the Mexican War. When his state seceded from the United States in 1861, Ewell resigned his commission, was given command of a regiment of Virginia infantry, and then successfully commanded a brigade at Manassas.
6. Bergeron, 149–150; Jones, 238, 240; Taylor, 39; James Gannon, *Irish Rebels/Confederate Tigers: The 6th Louisiana Volunteers, 1861–1865* (Campbell, California: Savas Publishing, 1998), x–xvi; James Nisbet, *Four Years on the Firing Line* (Chattanooga, Tennessee: Imperial Press, 1914), 112.
7. Bergeron, 150–151; Jones, 243.
8. Taylor, 24.
9. Handerson, 34.
10. William Trahern, *Memoir*, as cited in Krick, 413.
11. Randolph Shotwell, *The Papers of Randolph Shotwell*, ed. J. G. de Roulhac Hamilton (Raleigh, North Carolina: The North Carolina Historical Commission, 1879), 1:134.
12. Oates, 81.
13. Sally Putnam, *Richmond During the War* (New York: n.p., 1867), 35.
14. Theodore DeLeon, *Belles, Beaux, and Brains of the Sixties* (New York: n.p., 1909), 329.
15. Brooks, 98–99; *CSR*; Dufour, 153–54; Handerson, 90–91. These would include Simon Kiefner, James Lynch, Thomas Ryan, and John Young of the Walker Guards; James Brown, Patrick Deary, and Michael Lyman of the Tiger Rifles; James Carey, John Dougherty, and Edward Harris of the Delta Rangers; Zachariah Blackman, John O'Hara, Jesse Peebles, and Patrick Sweeney of the Catahoula Guerrillas; and James Barrett, Thomas Ford, and Daniel O'Neill of the Old Dominion Guards.
16. "Charles de Choiseul to Emma Louise Walton, September 5, 1861," as cited in Jones, 39.
17. Ibid.
18. Shotwell 1:134.
19. *CSR*. These would include Pvts. Charles Barnes, James Bawden, Charles Foster, Thomas Kilraine, John Tally, Charles Tidmarsh, and George Wrigley from the Walker Guards; Pvts. John Evans, John Reynolds, Daniel Ryan, John Smith, and Michael Sullivan from the Tiger Rifles; and Corp. Thomas Lennard and Pvts.

James Burnes, James Byrd, Thomas McGrath, Thomas Newell, and Sydney Vestphol from the Delta Rangers.

20. *CSR*.
21. *CSR*; Gannon, 14.
22. Niehaus, 29, 59–65.
23. Nisbet, 55–56.
24. Bergeron, 160.
25. New Orleans *Daily Crescent*, September 26, 1861; Dufour, 152. Lt. Col. de Choiseul returned to the 7th Louisiana and was mortally wounded at the battle of Port Republic on June 9, 1862.
26. Nisbet, 78; SHSP 9:54.
27. Brooks, 98; New Orleans *Daily Crescent*, November 15, 1861; New Orleans *Daily True Delta*, September 20 and November 8 and 16, 1861; Gannon, 7; Jones, 43; Handerson, 35; Taylor, 23, 25. The first slap to Seymour's face came when Walker, a Georgian, was appointed to command the brigade.
28. Brooks 99; *CSR*; Michael Parrish, *Richard Taylor: Soldier Prince of Dixie* (Chapel Hill, North Carolina: University of North Carolina Press, 1992), 142–46; Taylor, 25; James Harrold, "Surgeons of the Confederacy," 173; Michael Thomas, "Confederate Firing Squad at Centreville: First Military Execution in the Army of Northern Virginia," *Northern Virginia Heritage*, June 1980, 3–6.
29. Taylor, 25.
30. Dufour, 160–61; New Orleans *Commercial Bulletin*, December 20, 1861; *CV* 40:174; New Orleans *Daily Delta*, January 16, 1862; New Orleans *Daily Item*, August 25, 1896; Richmond *Dispatch*, December 14, 1861; Shotwell, 134; SHSP 9:485–86; Taylor, 25.
31. Shotwell, 134–35.
32. *CV* 40:174.
33. Parrish, 141.
34. New Orleans *Commercial Bulletin*, December 20, 1861; *CV* 40:174; New Orleans *Daily Item*, August 25, 1896. While half of the rifles were reportedly loaded with bullets, the other held blanks. In this way, a given member of the firing squad would not know if he had definitively killed one of his comrades.
35. New Orleans *Daily Item*, August 25, 1896.
36. McClendon, 37; Shotwell, 135.
37. Jones, 41.
38. Richmond *Dispatch*, December 14, 1861.
39. Shotwell, 135; Thomas, 8.
40. Dufour, 163.
41. Taylor, 25. Some people have claimed that Taylor executed the two Tigers simply because they were Irish. Taylor was part of the "Know Nothing" or American Party, a strong nativist movement that had opposed immigration and the miscegenation of Anglo-American culture.
42. Handerson, 92–93; Nisbet, 54–55.
43. Brooks, 98; *CSR*; Jones, 250; Sifakis, 62.
44. *CSR*.
45. Brooks, 99, 106–09, 111–12; New Orleans *Daily Item*, August 25, 1896; New Orleans *Daily Picayune*, October 4, 1861; New Orleans *Daily True Delta*, March 5 and June 27, 1862; *CV* 17:237, 31:295, 326, 40:173; Field, 52; SHSP 9:485–86; Taylor, 24, 49; May Wheat Shober, "The Louisiana Tigers," *Confederate Veteran* 19:520; William Andrews, *Footprints of a Regiment: A Recollection of the 1st Georgia Regulars 1861–65* (Atlanta: Longstreet Press, 1992), 48.
46. New Orleans *Daily Item*, August 25, 1896.
47. Harry Smith, *A Sporting Family in the Old South* (Albany, New York: J.B. Lyon, 1936), 320–25.
48. Handerson, 34.

Chapter 6

1. *B&L* 2:166–170; *OR* 5:55–56; 11, 1:5–50; 12, 1:7; 12, 3:51–53; 19, 2:725–26; Steven Sears, *To the Gates of Richmond: The Peninsula Campaign* (New York: Houghton Mifflin, 1992), 18, 31–33.
2. *OR* 5:1079–85, 1091–92; 11, 3:455–56, 99–505, 534–35; 47, 2:1305–06; Sears, 13–14; Jefferson Davis, *The Rise and Fall of the Confederate Government* (New York: D. Appleton, 1881) 2:87–88; Douglas Southall Freeman, *Lee's Lieutenants* (New York: Scribner's, 1944) 1:149–51; Joseph Harsh, *Confederate Tide Rising: Robert E. Lee and the Making of Southern Strategy, 1861–62* (Kent, Ohio: Kent State University Press, 1998), 26–35, 51–53; Joseph Johnston, *Narrative of Military Operations* (New York: D. Appleton, 1874), 114–16; Steven Newton, *The Battle of Seven Pines* (Lynchburg, Virginia: H. E. Howard, 1993), 1–18.
3. Handerson, 39; Taylor, 35, 39; "W. G. Ogden to father, March 24, 1862," as cited in Jones, 65.
4. SHSP 10:56.
5. Handerson, 40; *OR* 12, 1:729–733; Taylor, 36–38, 42.
6. "T.A. Tooke to wife, April 26, 1862," as cited in Jones, 67.
7. Taylor, 40.
8. "T.A. Tooke to wife, April 26, 1862," as cited in Jones, 67.
9. *OR* 12, 3:876; Taylor, 44.
10. *OR* 12, 3:878–892.
11. *OR* 12, 1:730, 523.
12. Handerson, 41; Taylor, 47.
13. *CSR*; Handerson, 40–41; Jones, 68; *OR* 12, 1:459–60; Taylor, 47.

14. *OR* 12, 1:701, 730, 12, 3:886, 897.
15. *OR* 12, 1:701, 730, 12, 3:886, 897; Taylor, 48–49.
16. Taylor, 48–49.
17. George Neese, *Three Years in the Confederate Horse Artillery* (New York: Neale Publishing, 1911), 55. Pvt. Neese misnamed the Tigers the "Mississippi Tigers ... from Louisiana." He was apparently drawn to their Mississippi rifles.
18. Taylor, 50.
19. E.P. Alexander, 3; Taylor, 50.
20. Nisbet, 78.
21. *OR* 12, 1:702; James Hall, *Diary*, May 22, 1862, as cited in Robert Tanner, Stonewall in the Valley: Thomas "Stonewall" Jackson's Shenandoah Valley Campaign, Spring, 1862 (Garden City, New York: Doubleday, 1976), 204.
22. Neese, 55.
23. Nisbet, 79; *OR* 12, 1:702; Taylor, 51.
24. *OR* 12, 1:559, 702, 778, 800; Taylor, 51.
25. *OR* 12, 1:555–56, 559, 564–65, 703; "Lieutenant Thompson's Account," as cited in Frank Moore, ed., *The Rebellion Record: Documents, Narratives, Illustrative Incidents, Poetry, etc.* (New York: Putnam, 1863) 5:140.
26. SHSP 10:54.
27. *OR* 12, 1:800.
28. *OR* 12, 1:702.
29. Lucy Buck, 78.
30. *OR* 12, 1:556.
31. Frank Moore 5:140.
32. Lucy Buck, 80.
33. *OR* 12, 1:702, 725, 800; SHSP 10:54–55; Taylor, 51.
34. *OR* 12, 1:556, 564.
35. *OR* 12, 1:702, 800; Taylor, 53.
36. Campbell Brown, *Reminiscences of the Civil War*, as cited in Steuart, "Wheat's Tigers," 57.
37. Taylor, 53.
38. Douglas, 60; *OR* 12, 1:557–59, 564–65, 702–03, 733.
39. *Lynchburg Republican*, May 27, 1862; *OR* 12, 1:555–57.
40. Lucy Buck, 82.
41. Buck, 80; *Lynchburg Republican*, May 27, 1862; *OR* 12, 1:703, 800.

Chapter 7

1. *OR* 12, 1:704, 779.
2. Douglas, 61; Neese, 56; *OR* 12, 1:703, 760; Taylor, 54.
3. Douglas, 61; *OR* 12, 1:574–75, 586.
4. Neese, 56.
5. *OR* 12, 1:703.
6. Neese, 56–57.
7. Douglas, 61–62; *OR* 12, 1:57; Edward Moore, *The Story of a Cannoneer under Stonewall Jackson* (New York: Neale Publishing, 1907), 53.
8. Handerson, 42; *OR* 12, 1:570, 703–04; Taylor, 55–56.
9. *OR* 12, 1:704; William Clark, *History of Hampton Battery F, Independent Pennsylvania Light Artillery* (Pittsburgh, Pennsylvania: Werner, 1909), 16–17.
10. *OR* 12, 1:568, 703; Taylor, 55; Robert Dabney, *Life and Campaigns of Lieutenant General T.J. Jackson* (New York: Blelock, 1866), 372.
11. Douglas, 62.
12. Neese, 57.
13. *OR* 12, 1:704.
14. Dabney, 373; Douglas, 63; Neese, 60; *OR* 12, 3:902.
15. *OR* 12, 1:704.
16. Douglas, 63.
17. Handerson, 42.
18. "Recollection of Robert Thomas Barton of the Rockbridge Artillery at the Battle of Winchester," as cited in Tanner, 224.
19. Douglas, 63–64; *OR* 12, 1:704, 736.
20. Douglas, 64; *OR* 12, 1:736, 776.
21. Handerson, 42.
22. Tanner, 1–161.
23. *OR* 12, 1:596, 736.
24. Douglas, 65; *OR* 12, 1:616, 704, 736.
25. Clark, 17–20; *OR* 12, 1:580, 595–96, 603, 610, 616, 619, 623, 625.
26. *OR* 12, 1:596, 617, 705, 736.
27. Douglas, 65; Taylor, 56.
28. *OR* 12, 1:705; Taylor, 56–57.
29. Dabney, 379; *OR* 12, 1:617, 801; Taylor, 85.
30. Dabney, 379; *OR* 12, 1:580, 596, 611, 617, 625, 801; Taylor, 85; W. W. Goldsborough, *The Maryland Line in the Confederacy, 1861–65* (Baltimore, Maryland: 1900), 45.
31. Douglas, 66.
32. Clark, 17–20; *OR* 12, 1:596, 611, 617, 619, 623, 625, 801; Taylor, 85.
33. Dabney, 379; John Worsham, *One of Jackson's Foot Cavalry* (New York: Neale Publishing, 1912), 87–88.
34. *OR* 12, 1:580, 596, 600, 611, 617, 619, 623, 625; Douglas, 66.
35. Douglas, 66–67; *OR* 12, 1:706; Taylor, 59; Worsham, 87.
36. *OR* 12, 1:617.
37. *CSR*; Douglas, 66–67; *OR* 12, 1:801; Taylor, 59; Worsham, 87. For its actions at the battle of Winchester, the Special Battalion surprisingly listed no casualties. For the rest of the Louisiana Brigade, however, which charged into the mouths of Federal musketry and cannon, 15 were killed and 88 were wounded.

Chapter 8

1. Douglas, 74; *OR* 12, 1:533, 628–33; Taylor, 61.
2. *OR* 12, 3:903; Alexander Boteler, "Stonewall Jackson in the Campaign of 1862," *Southern Historical Society Papers* 40:175.
3. *OR* 12, 1:531.
4. *OR* 12, 1:533, 643–44.
5. *OR* 12, 1:708, 12, 3:902; Tanner, 271–72.
6. *CSR; OR* 12, 1:694–95, 793. These would include Sgt. Andrew Murphy, Cpl. Morris Buckley and Pvts. Edward Buckley, J. Huff, Simon Lebrick, George Steele, and Charles Stratton from the Walker Guards; Pvts. James Arnold, Richard Kane, and Thomas Lee from the Delta Rangers; Pvt. James Shehan (who was wounded at the battle of Front Royal and left behind) from the Old Dominion Guards; and Lt. Robert Grinnel (who was also wounded during the previous battle and left behind), Cpl. Francis Foley, and Pvts. Edward Cummings, Thomas Caughlin, and John Murphy from Wheat's Life Guards.
7. Douglas, 77; Taylor, 37, 64.
8. Taylor, 37, 64.
9. Taylor, 61–62.
10. Taylor, 9–10. "Luther Martin, Patrick Henry and others" were famous Anti-Federalists who adamantly opposed the federation of states as articulated in the Constitution of 1787. They instead preferred a confederation of states as outlined in the Constitution of 1777 (the Articles of Confederation). The Anti-Federalists contended that the War for American Independence was a war to preserve local sovereignty—a war against strong central government; that the thirteen of the twenty-five-odd British American provinces seceded from the British Empire to ensure local control; that it wasn't simply "taxation without representation," but "taxation with fair and equal representation." Even if the British American provinces had been given representation per population in Parliament, they still would have always been outvoted by Britons and the rest of the empire. In other words, what good would democracy be if 40 percent of the people (British Americans) always lost? This war, the War for Southern Independence, was apparently no different, in most Southerners' eyes. Thirteen states seceded (or attempted to secede) from the United States just as thirteen British American provinces had seceded from the British Empire in 1776. As far as Taylor's openly anti-immigrant statement goes, some felt that his decision to execute Corcoran and O'Brien—two Irish immigrants—were fueled in part by his xenophobia.
11. Taylor, 238. President Lincoln would disagree. In his first inaugural address (March 4, 1861), he noted that he simply wished to stop the spread of slavery into the western territories and did not intend (nor had the power) to abolish it in the states where it already existed. This war was therefore a war to preserve the Union and the Constitution. In his second inaugural address (March 4, 1864), however, Lincoln changed his tone, focusing more on slavery as the root cause. He proclaimed: "Both parties deprecated war; but one of them would make war rather than let the nation survive [i.e., the Confederates]; and the other would accept war rather than let it perish [i.e., the Federals]. And the war came.... One eighth of the whole population were colored slaves, not distributed generally over the Union, but localized in the southern part of it. These slaves constituted a peculiar and powerful interest. All knew that this interest was, somehow, *the cause of the war*. To strengthen, perpetuate, and extend this interest was the object for which the insurgents would rend the Union, even by war; while [my] government claimed no right to do more than to restrict the territorial enlargement of it."
12. G.T. Beauregard, "The First Battle of Bull Run," *Battles and Leaders of the Civil War* (New York: The Century Company, 1884–87) Volume 1, Part 1, 222. The debate over "the cause" is of course well beyond the scope of this book. But according to most Southern soldiers, they said that they were fighting for the same right of secession as did their forefathers in 1776; that it was their legal and moral right to secede; that the North and the South were two distinct cultures and countries—slavery only being one of the differences. See Gary Gallagher's *The Confederate War: How Popular Will, Nationalism, and Military Strategy Could Not Stave Off Defeat* (Cambridge, Massachusetts: Harvard University Press, 1997).
13. Handerson, 21–22.
14. Niehaus, 49–53; Shugg, 41–42, 119–20, 174–75; SHSP, 56.
15. Taylor, 65.
16. Douglas, 77; Taylor, 65.
17. *OR* 12, 1:730–31; Taylor, 67.
18. Taylor, 67.
19. Taylor, 67–68; "J. K. Edmonson to his Wife, June 2, 1862," as cited in Tanner, 277.
20. Taylor, 70; "George Ring to wife, June 7, 1862," as cited in Gannon, 43.
21. Douglas, 84–85; Gannon, 37; Krick, 20–21; Taylor, 70.
22. *OR* 12, 1:712, 781; Taylor, 72.
23. *OR* 12, 1:712, 732, 781; Tanner, 287–288; Taylor, 72.
24. *OR* 12, 1:683, 781.
25. Alexander, 104; *OR* 12, 1:683, 699, 732.

26. Douglas, 92–93; *OR* 12, 1:683, 695, 699, 774, 801; Taylor, 72–73.
27. Douglas, 92–93; *OR* 12, 1:683, 695, 699, 774, 801; Taylor, 72–73.
28. *OR* 12, 1:645, 712; Edward Moore 5:107.
29. Nisbet, 93; Edward Moore 5:108.
30. *OR* 12, 1:796; Edward Moore 5:107.
31. *OR* 12, 1:664–65, 714, 782–84, 797, 802; Nisbet, 94–95.
32. Douglas, 95.
33. Nisbet, 95.

Chapter 9

1. Alexander, 105; Douglas, 94; *OR* 12, 1:665, 995, 714.
2. Douglas, 95–96; Krick, 289; *OR* 12, 1:728, 740.
3. *OR* 12, 1:732, 740.
4. Taylor, 73.
5. Krick, 311–312, 510; *OR* 12, 1:714, 740, 693–94.
6. *OR* 12, 1:695.
7. *OR* 12, 1:740.
8. Dabney, 421; *OR* 12, 1:693, 696, 743, 748.
9. Dabney, 421; Krick, 349; Taylor, 73–74.
10. Taylor, 74.
11. Henry Kelly, *The Battle of Port Republic* (Philadelphia, Pennsylvania: Lippincott, 1886), 16–17.
12. Macon, Georgia, *Daily Telegraph*, June 24, 1862, as cited in Krick, 350.
13. Kelly, 17–18; Taylor, 75, 84
14. New Orleans *Daily Picayune*, June 10, 1866; Kelly, 17; Krick, 408; Taylor, 74–75.
15. Neese, 74; *OR* 12, 1:697, 740–41, 750.
16. Taylor, 75.
17. New Orleans *Daily Picayune*, June 10, 1866.
18. Dabney, 429; Taylor, 75.
19. New Orleans *Daily Picayune*, June 10, 1866; Krick, 408, 411, 414–15; Neese, 74–75; Taylor, 75.
20. James Huntington, "Operations in the Shenandoah Valley, from Winchester to Port Republic," *Papers of the Military Historical Society of Massachusetts*, 1:334; Taylor, 75.
21. *Staunton Vindicator*, February 15, 1867.
22. Kelly, 19; *OR* 12, 1:695, 802.
23. Samuel Buck, *With the Old Confeds: Actual Experiences of a Captain in the Line* (Gaithersburg, Maryland: Butternut Press, 1983), 38. Pvt. Edmund Stevens of the 9th Louisiana similarly remembered: "Wheat was bloody as a butcher."
24. "Stevens to parents, June 14, 1862," as cited in Dufour, 187.
25. Krick, 422.
26. Krick, 423; *OR* 12, 1:693, 697, 802.
27. "Stevens to parents, June 14, 1862," as cited in Dufour, 187.
28. Neese, 75.
29. Kelly, 21; Neese, 75; *OR* 12, 1:786, 791; Taylor, 75.
30. Taylor, 76.
31. Richmond *Whig*, June 18, 1862.
32. *CSR*; *OR* 12, 1:787.
33. Douglas, 97; Neese, 76; *OR* 12, 1:716; Taylor, 76.
34. Douglas, 97.
35. Gannon, 14; *OR* 12, 1:802; Taylor, 77.
36. Dabney, 429–30; Douglas, 97; Henderson, 43; *OR* 12, 1:716 and Taylor, 77.
37. Taylor, 77–78.

Chapter 10

1. Joseph Harsh, *Confederate Tide Rising: Robert E. Lee and the Making of Southern Strategy, 1861–62* (Kent, Ohio: Kent State University Press, 1998), 1–46; Fitz-John Porter, "Hanover Court House and Gaines's Mill," *Battles and Leaders of the Civil War* (New York: Century Publishing, 1884) 2:324–25.
2. Harsh, 47–53, 84; *OR* 11, 2:489.
3. Clifford Dowdey, ed., *The Wartime Papers of Robert E. Lee* (Boston, Massachusetts: Little and Brown, 1961), 188.
4. Davis, 2:131; Harsh, 85–87; *OR* 11, 3:589–94, 12, 2:490, 12, 3:913; SHSP 40:175; Dowdey 2:188.
5. Douglas, 104–05; Henderson, 43; Nisbet, 108–09; *OR* 11, 2:483–87; 12, 3:915; Taylor, 83; Dowdey, 2:183–84.
6. Davis, 2:131; Douglas, 104–05; Henderson, 43; Nisbet, 108–09; *OR* 11, 2:483–87, 552, 12, 3:915; Taylor, 83; Dowdey, 183–84; D. H. Hill, "Lee Attacks North of the Chickahominy," *Battles and Leaders of the Civil War* (New York: Century Publishing, 1884) 2:347–49.
7. *OR* 11, 2:498–99.
8. *OR* 11, 2:483–89, 562.
9. Harsh, 81–84; *OR* 11, 2:483–89; Sifakis, 61–77.
10. Harsh, 84; *OR* 11, 2:490, 11, 3:238.
11. *OR* 11, 2:490–91.
12. Brown, 46; Taylor, 83.
13. Brown, 43; *B&L* 2:326, 396–99, 3:347, 352; Douglas, 105; *OR* 11, 2:490, 552–53, 562, 605, 614, 621.
14. *B&L* 2:352, 397; Douglas, 105; Harsh, 91–93; *OR* 11, 2:20–21, 222, 271, 384, 490, 552–55, 623, 834–35, 756.
15. Douglas, 105; Harsh, 93; *OR* 11, 2:555, 614.

Chapter 11

1. B&L 2:331; OR 11, 2:20–21, 222, 313.
2. B&L 2:331; OR 11, 2:223, 273, 386.
3. New Orleans *Daily Item*, August 25, 1896; SHSP, 57.
4. B&L 2:352; Douglas, 106; OR 11, 2:492, 553, 621; Taylor, 88.
5. Brown, 48–49; OR 11, 2:553.
6. Taylor, 88.
7. B&L 2:353; Douglas, 106; OR 11, 2:553, 621; Taylor, 88.
8. Handerson, 45; SHSP, 59.
9. OR 11, 2:492, 757–58, 836–37.
10. B&L 2:332; Brown, 47; OR 11, 2:20, 224, 236, 272, 348, 492, 554; Taylor, 88–89.
11. Nisbet, 109–110; OR 11, 2:553, 606, 624–5.
12. Douglas, 107–08.
13. New Orleans *Daily Item*, August 25, 1896.
14. Brown, 50; McClendon, 73; Nisbet, 110; OR 11, 2:553, 605–06, 614.
15. Naisawald, 69; OR 11, 2:420, 461; Edwin Bearss, "Richmond National Battlefield Park Map of the Battle of Gaines' Mill, 1965," Richmond National Battlefield Park Library.
16. Handerson, 46.
17. Handerson, 45.
18. New Orleans *Daily Item*, August 25, 1896; Dufour, 195; Handerson, 45–46; Jones, 104; SHSP, 50.
19. Handerson, 46.
20. Jones, 104.
21. New Orleans *Daily Item*, August 25, 1896; Nisbet, 110; OR 11, 2:614–15.
22. OR 11, 2:620.
23. Ibid.
24. Ibid.
25. Brown, 51–53.
26. Taylor, 84–85.
27. B&L 2:339–40; Douglas, 109; OR 11, 2:22, 224, 493, 556, 563, 570.
28. McClendon, 76–77.
29. B&L 2:339–40; OR 11, 2:22, 339–40, 388.
30. CSR; OR 11, 2:41, 609.
31. CSR; New Orleans *Daily True Delta*, September 7, 1862.

Chapter 12

1. Dufour, 196.
2. New Orleans *Daily Item*, August 25, 1896; Dufour, 196–97; SHSP, 427. Boyd said that Wheat was "one of the bravest of men, the gentlest and noblest of gentlemen, modest and refined as a woman, and the truest of friends." On July 4, 1862, Wheat's sister, Josephine Shober, visited his grave on that wooded ridge just south of Boatswain's Swamp. She wrote to her sister Selina: "I threw myself on his grave. I wept for us all but most of all for Ma. Oh that she should have to give up two such noble sons does seem so hard." In 1863, Wheat's body was disinterred because of the deteriorating condition of the gravesite. He was transported aboard a funeral dirge and accompanied by a caisson, a riderless horse and "escorted by a large military and civic procession" to Hollywood Cemetery in Richmond, where he was buried with full military honors. In 1933, an enormous headstone, which is still extant, was erected to mark Wheat's final resting place.
3. B&L 2:383; Handerson, 47; OR 11, 2:493, 607, 625, 662.
4. Douglas, 111; OR, 11, 2:493, 556, 607.
5. B&L 2:406–08; OR, 11, 2:22, 493, 555–556.
6. OR 11, 2:617; Taylor, 89.
7. B&L 2:362, 385–86.
8. OR 11, 2:50–51, 80–81, 430–31, 494, 663, 788–89; Taylor, 89.
9. Taylor, 89.
10. Handerson, 47–48.
11. Brown, 57; OR 11, 2:22, 80–81, 431, 495, 556, 565, 664; Taylor, 89.
12. B&L 2:386; OR 11, 2:625.
13. Brown, 57; OR 11, 2:556–57.
14. Alexander, 138; OR 11, 2:399, 906.
15. B&L 2:387–90; OR 11, 2:22, 51, 53, 81, 83, 99–100, 192, 387–90, 338–39, 431, 464, 495, 556–57, 565, 627, 664–65, 790, 906.
16. OR 11, 2:22, 53, 81, 100, 192, 339, 431, 464, 557.
17. OR 11, 2:495–96.
18. B&L 2:391; OR 11, 2:496.
19. B&L 2:391.
20. B&L 2:391–92; OR 11, 2:557, 607, 666.
21. B&L 2:391–92; OR 11, 2:557, 607, 611.
22. Brown, 60, 64–65, 67; Taylor, 92.
23. Handerson, 48–49.
24. OR 11, 2:23, 192, 228, 237, 496; Sears, 311–321.
25. OR 11, 2:557.
26. Alexander, 160–63; OR 11, 2:23, 496, 625, 665, 908; Taylor, 92.
27. Brown, 60; Handerson, 49; OR 11, 2:557–558; Taylor, 92.
28. OR 11, 2:620.
29. Ibid.
30. CSR; OR 11, 2:609.
31. Douglas, 114.
32. CSR.
33. Handerson, 49.
34. Ibid., 50.
35. Taylor, 86–87, 93.
36. Alexander, 168–70; Brown, 67–68; Douglas, 114–115; OR 11, 2:559.

37. Alexander, 168–69; Taylor, 93.
38. Douglas, 116; Brown, 67–68; Handerson, 50–51.
39. Alexander, 170–71; Brown, 68–69; Douglas, 112.
40. Brown, 69; Douglas, 112.

Chapter 13

1. *OR* 11, 2:41, 501–10.
2. Taylor, 117.
3. Alexander, 176.
4. John Hennessy, *Return to Bull Run: The Campaign and Battle of Second Bull Run* (New York: Simon and Schuster, 1993), 10.
5. *OR* Series 4, 2:198. This did not officially come to pass until after the battle of Sharpsburg in September 1862. Jackson would be rewarded for his actions in the Valley and Longstreet for his actions during the Seven Days.
6. Taylor, 93. In the introduction to Taylor's *Destruction and Reconstruction*, editor Mike Parrish (1995) writes: "The Army of Northern Virginia needed young general officers with Taylor's manifold talents. Although no other Confederate officer could have achieved the results Taylor did in protecting Louisiana from enemy invasion, had he remained with Lee in Virginia he would have made an excellent divisional commander, and most likely he would have emerged as an equally fine corps commander." Douglas Southall Freeman, the leading modern historian of the Army of Northern Virginia, said: "The army was poorer for Taylor's departure." See Freeman, 1:669.
7. Jones, 111–112.
8. *OR* 51, 2:597.
9. *OR* 12, 2:548–50. D'Aquin's battery of Louisiana Guard Artillery was also added to Ewell's division.
10. Jones, 112; *OR* 11, 3:448, 656, 12, 3:918–19. Starke's promotion, like Taylor's a year before, caused quite a ruckus. Starke had been commanding Virginians before his promotion, and not Louisianans.
11. Jones, 112; Sifakis, 98.
12. Sifakis, 98.
13. *OR* 51, 2:597.
14. Dufour, 199.
15. *CSR*.
16. Brooks, 99, 113 (see note 22); *CSR*.
17. Jones, 111. General Hays was not able to join the brigade until the Fredericksburg Campaign (December 1862) because he was still convalescing from the wound he received at Port Republic. Therefore, Col. Henry Forno of the 5th Louisiana Regiment, the ranking officer in the brigade, commanded the 1st Louisiana "Tiger" Brigade through its horrendous trials at 2nd Manassas and Sharpsburg.
18. *CSR* 31:213.
19. New Orleans *Daily Item*, August 25, 1896; McClendon, 37.

Bibliography

Primary and Secondary Works

Alexander, E. Porter. *Military Memoirs of a Confederate.* New York: Da Capo Press, 1983.

Andrews, William. *Footprints of a Regiment: A Recollection of the First Georgia Regulars 1861–65.* Atlanta: Longstreet Press, 1992.

Ashkenaski, Elliot, ed. *The Civil War Diary of Clara Solomon: Growing Up in New Orleans, 1861–62.* Baton Rouge: Louisiana State University Press, 1995.

Barney, William. *The Passage of the Republic: An Interdisciplinary History of Nineteenth-Century America.* Lexington, Massachusetts: Heath, 1987.

Bartlett, Napier. *Military Record of Louisiana.* Baton Rouge: Louisiana State University Press, 1964.

Battles and Leaders of the Civil War. New York: Century, 1887.

Bergeron, Arthur. *Guide to Louisiana Confederate Units, 1861–65.* Baton Rouge: Louisiana State University Press, 1989.

Booth, Andrew. *Record of Louisiana Confederate Soldiers and Louisiana Confederate Commands.* Baton Rouge: Louisiana State University Press, 1984.

Bragg, Jefferson Davis. *Louisiana in the Confederacy.* Baton Rouge: Louisiana State University Press, 1952.

Brown, Campbell. "Memoirs," ed. Terry Jones. In *The Peninsula Campaign of 1862.* Campbell, California: Savas-Woodbury Publishers, 1995.

Brown, Charles. *Agents of Manifest Destiny: The Lives and Times of the Filibusters.* Chapel Hill: University of North Carolina Press, 1980.

Brown, Stuart. *The Guns of Harpers Ferry.* Virginia Book, 1968.

Buck, Samuel. *With the Old Confeds: Actual Experiences of a Captain in the Line.* Gaithersburg, Maryland: Butternut Press, 1983.

Buck, William, ed. *Sad Earth, Sweet Heaven: The Diary of Lucy Rebecca Buck During the War Between the States.* Birmingham, Alabama: Buck, 1992.

Carr, Albert. *The World and William Walker.* New York: Harper and Row, 1963.

Catlett, James M., and T. B. Warder. *Battle of Young's Branch or, Manassas Plain, Fought July 21, 1861.* Richmond: Enquirer Book and Job Press, 1862.

Clark, William. *History of Hampton Battery F, Independent Pennsylvania Artillery.* Pittsburgh: Werner, 1909.

Company of Military Historians. *Military Uniforms in America.* Volume 3: *Long Endure: The Civil War Period, 1852–1867.* 3 vols. Novato, California: Presidio Press, 1982.

Cummer, Clyde, ed. *Yankee in Gray: The Civil War Memoirs of Henry Handerson with a Selection of His Wartime Letters.* Cleveland: Western Case University, 1962.

Dabney, Robert. *Life and Campaigns of Lieutenant General T.J. Jackson.* New York: Blelock, 1866.

Davis, Jefferson. *The Rise and Fall of the Confederate Government.* New York: D. Appleton, 1881.

203

DeLeon, Theodore. *Belles, Beaux, and Brains of the Sixties*. New York: n.p., 1909.

Doubleday, Charles. *Reminiscences of the "Filibuster" War in Nicaragua*. New York: Putnam's, 1886.

Douglas, Henry. *I Rode with Stonewall*. Chapel Hill: University of North Carolina Press, 1940.

Dowdey, Clifford, ed. *The Wartime Papers of Robert E. Lee*. Boston: Little and Brown, 1961.

Dufour, Charles. *Gentle Tiger: The Gallant Life of Roberdeau Wheat*. Baton Rouge: Louisiana State University Press, 1957.

Field, Ron. *The American Civil War: Confederate Army*. London: Brassey's, 1998.

Franklin, John. *The Militant South: 1800–1860*. Cambridge: Harvard University Press, 1956.

Freehling, William. *The Road to Disunion: Secessionists at Bay, 1776–1854*. New York: Oxford University Press, 1990.

Freeman, Douglas Southall. *Lee's Lieutenants*. 3 vols. New York: Scribner's, 1944.

Gallagher, Gary. *The Confederate War: How Popular Will, Nationalism, and Military Strategy Could Not Stave Off Defeat*. Cambridge: Harvard University Press, 1997.

Gannon, James. *Irish Rebels, Confederate Tigers: A History of the Sixth Louisiana Volunteers, 1861–65*. Campbell, California: Savas Publishing, 1998.

Goldsborough, W.W. *The Maryland Line in the Confederacy, 1861–65*. Baltimore, Maryland: n.p., 1900.

Handerson, Henry E. *Yankee in Gray: the Civil War Memoirs of Henry E. Handerson, with a Selection of His Wartime Letters*. Cleveland: Press of Western Reserve University, 1962.

Harsh, Joseph. *Confederate Tide Rising: Robert E. Lee and the Making of Southern Strategy, 1861–62*. Kent, Ohio: Kent State University Press, 1998.

Haynes, Martin. *A History of the Second Regiment, New Hampshire Volunteer Infantry*. Lakeport, New Hampshire: n.p., 1896.

Hearn, Chester. *The Capture of New Orleans*. Baton Rouge: Louisiana State University Press, 1995.

Heidler, David. *Pulling Down the Temple: The Fire-Eaters and the Destruction of the Union*. Mechanicsburg, Pennsylvania: Stackpole Books, 1994.

Hennessy, John. *The First Battle of Manassas: An End to Innocence*. Lynchburg, Virginia: Howard Company, 1989.

_____. *Return to Bull Run: The Campaign and Battle of Second Bull Run*. New York: Simon and Schuster, 1993.

Hewitt, Janet, ed. *Supplement of the Official Records of the Union and Confederate Armies: "Louisiana Troops (Confederate)."* Wilmington, North Carolina: Broadfoot Publishing, 1992.

Huntington, James. "Operations in the Shenandoah Valley, from Winchester to Port Republic." *Papers of the Military Historical Society of Massachusetts*.

Johnston, Joseph. *Narrative of Military Operations*. New York: D. Appleton, 1874.

Jones, Terry. *Lee's Tigers: The Louisiana Infantry in the Army of Northern Virginia*. Baton Rouge: Louisiana State University Press, 1987.

Kelly, Henry. *The Battle of Port Republic*. Philadelphia: Lippincott, 1886.

Krick, Robert. *Conquering the Valley: Stonewall Jackson at Port Republic*. New York: William Morrow, 1996.

Lonn, Ella. *Foreigners in the Confederacy*. Chapel Hill: University of North Carolina Press, 1940.

May, Robert. *The Southern Dream of a Caribbean Empire, 1854–1861*. Baton Rouge: Louisiana State University Press, 1973.

McAfee, Michael. *Zouaves: The First and the Bravest*. Gettysburg: Thomas Publications, 1991.

McClendon, William. *Recollections of War-Times by an Old Veteran While Under Stonewall Jackson and Lieutenant General James Longstreet: How I Got In and How I Got Out*. Montgomery, Alabama: Paragon Press, 1909.

McElfresh, Earl. *The Manassas Battlefields*. Olean, New York: McElfresh Map, 1996.

McPherson, James. *Battle Cry of Freedom: The Civil War Era*. New York: Oxford University Press, 1988.

_____. *Drawn with the Sword*. New York: Oxford University Press, 1996.

McWhiney, Grady, and Perry Jamieson. *Attack and Die: Civil War Military Tactics and the Southern Military Heritage. Montgomery: The University of Alabama Press, 1982.

Moore, Allison. He Died Furious. Baton Rouge: Ortlieb Press, 1983.

Moore, Edward. The Story of a Cannoneer Under Stonewall Jackson. New York: n.p., 1907.

Moore, Frank, ed. The Rebellion Record: Documents, Narratives, Illustrative Incidents, Poetry, etc. New York: Putnam, 1863.

Naisawald, Vanhorn. Grape and Canister: The Story of the Field Artillery of the Army of the Potomac, 1861–65. Mechanicsburg, Pennsylvania: Stackpole Books, 1999.

Neese, George. Three Years in the Confederate Horse Artillery. New York: Neale Publishing, 1911.

Newton, Steven. The Battle of Seven Pines. Lynchburg, Virginia: H.E. Howard, 1993.

Niehaus, Earl. The Irish in New Orleans, 1800–1860. Baton Rouge: Louisiana State University Press, 1965.

Nisbet, James. Four Years on the Firing Line. Chattanooga: Imperial Press, 1914.

Oates, William. The War Between the Union and Confederacy and Its Lost Opportunities with a History of the Fifteenth Alabama [Infantry] Regiment and the Forty-Eight Battles in Which It Was Engaged. Dayton, Ohio: Morning Side Publishing, 1974.

Oliphant, Laurence. Patriots and Filibusters. London: William Blackwood and Sons, 1860.

Olmstead, Frederick Law. The Cotton Kingdom: A Traveller's Observations on Cotton and Slavery in the American Slave States, 1853–1861. Ed. Arthur Schlesinger. New York: Da Capo Press, 1996.

Parrish, Michael. Richard Taylor: Soldier Prince of Dixie. Chapel Hill: University of North Carolina Press, 1992.

Powell, Alexander. Gentlemen Rovers. New York: Scribner's, 1913.

Putnam, Sally. Richmond During the War. New York: n.p., 1867.

Rhodes, Elijah. All for Union: A History of the Second Rhode Island Infantry in the War of the Great Rebellion. Lincoln: University of Nebraska Press, 1986.

Rosengarten, Frederic. Freebooters Must Die! The Life and Death of William Walker, the Most Notorious Filibuster of the Nineteenth Century. Wayne, Pennsylvania: Haverford House, 1976.

Scroggs, William. Filibusters and Financiers: The Story of William Walker and His Associates. New York: Russell and Russell, 1916.

Sears, Stephen. George B. McClellan: The Young Napoleon. New York: Da Capo Press, 1999.

_____. To the Gates of Richmond: The Peninsula Campaign. New York: Houghton Mifflin, 1992.

Shotwell, Randolph. The Papers of Randolph Shotwell. Edited by J.G. de Roulhac Hamilton. Raleigh: The North Carolina Historical Commission, 1879.

Shugg, Robert. Origins of Class Struggle in Louisiana: A Social History of White Farmers and Laborers During Slavery and After, 1840–1875. Baton Rouge: Louisiana State University Press, 1965.

Sifakis, Stewart. Compendium of Confederate Armies: Louisiana. New York: Facts on File, 1995.

Smith, Harry. A Sporting Family in the Old South. Albany, New York: n.p., 1936.

Smith, Robin. American Civil War Zouaves. London: Osprey Publishing, 1996.

Soule, Leon. The Know Nothing Party in New Orleans: A Reappraisal. Baton Rouge: Louisiana Historical Association, 1962.

Stampp, Kenneth. The Causes of the Civil War. New York: Simon and Schuster, 1991.

Stout, Joseph. The Liberators: Filibustering Expeditions into Mexico, 1848–62 and the Last Thrust of Manifest Destiny. Los Angeles: Westernlore Press, 1973.

Sullivan, Edward. Rambles and Scrambles in North and South America. London: n.p., 1852.

Tanner, Robert. Stonewall in the Valley: Thomas "Stonewall" Jackson's Shenandoah Valley Campaign, Spring, 1862. Garden City, New York: Doubleday, 1976.

Taylor, Richard. Destruction and Reconstruction: Personal Experiences of the Civil War. Ed. Michael Parrish. New York: Da Capo Press, 1995.

Time Life Books. Echoes of Glory: Arms and

Equipment of the Confederacy. Alexandria, Virginia: Time-Life Books, 1991.

Todd, William. *The Seventy-Ninth Highlanders, New York Volunteers, in the War of the Rebellion, 1861–65*. Albany, New York: Press of Brandon, Baton, 1886.

Uniform Regulations for the Army of the United States: 1861. Washington, D.C.: Smithsonian Institute, 1961.

Walker, William. *The War in Nicaragua*. Mobile, Alabama: S. H. Goetzel, 1860.

Wallace, Edward. *Destiny and Glory*. New York: Coward-McCann, 1957.

War of the Rebellion: A Compilation of the Official Records of the Union and Confederate Armies, 1861–65. 130 vols. Washington, D.C.: Government Printing Office, 1880–1901.

Withers, Robert. *Autobiography of an Octogenarian*. Roanoke, Virginia: The Stone Printing and Manufacturing Company Press, 1907.

Worsham, John. *One of Jackson's Foot Cavalry*. New York: Neale Publishing, 1912.

Zettler, Berrien. *War Stories and School Days Incidents for Children*. New York: Neale Publishing, 1912.

Magazines and Journals

Boteler, Alexander. "Stonewall Jackson in Campaign of 1862." *Southern Historical Society Papers* 40 (September 1915): 162–83.

Bridges, Charles. "The Knights of the Golden Circle: A Filibustering Fantasy." *Southwestern Historical Quarterly*, January 1941, 286–91.

Brooks, Ross. "'Part Irish and the Rest the Flower of Southern Chivalry': Clothing, Arms, and Equipment of the First Special Battalion, Louisiana Infantry 1861–62." *Military Collector and Historian*, Fall 1999, 98–115.

De Bow, John. "Advancement of Agricultural Interest of the South." *De Bow's Review*, February 1859, 14–15.

———. "The Walker Expedition, 1856: The Regenerator of Central America." *De Bow's Review*, February 1858, 1–2.

"First (Wheat's) Special Battalion, Infantry." *Compiled Service Records of Confederate Soldiers Who Served in Organizations from the State of Louisiana*. Record Group 108, M320, rolls 100 and 101. National Archives, Washington, D.C.

Fitzhugh, George. "Acquisition of Mexico—Filibustering." *De Bow's Review*, December 1858, 36–40.

Fremaux, Leon. "The Tiger Rifles: Wheat's Battalion [drawing]." N.d. Natalie Nelson Collection, Manassas National Battlefield Park Library.

Harrold, James. "Surgeons of the Confederacy." *Confederate Veteran* 40 (May 1932): 172–75.

Holmes, Jack. "The Not So Gentle Louisiana Tigers." *Civil War Times Illustrated*, May 1963, 22–25.

Howison, Robert. "History of the War, Chapter VI." *Southern Literary Messenger* 37.5 (1863): 255–84.

Johnson, Bradley T. "Memoir of the First Maryland [Infantry] Regiment [C.S.]." *Southern Historical Society Papers* 10 (January and February 1882): 46–56.

Jones, Michael. "Chatham Roberdeau Wheat and His Louisiana Tigers." *Blue and Gray Magazine*, November 1985, 24–30.

Jones, Terry. "Wheat's Tigers." *Civil War Times Illustrated*, March-April 1994, 21–32.

Lawrence, Debra. "Drury Gibson: Letters from a North Louisiana Tiger." *North Louisiana Historical Association*, Fall 1979, 130–31.

Minnich, J. W. "Picturesque Soldiery." *Confederate Veteran* 31 (August 1923): 295.

Ollinger, Crenshaw. "The Knights of the Golden Circle." *American Historical Review*, October 1941, 32–51.

"Phasalia and Manassas." *Southern Literary Messenger* 33 (1863): 295–98.

Roden, J. B. "Trip from New Orleans to Louisville in 1861." *Confederate Veteran* 18 (May 1910): 236–37.

Shober, May Wheat. "The Louisiana Tigers." *Confederate Veteran* 19 (November 1911): 520.

Steffen, Randy, and Ronald E. Youngquist. "First Special Battalion, Louisiana Infantry (Wheat's Tigers), 1861–1862." *Military Collector and Historian*, Spring 1959, 12–16.

Steuart, Richard D. "Wheat's Tigers and Others." *Confederate Veteran* 31 (September 1923): 326.

Thomas, Michael. "Unearthing the Tigers' Graves." *Northern Virginia Heritage*, June 1980, 2–10.

Walker, William. "General Walker's Policy in Central America." *De Bow's Review*, August 1860, 5–25, 160–65.

———. "Walker's Expedition of 1856." *De Bow's Review*, February 1858.

Wheat, Leo. "Memoir of Gen. C. R. Wheat, Commander of the 'Louisiana Tiger Battalion.'" *Southern Historical Society Papers* 17 (January–December 1889): 47–59.

Newspapers

Baltimore *Sun*
London *Times*
Lynchburg *Republican*
New Orleans *Bee*
New Orleans *Commercial Bulletin*
New Orleans *Daily Crescent*
New Orleans *Daily Delta*
New Orleans *Daily Picayune*
New Orleans *Orleanian*
New York *Daily News*
New York *Times*
Providence *Evening Press*
Richmond *Dispatch*
Richmond *Examiner*
Staunton *Vindicator*
Washington *Evening Star*

Special Collections

Beares, Edwin. Richmond National Battlefield Park Map of the Battle of Gaines' Mill, 1965. Richmond National Battlefield Park.

Brezeale, B.B. Co. J, Fourth South Carolina Infantry at the Battle of First Manassas. N.d. Manassas Battlefield National Park.

Index

Accessory Transit Route 15
Adrian, Thomas 56, 66–67, 72–73, 76, 81, 86, 155, 157, 169, 174, 187
Africa 8–9, 11, 22, 122–123, 129, 147
Alabama troops: 4th Regiment 64, 67, 74, 194; 15th Regiment 1, 80, 126, 154, 170
Alexander, John 48, 51, 55–57
Alvarez, Juan 13–14, 29
American Phalanx 17–19
Anderson, Frank 16, 20, 27, 29
Ashby, Turner 100, 106, 108–112, 115, 117, 119–120, 124, 126
Atkins, Robert Going 30, 51, 89, 155, 157, 169–170, 180–181, 186–87
Avegno, Anatole 34

Banks, Nathaniel 93, 95–101, 104, 107–112, 116, 119, 121, 140, 167
Bartow, Francis 67, 69, 74
Beauregard, P.G.T. 49, 51, 53, 56, 66, 68–69, 71–75, 77–78, 81, 91–92, 122, 193
Bee, Bernard 64, 67, 69, 72, 74
Boyd, David French 1, 47, 86, 91, 138, 145–146, 150, 156, 167, 170, 200
Buhoup, Jonathan W 46–47, 58, 65, 82, 177, 186–187
Burnside, Ambrose 58, 60, 62–65, 67, 194

Camp Beauregard 81, 92
Camp Buchanan 96
Camp Carondolet 89, 96, 104
Camp Davis 2, 36, 38, 41, 180
Camp Florida 1, 83, 174–175
Camp Moore 42, 46–47, 89, 177–178, 180
Camp Walker 42, 45, 171
Carroll, Samuel 126–127, 129
Carvajal, Jose 13
Castellon, Francisco 14–19, 21, 24
Catahoula Guerrillas 46, 50, 55, 57–58, 61, 63, 76, 82, 89, 168, 171, 177–179, 184
Chamorro, Fruto 14–19, 24
Chasseur à Pied 34
Chinandega 17–18, 21, 27

Cocke, Philip St. George 48, 56, 68, 72
Connecticut troops: 5th Regiment 113
Connor, Zachary 120
Corcoran, Dennis 83–87
Cuba 2, 5, 8, 12, 31, 78

Delta Rangers 2, 35–36, 41–45, 58, 63, 65, 73, 76, 89, 107, 137, 155, 169, 171–172, 175–179, 184–185
Douglas, Henry Kyd 106, 110–111, 114, 127–128, 137, 148, 156, 164

Elzey, Arnold 79, 84–85, 108, 117, 121, 126–129, 146, 148, 150, 153, 161
Ewell, Richard 79, 81, 83, 84–85, 89, 96–100, 106–108, 111–112, 117, 120–121, 123–124, 126–128, 136, 141–143, 147,-148, 150, 153–154, 157, 159, 161, 163, 165, 166–168, 195
Executions 12, 77, 84–86

Filibusters 2, 5, 9, 11–17, 19–31, 36, 39–40, 46, 51, 55, 61, 64–66, 73, 76–77, 92, 98, 105, 107, 110, 115, 134–135, 147, 151, 156, 171–172
Flournoy, Thomas 96–98, 100–101, 105–106, 124, 126, 129
Frémont, John Charles 93, 96–98, 120–121, 124–128, 129, 137–138, 140, 167
Frying Pan Church 48
Fulkerson, Sam 111, 127

Gardner, Henry 2, 35, 37–38, 41, 67, 107, 155, 175, 179, 185
Garibaldi, Giuseppi 2, 30, 41, 78, 180–181, 183–185
Georgia troops: 7th Regiment 74; 8th Regiment 67; 18th Regiment 120; 21st Regiment 82, 100, 128

Handerson, Harry 80, 83, 92, 111, 122–123, 150–151, 153, 158, 161, 164–165
Hays, Harry 74, 79–80, 83–84, 98, 132, 154, 169–170, 201

Index

Heintzelman, Samuel 53, 67, 69–72, 160
Hunter, David 53, 58, 60, 64, 69, 194

Imboden, John 64, 69–70
Indiana troops: 7th Regiment 130; 13th Regiment 98; 27th Regiment 101, 113

Jackson, Thomas Jonathan 3, 68–72, 74, 96–102, 104–114, 116–121, 123–134, 137–149, 157–161, 165–170
Johnston, Bradley 100, 103
Johnston, Joseph 64, 68, 78–79, 81, 83, 89, 91, 93–94, 96, 112, 126, 139–140, 193, 203

Kenly, John Reese 100–101, 103–106
Knights of the Golden Circle 8–13

Lee, Robert Edward 94, 97, 119, 139–142, 144, 146–148, 150, 155, 157–168
Lopez, Narcisco 11–12, 78
Louisiana troops: 1st Battalion (Dreux's) 168; 1st Regiment 47, 168, 170; 1st Zouave Battalion (Coppens's) 34, 168; 2nd Regiment 47, 168; 3rd Battalion (Bradford's) 168; 5th Regiment 47, 168–169; 6th Regiment 46–47, 79–80, 82, 104, 114, 124–125, 128, 132–135, 163, 168–169; 7th Battalion (St. Paul's) 82, 168, 177; 7th Regiment 47, 74, 79–82, 84, 98, 110, 128, 132–133, 154, 163, 168–169; 8th Regiment 43, 46–47, 79–80, 84, 86, 90, 128, 132–133, 135, 154, 163, 168–169, 177; 9th Regiment 47, 79, 80, 83, 86, 91–92, 98, 111, 122, 128, 132–133, 135–136, 145, 150, 154, 158, 161, 163–165, 168, 170; 10th Regiment 168; 14th Regiment 168–169; 15th Regiment 82, 168, 177

Maine troops: 1st Cavalry 108; 2nd Regiment 150
Maryland troops: 1st Regiment (C.S.) 100–106, 114, 143; 1st Regiment (U.S.) 100–106
Massachusetts troops: 2nd Regiment 101, 113, 117; 5th Regiment 72; 9th Regiment 145; 11th Regiment 72
McClellan, George Brinton 6, 34, 93, 94, 97, 99, 119–120, 139–142, 144–146, 154–155, 157–160, 164–168
McDowell, Irvin 53, 58, 69–70, 74–75, 93, 96–99, 119–120, 125, 138–140, 147, 165, 167
Michigan troops: 4th Cavalry 113–116
Miller, Obedia Plummer 35, 42, 76, 78, 89, 123, 155, 172, 179–180, 195
Minnesota troops: 1st Regiment 70–72
Mississippi troops: 1st Rifles (Mexican War) 46; 2nd Regiment 64, 72, 74
Missouri Compromise 7–8, 122
Munford, Thomas 96–97, 100, 119, 120, 124, 126, 129, 138

Neese, George 93, 99–100, 109, 111, 133, 136
New Hampshire troops 2nd Regiment 58, 64–65, 194
New York troops: M/1st Artillery 113; 5th Cavalry 101, 104; 8th Regiment 58, 128; 11th Regiment 70–71, 73; 13th Regiment 74; 14th Regiment 58, 71–73; 27th Regiment 58; 28th Regiment 113, 115; 32nd Regiment 150; 33rd Regiment 150; 38th Regiment 74; 69th Regiment 74; 71st Regiment 58, 63, 65; 79th Regiment 74
North Carolina troops: 1st Battalion 80–81, 84; 6th Regiment 72

Ohio troops: H/1st Artillery 130–131, 134–135; L/1st Artillery 130, 134; 5th Regiment 130–131, 135–136; 7th Regiment 130, 135–136; 29th Regiment 130; 66th Regiment 135; 69th Regiment 130–131, 135–136
Old Dominion Guards 2, 35–36, 39, 41–43, 45, 58, 63, 73, 76, 89, 137, 155, 169, 171–172, 179–180
O'Sullivan, John 13

Patton, John 100, 113, 117
Pennsylvania troops 29th Regiment 101, 104, 113; 33rd Regiment 150–151; 84th Regiment 130, 133; 95th Regiment 150–152; 110th Regiment 130, 133; Collis's Zouaves 110; Independent Battery C 113; Independent Battery E 101, 113; Independent Battery F 110, 113
Porter, Andrew 58, 65, 67, 69–71, 194
Porter, Fitz-John 141–143, 145–147, 150, 154, 157, 160, 163

Quitman, John 6–8, 12–13

Rhode Island troops: 1st Regiment 58, 61, 63; 2nd Regiment 57–63, 65–66, 193–194; Reynolds's Battery A 58, 63
Ricketts, James 67, 69–72, 74, 194
Rough and Ready Rangers 2, 36, 41, 45, 47, 89, 171, 180–182

Scott, William 100, 108, 117, 121, 126, 127–129
Scott, Winfield 6–7, 78
Seymour, Isaac 79, 83, 104, 114, 132–133, 142, 150–151, 153–154, 196
Shields, James 97, 99, 120–121, 125–126, 129–130, 138
Slavery 8–9, 11–12, 22, 30, 121, 122–123, 198
Somerville, battle of 98, 102
Soule, Pierre 8, 29, 31
South Carolina troops: 2nd Regiment 74; 4th Regiment 48, 51, 54–56, 58, 64, 69; 8th Regiment 74; Hampton's Legion 68
Stafford, Leroy 145, 153, 163, 165
Steuart, George "Maryland" 126–127, 129–130, 165
Stuart, James Ewell Brown 71, 112, 157, 160, 165

Taliaferro, William 100, 111, 113–115, 117, 127, 129

Index

Taylor, Richard 6, 79–80, 83–85, 89–91, 96, 99–102, 104–106, 108, 110, 113–118, 121–139, 142, 146, 150, 153–154, 158, 165, 167–170, 174
Taylor, Zachary 6–8
Tennessee Mounted Rifles 5–6
Tiger Rifles 2, 35–37, 40–41, 43–45, 47, 51, 55–58, 61, 73, 76–77, 80, 82–84, 86, 89, 91, 100, 109, 135, 137, 155, 164, 169, 171, 173–175
Trimble, Isaac Ridgeway 79–82, 84–85, 100, 108, 117, 121, 126–129, 137, 148, 150, 153–154, 161
Tyler, Daniel 53–55, 66, 69
Tyler, Erastus 127, 129–130, 133, 135–136

United States troops: I/1st Artillery 76, 78–80, 86; E/2nd Artillery 63; L-M/3rd Artillery 183; E/4th Artillery 156, 163; D/5th Artillery 66, 78–80; cavalry 58; infantry 58; Marines 58, 70–71

Vanderbilt, Cornelius 14–16, 18, 21, 24, 26–28
Vermont troops: 1st Cavalry 98
Virginia troops: 1st Cavalry 71; 1st Regiment (C.S.) 91; 1st Regiment (U.S.) 130; 2nd Cavalry 96, 120, 124, 126, 129; 2nd Regiment 72, 129, 131, 133–134, 138; 4th Regiment 27, 72, 131, 133–134; 5th Regiment 74, 131, 134; 6th Cavalry 96, 98, 101, 112, 124, 126; 7th Cavalry 100, 106, 108, 124, 126–127; 8th Regiment 68; 10th Regiment 115; 11th Cavalry 100, 106, 108, 126–127; 13th Regiment 128, 143; 18th Regiment 48, 72, 74, 86; 21st Regiment 115; 23rd Regiment 115; 25th Regiment 128; 27th Regiment 72, 131, 134; 33rd Regiment 71–72; 37th Regiment 127; 44th Regiment 136; 49th Regiment 68, 72; 58th Regiment 136; Chew's Artillery 98; Culpeper Artillery 74; Lynchburg Artillery 51; Rockbridge Artillery 108; Staunton Artillery 69

Walker, William 9, 11, 14–31
Walker Guards 2, 14, 35–36, 40–41, 43, 45, 61, 73, 76, 81–83, 89, 137, 155, 164, 169, 171–173
Wheat, Chatham Roberdeau 1–3, 5–15, 22, 27–32, 34–48, 50–51, 54–65, 75–83, 89, 91–92, 97–98, 101–111, 114–115, 121, 123–125, 128, 132–138, 142, 145–157, 164, 167, 168–171, 186
Wheat's Life Guards 89, 137, 169, 172, 180
White, Alexander 2, 35, 37–41, 44, 51, 57–58, 73, 76–78, 89–90, 109, 137, 155, 169, 173
Winder, Charles 100, 108, 112–114, 117, 120, 126–127, 129–130, 132–134, 141–142, 154, 161, 168
Wisconsin troops: 2nd Regiment 74; 3rd Regiment 101, 113

Zouaves 2, 33, 34, 55, 58